TOP
STOCKS

TWENTY-NINTH EDITION

2023

MARTIN ROTH'S

BEST-SELLING ANNUAL

TOP
STOCKS

TWENTY-NINTH EDITION

2023

A SHAREBUYER'S GUIDE TO
LEADING AUSTRALIAN
COMPANIES

WILEY

The author and publisher would like to thank Alan Hull (author of *Active Investing*, Revised Edition, *Trade My Way* and *Invest My Way*; www.alanhull.com) for generating the five-year share-price charts.

This twenty-ninth edition first published in 2023 by Wrightbooks, an imprint of John Wiley & Sons Australia, Ltd

Level 1, 155 Cremorne Street, Richmond VIC 3121

Typeset in Adobe Garamond Pro Regular by 10/12 pt

First edition published as *Top Stocks* by Wrightbooks in 1995

New edition published annually

ISBN: 978-1-119-88864-2

A catalogue record for this book is available from the National Library of Australia

Cover design: Wiley

Cover image: Stock market graph © Phongphan/Shutterstock

Charts created using MetaStock

Disclaimer
The material in this publication is of the nature of general comment only, and does not represent professional advice. It is not intended to provide specific guidance for particular circumstances and it should not be relied on as the basis for any decision to take action or not take action on any matter which it covers. Readers should obtain professional advice where appropriate, before making any such decision. To the maximum extent permitted by law, the author and publisher disclaim all responsibility and liability to any person, arising directly or indirectly from any person taking or not taking action based on the information in this publication.

Contents

PART II: the tables

Preface

This latest edition of *Top Stocks* arrives at a time when many investors are concerned about the direction of the stock market. Reasons for continuing volatility seem to abound.

Interest rates and inflation have been rising. Energy prices are a particular concern. House prices have been falling. Consumer confidence seems to be ebbing. The war in Ukraine has brought political instability to Europe. Recession could follow. And is the COVID pandemic really coming to an end?

As I have noted in earlier editions, *Top Stocks* is written for times such as these, when the future is cloudy. Because, no matter the direction of the stock market, numerous fine companies continue to emerge in Australia, offering investors great prospects. *Top Stocks 2023* showcases many such companies.

They are often smaller to medium-sized corporations. Some will be unfamiliar to investors. But all meet the stringent *Top Stocks* criteria, including solid profits and moderate debt levels.

Of course, such stocks could not withstand the tidal wave of a substantial market sell-off. They too would be affected. But they should be affected less. And if they are good companies they will continue to thrive and to pay dividends. And they will bounce back faster than many others.

This is the 29th annual edition of *Top Stocks*, and guiding investors towards value stocks has been one of the paramount aims of the book from the very first edition. Indeed, one of the rationales for the book has always been to highlight the truth that Australia boasts many excellent companies that enjoy high profits — and growing profits — regardless of the direction of the markets. Despite the title, *Top Stocks* is actually a book about companies.

Right from the start it has been an attempt to help investors find the best public companies in Australia, using strict criteria. These criteria are explained fully later. But, in essence, all companies in the book must have been publicly listed for at least five years and must have been making a profit and paying a dividend for each of those five years. They must also meet tough benchmarks of profitability and debt levels. It is completely objective. The author's own personal views count for nothing. In addition, share prices have never been relevant.

Of the 93 companies in *Top Stocks 2023* — two more than in last year's edition — fully 69 reported a higher after-tax profit in the latest financial year (June 2022 for most of them), including eight that achieved triple-digit profit growth and a further 53 with double-digit growth. In addition, 69 achieved higher earnings per share and 73 paid a higher dividend.

And though, as I have noted, share prices are not relevant for selection to *Top Stocks*, 60 of the companies in the book have provided investor returns — share price appreciation plus dividends — of an average of at least 10 per cent per year over a five-year period.

Electric vehicles and clean energy

Each year I try to identify trends among the companies of *Top Stocks*. Certainly one of the biggest recently has been the move towards electric vehicles, and clean energy more generally. This suggests that demand is going to rise significantly for a range of specific minerals and metals, including copper, nickel, lithium and cobalt. Australian mines are among the world's leading producers of these.

Here are companies from this edition of *Top Stocks* with exposure to this trend:

- BHP Group has declared that it sees its greatest potential in 'future-facing' commodities, such as copper and nickel for electrification, renewable power and electric vehicles, and potash for fertiliser. It is ending its exposure to thermal coal.
- Fortescue Metals has launched Fortescue Future Industries, a global green energy business, with a particular focus on green hydrogen, which the company predicts could become a US$12 trillion market by 2050.
- IGO is working to transform itself into a major producer of commodities related to clean energy. Having acquired nickel miner Western Areas and a 49 per cent stake in Tianqi Lithium Energy Australia it is now a significant producer of nickel and lithium, and it also mines copper and cobalt.
- Iluka Resources is a global leader in the mining and processing of a range of rare earth minerals that are key components for a growing number of high-tech industries.
- Mineral Resources has a substantial exposure to lithium through its holdings in the Wodgina lithium mine and the Mount Marion lithium project.

- OZ Minerals is a significant copper miner, with interests also in nickel.
- Rio Tinto is working to resume development of its US$2.4 billion Jadar lithium project in Serbia, and is also involved in the massive Oyu Tolgoi copper–gold mine development in Mongolia.
- Wesfarmers is constructing a $1.9 billion lithium mine and refinery through its Covalent Lithium joint venture.

High-tech companies

For some years in *Top Stocks* I have been talking about the rise and rise of high-tech companies in Australia. They are generally small companies — though large enough to be in the All Ordinaries Index of Australia's 500 largest stocks — and it can sometimes be difficult for outsiders to understand just how they make their money. Thus, many investors avoid them.

But technology is steadily infiltrating every facet of our lives, and the best of these companies are set to continue growing. It is worth taking the time to learn more about them.

Increasingly they are selling what has come to be known as software as a service. This means they will often charge an initial fee and then a subscription, so they have a high degree of recurring revenue. It gives a degree of consistency and predictability to their earnings. They can also generate high profits from a relatively small increase in sales, given that they are dealing especially in software.

Profit growth (and share price acceleration) for many of these companies has been outstanding. They are often on high price-earnings ratios, but that reflects the market's belief that high levels of growth will continue. They should be on the radar of all serious investors.

Information technology companies

	Dividend yield (%)	5-year share price return (% p.a.)
Altium	1.3	26.7
Codan	4.6	24.4
Computershare	2.2	11.9
Data#3	2.8	29.9
Hansen	2.4	8.1
IRESS	4.0	3.4
Objective	0.7	41.3
Technology One	1.2	19.4
Wisetech	0.2	38.4

Healthcare companies

Australia boasts quite a dynamic healthcare industry. In fact, Healthcare is the third largest major sector on the ASX, after Financials and Materials. Some of these companies are showing excellent growth, although dividend yields are generally small. Here are healthcare companies in this edition of *Top Stocks*.

Healthcare companies

	Dividend yield (%)	5-year share price return (% p.a.)
Ansell	2.9	5.0
Clinuvel Pharmaceuticals	0.2	24.9
Cochlear	1.4	5.6
CSL	1.1	17.8
Healius	4.4	4.7
Pro Medicus	0.4	53.1
Sonic Healthcare	3.1	11.3

Small stocks

A particular attraction of *Top Stocks* is the manner in which the book places the spotlight on smaller, emerging companies, many of which have just ascended into the rankings of the top 500 stocks. Some of these companies continue to rise, offering solid gains to astute investors.

A special example is the medical imaging software company Pro Medicus. It entered the book in *Top Stocks 2006* at a share price of $1.15 and a market capitalisation of $108.5 million. It appears in this latest edition of the book at a price of $55.70 — having been as high as $70.00 — and a market capitalisation of $5.8 billion.

Another, less spectacular, example is Objective Corporation, a developer of software used extensively by local authorities and governmental bodies. It entered the book in *Top Stocks 2007* at a share price of $1.05 and a market capitalisation of $145.2 million. It appears in this latest edition of the book at a price of $15.10 — having been as high as $20.83 — and a market capitalisation of $1.4 billion.

Two recent examples: The first is Supply Network, a provider of truck and bus parts for transport companies, with operations throughout Australia and New Zealand. It entered the book in *Top Stocks 2020* at a price of $3.99. It appears in *Top Stocks 2023* at a price of $10.53, and has been as high as $11.49.

The other is Australian Ethical Investment. It too entered the book in *Top Stocks 2020*, priced at $2.18. It has since been as high as $15.08, although in line with other money management companies it has fallen considerably, and in *Top Stocks 2023* it is priced at $6.02.

Here are some of the companies that are appearing in *Top Stocks* for the first time:

- Clinuvel Pharmaceuticals has received acclaim for its breakthrough skincare products.
- Enero Group occupies strong positions in several countries in niche areas of the marketing, PR, communications and advertising sectors.
- IGO is working to transform itself into a major producer of commodities related to clean energy, with particular interests in nickel and lithium.
- Johns Lyng Group is a rapidly expanding construction company, with a special interest in building and restoration work for insurance claims.
- Netwealth Group has been gaining market share for its wealth management platform, which is designed to help financial advisors track their investment portfolios.
- PeopleIn is a recruitment agency that is benefiting from the inability of many companies to find sufficient numbers of qualified staff.
- Wisetech Global is a global leader in international logistics software, with customers that include most of the world's largest freight forwarders and logistics providers.

Who is *Top Stocks* written for?

Top Stocks is written for all those investors wishing to exercise a degree of control over their portfolios. It is for those just starting out, as well as for those with plenty of experience but who still feel the need for some guidance through the thickets of more than 2000 listed stocks.

It is not a how-to book. It does not give step-by-step instructions to 'winning' in the stock market. Rather, it is an independent and objective evaluation of leading companies, based on rigid criteria, with the intention of yielding a large selection of stocks that can become the starting point for investors wishing to do their own research.

A large amount of information is presented on each company, and another key feature of the book is that the data is presented in a common format, to allow readers to make easy comparisons between companies.

It is necessarily a conservative book. All stocks must have been listed for five years even to be considered for inclusion. It is especially suited for those seeking out value stocks for longer-term investment.

Yet, perhaps ironically, the book is also being used by short-term traders seeking a goodly selection of financially sound and reliable companies whose shares they can trade.

In addition, there are many regular readers, who buy the book each year, and to them in particular I express my thanks.

What are the entry criteria?

The criteria for inclusion in *Top Stocks* are strict:

- All companies must be included in the All Ordinaries Index, which comprises Australia's 500 largest stocks (out of more than 2000). The reason for excluding smaller companies is that there is often little investor information available on many of them and some are so thinly traded as to be almost illiquid. In fact, the 500 All Ordinaries companies comprise, by market capitalisation, more than 95 per cent of the entire market.
- It is necessary that all companies be publicly listed since at least the end of 2017, and have a five-year record of profits and dividend payments, each year.
- All companies are required to post a return-on-equity ratio of at least 10 per cent in their latest financial year.
- No company should have a debt-to-equity ratio of more than 70 per cent.
- It must be stressed that share price performance is NOT one of the criteria for inclusion in this book. The purpose is to select companies with good profits and a strong balance sheet. These may not offer the spectacular share price returns of a high-tech start-up or a promising lithium miner, but they should also present less risk.
- There are several notable exclusions. Listed managed investments are out, as these mainly buy other shares or investments. Examples are Australian Foundation Investment Company and all the real estate investment trusts.
- A further exclusion are the foreign-registered stocks listed on the ASX. There is sometimes a lack of information available about such companies. In addition, their stock prices tend to move on events and trends in their home countries, making it difficult at times for local investors to follow them.

It is surely a tribute to the strength and resilience of Australian corporations that, once again, despite the volatility of recent years, so many companies have qualified for the book.

Changes to this edition

A total of 22 companies from *Top Stocks 2022* have been omitted from this new edition.

Two corporations, CIMIC Group and Virtus Health, were acquired during the year. One, OFX Group, did not pay a dividend.

Seven companies saw their debt-to-equity ratio rise above the 70 per cent limit for this book:

ALS
Brambles
Dicker Data
Money3 Corporation
Orora

Seven Group Holdings
SG Fleet Group

The remaining 12 excluded companies had return-on-equity ratios that fell below the required 10 per cent:

Accent Group
Austal
Bravura Solutions
Costa Group Holdings
Evolution Mining
Infomedia
Integral Diagnostics
Newcrest Mining
Orica
Pacific Smiles Group
Regis Resources
Sandfire Resources

There are 24 new companies in this book (although 13 of them have appeared in earlier editions of the book, but were not in *Top Stocks 2022*). One of these is Telstra, which was in *Top Stocks 2004*, but otherwise has not been in the book, due to its heavy borrowings.

The new companies in this book are:

Alumina
ANZ Banking Group
Aurizon Holdings*
Brickworks
Clinuvel Pharmaceuticals*
Computershare
Enero Group*
Globe International*
Healius
IGO*
Iluka Resources
Johns Lyng Group*
Lifestyle Communities
National Australia Bank
Netwealth Group*
Nine Entertainment Company Holdings*
NRW Holdings
OZ Minerals*
PeopleIn*
Ridley Corporation
Seek

Telstra Corporation
Wisetech Global*
Woolworths Group

* Companies that have not appeared in any previous edition of *Top Stocks*.

Companies in every edition of *Top Stocks*

This is the 29th edition of *Top Stocks*. Just one company has appeared in every edition: Commonwealth Bank of Australia.

Once again it is my hope that *Top Stocks* will serve you well.

Martin Roth
Melbourne
September 2022

Introduction

The 93 companies in this book have been placed as much as possible into a common format, for ease of comparison. Please study the following explanations in order to get as much as possible from the large amount of data.

The tables have been made as concise as possible, though they repay careful study, as they contain large amounts of information.

Note that the tables for the banks have been arranged a little differently from the others. Details of these are given later in this Introduction.

Head
At the head of each entry is the company name, with its three-letter ASX code and the website address.

Share-price chart
Under the company name is a long-term share-price chart, to September 2022, provided by Alan Hull (www.alanhull.com), author of *Invest My Way*, *Trade My Way* and *Active Investing*.

Small table
Under the share-price chart is a small table with the following data.

Sector
This is the company's sector as designated by the ASX. These sectors are based on the Global Industry Classification Standard — developed by S&P Dow Jones Indices and Morgan Stanley Capital International — which was aimed at standardising global industry sectors. You can learn more about these at the ASX website.

Share price
This is the closing price on 8 September 2022. Also included are the 12-month high and low prices, as of the same date.

Market capitalisation

This is the size of the company, as determined by the stock market. It is the share price multiplied by the number of shares in issue. All companies in this book must be in the All Ordinaries Index, which comprises Australia's 500 largest stocks, as measured by market capitalisation.

Price-to-NTA-per-share ratio

The NTA-per-share figure expresses the worth of a company's net tangible assets — that is, its assets minus its liabilities and intangible assets — for each share of the company. The price-to-NTA-per-share ratio relates this figure to the share price.

A ratio of one means that the company is valued exactly according to the value of its assets. A ratio below one suggests that the shares are a bargain, though usually there is a good reason for this. Profits are more important than assets.

Some companies in this book have a negative NTA-per-share figure — as a result of having intangible assets valued at more than their net assets — and a price-to-NTA-per-share ratio cannot be calculated.

See Table M, in the second part of this book, for a little more detail on this ratio.

Five-year share price return

This is the approximate total return you could have received from the stock in the five years to September 2022. It is based on the share price appreciation or depreciation plus dividends, and is expressed as a compounded annual rate of return.

Dividend reinvestment plan

A dividend reinvestment plan (DRP) allows shareholders to receive additional shares in their company in place of the dividend. Usually — though not always — these shares are provided at a small discount to the prevailing price, which can make them quite attractive. And of course no broking fees apply.

Many large companies offer such plans. However, they come and go. When a company needs finance it may introduce a DRP. When its financing requirements become less pressing it may withdraw it. Some companies that have a DRP in place may decide to deactivate it for a time.

The information in this book is based on up-to-date information from the companies. But if you are investing in a particular company in expectations of a DRP be sure to check that it is still on offer. The company's own website will often provide this information.

Price/earnings ratio

The price/earnings ratio (PER) is one of the most popular measures of whether a share is cheap or expensive. It is calculated by dividing the share price — in this case the closing price for 8 September 2022 — by the earnings per share figure. Obviously the share price is continually changing, so the PER figures in this book are for guidance only. Many newspapers publish each morning the latest PER for every stock.

Dividend yield

This is the latest full-year dividend expressed as a percentage of the share price. Like the price/earnings ratio, it changes as the share price moves. It is a useful figure, especially for investors who are buying shares for income, as it allows you to compare this income with alternative investments, such as a bank term deposit or a rental property.

Company commentary

Each commentary begins with a brief introduction to the company and its activities. Then follow the highlights of its latest business results. For the majority of the companies these are their June 2022 results, which were issued during July and August 2022. Finally, there is a section on the outlook for the company.

Main table

Here is what you can find in the main table.

Revenues

These are the company's revenues from its business activities, generally the sale of products or services. However, it does not usually include additional income from such sources as investments, bank interest or the sale of assets. If the information is available, the revenues figure has been broken down into the major product areas.

As much as possible, the figures are for continuing businesses. When a company sells a part of its operations the financial results for the sold activities are separated from the core results and reported as a separate item. This can mean that the previous year's results are restated — also excluding the sold business — to make year-on-year comparisons more valid.

Earnings before interest and taxation

Earnings before interest and taxation (EBIT) is the firm's profit from its operations before the payment of interest and tax. This figure is often used by analysts examining a company. The reason is that some companies have borrowed extensively to finance their activities, while others have opted for alternative means. By expressing profits before interest payments it is possible to compare more precisely the performance of these companies. The net interest figure — interest payments minus interest receipts — has been used for this calculation.

You will also find many companies using a measure called EBITDA, which is earnings before interest, taxation, depreciation and amortisation.

EBIT margin

This is the company's EBIT expressed as a percentage of its revenues. It is a gauge of a company's efficiency. A high EBIT margin suggests that a company is achieving success in keeping its costs low.

Gross margin

The gross margin is the company's gross profit as a percentage of its sales. The gross profit is the amount left over after deducting from a company's sales figure its cost of sales: that is, its manufacturing costs or, for a retailer, the cost of purchasing the goods it sells. The cost of goods sold figure does not usually include marketing or administration costs.

As there are different ways of calculating the cost of goods sold figure, this ratio is better used for year-to-year comparisons of a single company's efficiency, rather than in comparing one company with another.

Many companies do not present a cost of goods sold figure, so a gross margin ratio is not given for every stock in this book.

The revenues for some companies include a mix of sales and services. Where a breakdown is possible, the gross profit figure will relate to sales only.

Profit before tax/profit after tax

The profit before tax figure is simply the EBIT figure minus net interest payments. The profit after tax figure is, of course, the company's profit after the payment of tax, and also after the deduction of minority interests. Minority interests are that part of a company's profit that is claimed by outside interests, usually the other shareholders in a subsidiary that is not fully owned by the company. Many companies do not have any minority interests, and for those that do it is generally a tiny figure.

As much as possible, I have adjusted the profit figures to exclude non-recurring profits and losses, which are often referred to as significant items. It is for this reason that the profit figures in *Top Stocks* sometimes differ from those in the financial media or on financial websites, where profit figures normally include significant items.

Significant items are those that have an abnormal impact on profits, even though they happen in the normal course of the company's operations. Examples are the profit from the sale of a business, or expenses of a business restructuring, the write-down of property, an inventory write-down, a bad-debt loss or a write-off for research and development expenditure.

Significant items are controversial. It is often a matter of subjective judgement as to what is included and what excluded. After analysing the accounts of hundreds of companies while writing the various editions of this book, it is clear that different companies use varying interpretations of what is significant.

Further, when they do report a significant item there is no consistency as to whether they use pre-tax figures or after-tax figures. Some report both, making it easy to adjust the profit figures in the tables in this book. But difficulties arise when only one figure is given for significant items.

In normal circumstances most companies do not report significant items. But investors should be aware of this issue. It sometimes causes consternation for readers of *Top Stocks* to find that a particular profit figure in this book is substantially different from that given by some other source. My publisher occasionally receives emails from readers enquiring why a profit figure in this book is so different from that reported elsewhere. In virtually all cases the reason is that I have stripped out a significant item.

It is also worth noting my observation that a growing number of companies present what they call an underlying profit (called a cash profit for the banks), or even a so-called normalised profit, in addition to their reported (statutory) profit. This underlying profit will exclude not only significant items but also discontinued businesses and sometimes other related items. Where all the relevant figures are available, I have generally used these underlying figures for the tables in this book.

As already noted, when a company sells or terminates a significant business it will now usually report the profit or loss of that business as a separate item. It will also usually backdate its previous year's accounts, to exclude that business, so that worthwhile comparisons can be made of continuing businesses.

The tables in this book usually refer to continuing businesses only.

Earnings per share
Earnings per share is the after-tax profit divided by the number of shares. Because the profit figure is for a 12-month period the number of shares used is a weighted average of those on issue during the year. This number is provided by the company in its annual report and its results announcements.

Cashflow per share
The cashflow per share ratio tells — in theory — how much actual cash the company has generated from its operations.

In fact, the ratio in this book is not exactly a true measure of cashflow. It is simply the company's depreciation and amortisation figures for the year added to the after-tax profit, and then divided by a weighted average of the number of shares. Depreciation and amortisation are expenses that do not actually utilise cash, so can be added back to after-tax profit to give a kind of indication of the company's cashflow.

By contrast, a true cashflow — including such items as newly raised capital and money received from the sale of assets — would require quite complex calculations based on the company's statement of cashflows.

However, many investors use the ratio as I present it, because it is easy to calculate, and it is certainly a useful guide to approximately how much funding the company has available from its operations.

Dividend
The dividend figure is the total for the year, interim and final. It does not include special dividends. The level of franking is also provided.

Net tangible assets per share
The NTA per share figure tells the theoretical value of the company — per share — if all assets were sold and then all liabilities paid. It is very much a theoretical figure, as there is no guarantee that corporate assets are really worth the price put on them in the balance sheet. Intangible assets such as goodwill and patent rights are excluded because of the difficulty in putting a sales price on them, and also because they may in fact not have much value if separated from the company.

As already noted, some companies in this book have a negative NTA, due to the fact that their intangible assets are so great, and no figure can be listed for them.

Where a company's most recent financial results are the half-year figures, these are used to calculate this ratio.

Interest cover

The interest cover ratio indicates how many times a company could make its interest payments from its pre-tax profit. A rough rule of thumb says a ratio of at least three times is desirable. Below that and fast-rising interest rates could imperil profits. The ratio is derived by dividing the EBIT figure by net interest payments. Some companies have interest receipts that are higher than their interest payments, which turns the interest cover into a negative figure, and so it is not listed.

Return on equity

Return on equity is the after-tax profit expressed as a percentage of the shareholders' equity. In theory, it is the amount that the company's managers have made for you — the shareholder — on your money. The shareholders' equity figure used is an average for the year.

Debt-to-equity ratio

This ratio is one of the best-known measures of a company's debt levels. It is total borrowings minus the company's cash holdings, expressed as a percentage of the shareholders' equity. Some companies have no debt at all, or their cash position is greater than their level of debt, which results in a negative ratio, so no figure is listed for them.

Where a company's most recent financial results are the half-year figures, these are used to calculate this ratio.

Current ratio

The current ratio is simply the company's current assets divided by its current liabilities. Current assets are cash or assets that can, in theory, be converted quickly into cash. Current liabilities are normally those payable within a year. Thus, the current ratio measures the ability of a company to repay in a hurry its short-term debt, should the need arise. The surplus of current assets over current liabilities is referred to as the company's working capital.

Where a company's most recent financial results are the half-year figures, these are used to calculate this ratio.

Banks

The tables for the banks are somewhat different from those for most other companies. EBIT and debt-to-equity ratios have little relevance for them, as they have such high interest payments (to their customers). Other differences are examined below.

Operating income

Operating income is used instead of sales revenues. Operating income is the bank's net interest income — that is, its total interest income minus its interest expense — plus other income, such as bank fees, fund management fees and income from businesses such as corporate finance and insurance.

Net interest income

Banks borrow money — that is, they accept deposits from savers — and they lend it to businesses, homebuyers and other borrowers. They charge the borrowers more than they pay those who deposit money with them, and the difference is known as net interest income.

Operating expenses

These are all the costs of running the bank. Banks have high operating expenses, and one of the keys to profit growth is cutting these expenses.

Non-interest income to total income

Banks have traditionally made most of their income from savers and from lending out money. But they are also working to diversify into new fields, and this ratio is an indication of their success.

Cost-to-income ratio

As noted, the banks have high costs — numerous branches, expensive computer systems, many staff, and so on — and they are all striving to reduce these. The cost-to-income ratio expresses their expenses as a percentage of their operating income, and is one of the ratios most often used as a gauge of efficiency. The lower the ratio drops the better.

Return on assets

Banks have enormous assets, in sharp contrast to, say, a high-tech start-up whose main physical assets may be little more than a set of computers and other technological equipment. So the return on assets — the after-tax profit expressed as a percentage of the year's average total assets — is another measure of efficiency.

PART I

THE COMPANIES

Adairs Limited

ASX code: ADH www.adairs.com.au

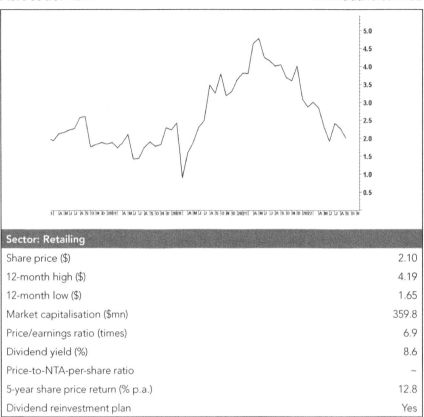

Sector: Retailing	
Share price ($)	2.10
12-month high ($)	4.19
12-month low ($)	1.65
Market capitalisation ($mn)	359.8
Price/earnings ratio (times)	6.9
Dividend yield (%)	8.6
Price-to-NTA-per-share ratio	~
5-year share price return (% p.a.)	12.8
Dividend reinvestment plan	Yes

Melbourne-based home furnishings specialist Adairs dates back to 1918 and the opening of a store in Chapel Street in Prahran, Melbourne. It has since grown into a nationwide chain of stores specialising in bed linen, bedding, towels, homewares, soft furnishings, children's furnishings and some bedroom furniture. It has also expanded to New Zealand, and it manages a flourishing online business. It operates the Mocka online furniture business, and in December 2021 it acquired Melbourne-based retailer Focus on Furniture. At June 2022 it operated 172 Adairs stores and 23 Focus stores.

Latest business results (June 2022, full year)

Revenues rose, thanks especially to a seven-month contribution from Focus, but underlying profits fell as the company was buffeted by COVID-related store closures, supply delays and higher costs. Like-for-like sales fell 2 per cent, having risen 16.5 per cent in the previous year. Online sales of $195.4 million were up 4.5 per cent. Debt levels rose significantly to pay for the Focus on Furniture acquisition. Sales at Adairs stores fell 6.1 per cent, with management estimating that COVID-mandated store closures reduced sales by around $35 million. Rising supply chain and delivery costs, and an increase in promotional activity, weakened profit margins. Mocka performed particularly poorly, with sales up but EBIT crashing by more than 70 per cent as supply delays led to order cancellations, compounded by inventory issues and rising costs. Focus contributed sales of $81.7 million and underlying EBIT of $17.2 million.

Outlook

Adairs manages popular brands with high levels of customer recognition and loyalty. With an addressable Australian home furnishings market of some $12 billion it sees great scope for growth. Following its poor June 2022 performance it is optimistic of a rebound in demand for June 2023, with a forecast of sales of $625 million to $665 million and EBIT of $75 million to $85 million. It also has a target of total annual company sales of at least $1 billion within five years. It has introduced new management to Mocka, aiming to put this business on a solid foundation for long-term growth. It sees great potential in its $80 million Focus acquisition, which significantly expands its exposure to the $8.3 billion bulky furniture sector. Adairs believes that through a modest investment in lighting, layout and styling it can boost sales at Focus stores, and it has begun a refurbishment program. It also plans to launch a rollout of new Focus stores, with a target of $250 million in annual Focus sales within five years.

Year to 26 June*	2021	2022
Revenues ($mn)	499.8	564.5
Adairs (%)	88	74
Focus (%)	0	14
Mocka (%)	12	12
EBIT ($mn)	109.0	76.3
EBIT margin (%)	21.8	13.5
Gross margin (%)	60.7	54.7
Profit before tax ($mn)	107.8	73.3
Profit after tax ($mn)	75.4	51.6
Earnings per share (c)	44.60	30.32
Cash flow per share (c)	70.96	60.45
Dividend (c)	23	18
Percentage franked	100	100
Net tangible assets per share ($)	~	~
Interest cover (times)	88.1	25.3
Return on equity (%)	49.4	28.5
Debt-to-equity ratio (%)	~	47.1
Current ratio	0.7	1.2

*27 June 2021

Altium Limited

ASX code: ALU

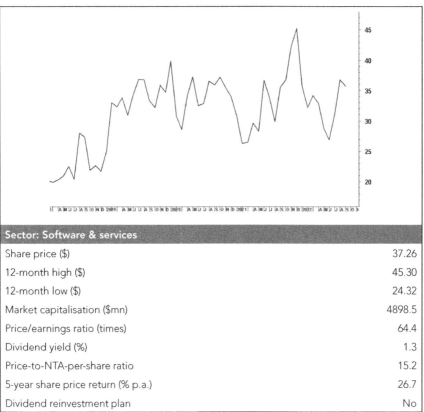

Sector: Software & services	
Share price ($)	37.26
12-month high ($)	45.30
12-month low ($)	24.32
Market capitalisation ($mn)	4898.5
Price/earnings ratio (times)	64.4
Dividend yield (%)	1.3
Price-to-NTA-per-share ratio	15.2
5-year share price return (% p.a.)	26.7
Dividend reinvestment plan	No

Sydney-based software company Altium was founded in Tasmania in 1985. It was originally named Protel. Its specialty is the provision of software that allows engineers to design printed circuit boards (PCBs). Its core product is Altium Designer. A much smaller division provides the Nexar cloud platform for connecting Altium customers with software, suppliers and manufacturers. Altium has most of its operations abroad but retains its Sydney headquarters and its ASX listing.

Latest business results (June 2022, full year)

Altium rebounded from the previous year's disappointing result with a double-digit increase in sales and profits. The core PCB business saw revenues up 12 per cent, with double-digit growth in all regions except China, constrained by COVID-related lockdowns. In recent years China had been providing some of the company's strongest growth. The Nexar division achieved a 76 per cent jump in revenues, underpinned by increased search activity for integrated circuits due to global shortages. Thanks to strongly rising demand for its products, Altium was also able to benefit by pushing through price rises, with discounting at its lowest level for many years. Note that

Altium reports its finances in US dollars. All figures in this book are converted to Australian dollars using prevailing exchange rates and are for guidance only.

Outlook

Printed circuit boards are incorporated in most electronic devices, and demand for them continues to grow. Altium has a strong reputation for its PCB design software, with high profit margins and a growth rate higher than the industry average. The strong rise in smart electronic connected devices is partly behind this trend. The company claims that as smart products increase in complexity its multi-board design processes allow the creation of electronic systems comprising multiple PCBs, and it expects this will help drive significant future growth in demand. It also sees particular potential for its Altium 365 product, the world's first cloud platform for PCB design and realisation. It is expensive for a customer to switch once it makes a decision to employ Altium software. The company is working to transition to a subscription-based business, and subscriptions grew 42.2 per cent in the June 2022 year to represent 75.4 per cent of total income, up from 65 per cent in the prior year. It has set itself a June 2026 target of US$500 million in total revenues. For June 2023 it forecasts revenue growth of 15 per cent to 20 per cent. At June 2022 Altium had no debt and nearly US$200 million in cash holdings.

Year to 30 June	2021	2022
Revenues ($mn)	237.1	302.5
EBIT ($mn)	62.4	92.1
EBIT margin (%)	26.3	30.4
Profit before tax ($mn)	62.7	93.0
Profit after tax ($mn)	46.4	76.0
Earnings per share (c)	35.38	57.84
Cash flow per share (c)	47.33	70.06
Dividend (c)	40	47
Percentage franked	8	100
Net tangible assets per share ($)	2.02	2.46
Interest cover (times)	~	~
Return on equity (%)	15.3	20.6
Debt-to-equity ratio (%)	~	~
Current ratio	2.4	3.1

Alumina Limited

ASX code: AWC www.aluminalimited.com

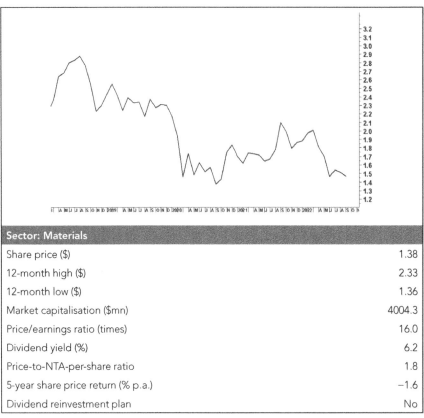

Sector: Materials	
Share price ($)	1.38
12-month high ($)	2.33
12-month low ($)	1.36
Market capitalisation ($mn)	4004.3
Price/earnings ratio (times)	16.0
Dividend yield (%)	6.2
Price-to-NTA-per-share ratio	1.8
5-year share price return (% p.a.)	−1.6
Dividend reinvestment plan	No

Melbourne-based Alumina traces its origins to the late 1950s and the mining of bauxite by WMC Limited. This led in 1961 to the establishment of a joint venture company between WMC and the Aluminium Company of America (Alcoa). In 2002 WMC spun off its interest in this business into a separate company, Alumina. Today Alumina's sole business activity is ownership of 40 per cent of the equity of Alcoa World Alumina and Chemicals (AWAC), in partnership with Alcoa, which holds the other 60 per cent. AWAC is an international business, responsible for about 10 per cent of global alumina production. It manages bauxite mines in Western Australia, Brazil, Saudi Arabia and Guinea. It also operates alumina refineries in Western Australia, Brazil, Saudi Arabia and Spain. Other businesses include the Alcoa Steamship operation and the Portland aluminium smelter in Victoria, in which it holds a 55 per cent equity share.

Latest business results (June 2022, half year)

Supply disruptions sent global alumina prices higher, generating a substantial upturn in revenues and profits for the company. Alumina divides its operations into three segments, bauxite mining, alumina refining and Portland aluminium smelting. The mining business produced 20.1 million tonnes of bauxite, down from 22.8 million tonnes in the June 2021 half. The average cash cost of US$13.10 per tonne was up from US$11.20. It refined 6.1 million tonnes of alumina at its own refineries, down from 6.4 million tonnes in June 2021. The average cash cost of US$304 per tonne was substantially up from US$230 in June 2021, due especially to higher energy prices. However, the average price received of US$398 per tonne was a big jump from US$290 a year before, delivering higher margins. The Portland smelter produced 75 000 tonnes of aluminium, down from 78 000 tonnes in June 2021. Note that Alumina reports its results in US dollars. The Australian dollar figures in this book — converted at prevailing exchange rates — are for guidance only.

Outlook

Alumina benefits from high-quality bauxite reserves and low-cost alumina refining operations. Its shares have attracted attention for a high dividend yield. However, its financial results are directly linked to global alumina and aluminium prices, which continue to be volatile, due in part to the war in Ukraine. In addition, energy costs remain high. Nevertheless, the company is optimistic about the longer-term outlook, believing that continuing industrial growth and a decarbonising world mean that current global levels of alumina production will be insufficient to meet the expected strong rise in demand, boosting prices.

Year to 31 December	2020	2021
Revenues ($mn)	238.7	272.8
EBIT ($mn)	220.7	255.1
EBIT margin (%)	92.5	93.5
Profit before tax ($mn)	213.2	250.1
Profit after tax ($mn)	212.3	250.1
Earnings per share (c)	7.36	8.62
Cash flow per share (c)	7.37	8.63
Dividend (c)	7.55	8.55
Percentage franked	100	100
Interest cover (times)	29.3	51.7
Return on equity (%)	8.8	11.0
Half year to 30 June	2021	2022
Revenues ($mn)	107.0	244.2
Profit before tax ($mn)	95.6	233.2
Profit after tax ($mn)	95.6	233.2
Earnings per share (c)	3.25	8.06
Dividend (c)	4.65	6.12
Percentage franked	100	100
Net tangible assets per share ($)	0.69	0.76
Debt-to-equity ratio (%)	0.3	~
Current ratio	11.1	12.8

Ansell Limited

ASX code: ANN   www.ansell.com

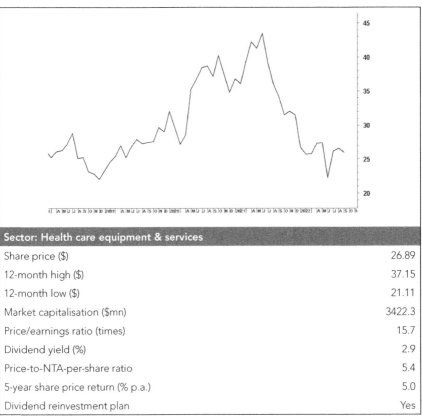

Sector: Health care equipment & services	
Share price ($)	26.89
12-month high ($)	37.15
12-month low ($)	21.11
Market capitalisation ($mn)	3422.3
Price/earnings ratio (times)	15.7
Dividend yield (%)	2.9
Price-to-NTA-per-share ratio	5.4
5-year share price return (% p.a.)	5.0
Dividend reinvestment plan	Yes

Melbourne-based Ansell has roots that stretch back to the manufacture of pneumatic bicycle tyres in the 19th century. It is today a global leader in a variety of safety and healthcare products. It makes a wide range of examination and surgical gloves for the medical profession. It also makes gloves and other hand and arm protective products for industrial applications, including for single use, along with household gloves. It has offices and production facilities in 55 countries, and more than 90 per cent of company revenues derive from abroad. Though still based in Australia, the company has its operational headquarters in the US.

Latest business results (June 2022, full year)

Ansell became a significant beneficiary of the COVID pandemic during the previous year, with demand soaring for its single-use gloves and personal protective equipment. However, this demand declined more sharply than anticipated during the June 2022 year, and profits fell. Revenues too edged down, although Ansell reports its financial results in US dollars, and the sales amount actually rose slightly when converted to Australian dollars for this book. Against this trend, emerging market sales remained strong. The Healthcare division saw EBIT crash 39 per cent, with sales down 4 per cent, as reduced demand forced the company to cut prices, compounded by higher freight costs and COVID-related manufacturing disruptions. In the previous year Healthcare division sales had risen 38 per cent, with EBIT surging 66 per cent. The Industrial division saw sales down 4 per cent and EBIT falling 5 per cent. As noted, Ansell reports its results in US dollars. The Australian dollar figures in this book — converted at prevailing exchange rates — are for guidance only.

Outlook

Ansell has a strong portfolio of products. It has achieved success in its research and development efforts, with a continuing stream of innovative and high-margin products. It operates 14 manufacturing facilities globally, and is spending US$80 million over three years on a new surgical products manufacturing site in India. It also continues to seek appropriate acquisition opportunities. It expects continuing solid demand for products such as its specialist protective gloves for the automotive industry, and Ansell enjoys a particularly strong relationship with electric vehicle manufacturers. It believes it can raise some prices further to meet rising costs. It has withdrawn from Russia, which means that US$9 million EBIT in June 2022 will not reoccur in June 2023. Ansell's early forecast is for a June 2023 EPS of US$1.15 to US$1.35, compared with US$1.25 in June 2022.

Year to 30 June	2021	2022
Revenues ($mn)	2667.0	2674.1
Healthcare (%)	61	61
Industrial (%)	39	39
EBIT ($mn)	444.7	312.5
EBIT margin (%)	16.7	11.7
Gross margin (%)	40.0	34.1
Profit before tax ($mn)	418.6	285.5
Profit after tax ($mn)	324.6	217.4
Earnings per share (c)	252.81	171.45
Cash flow per share (c)	318.49	241.99
Dividend (c)	101.34	78.85
Percentage franked	0	0
Net tangible assets per share ($)	4.30	4.97
Interest cover (times)	22.4	15.7
Return on equity (%)	15.9	10.1
Debt-to-equity ratio (%)	13.5	14.1
Current ratio	2.1	2.7

ARB Corporation Limited

ASX code: ARB　　　　　　　　　　　　　　　　www.arb.com.au

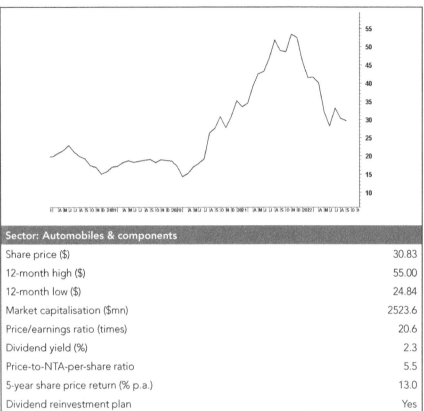

Sector: Automobiles & components	
Share price ($)	30.83
12-month high ($)	55.00
12-month low ($)	24.84
Market capitalisation ($mn)	2523.6
Price/earnings ratio (times)	20.6
Dividend yield (%)	2.3
Price-to-NTA-per-share ratio	5.5
5-year share price return (% p.a.)	13.0
Dividend reinvestment plan	Yes

Melbourne-based ARB, founded in 1975, is a prominent manufacturer of specialty automotive accessories, and an international leader in the design and production of specialised equipment for four-wheel-drive vehicles. These include its Air Locker air-operated locking differential system. It also makes and distributes a wide range of other products, including bull bars, roof racks, tow bars, canopies and the Old Man Emu range of suspension products. It operates a network of 74 ARB-brand stores throughout Australia, including 30 that are company-owned. It has established manufacturing facilities in Thailand and it exports to more than 100 countries.

Latest business results (June 2022, full year)

ARB goes from strength to strength and posted another firm result. Sales growth of 11.5 per cent built upon the 34 per cent increase of the previous year, and was particularly impressive as it came in an environment of constraints on new vehicle availability and continuing staffing and supply chain challenges. Nevertheless, the company reported a notable slowdown in the second half. The Australian aftermarket represents more than half the company's business, and sales grew 9.2 per cent. Exports were up 17.4 per cent and now comprise more than 38 per cent of total company turnover. Original equipment manufacturer sales to Australian vehicle makers were generally flat for the year. This business is less than 8 per cent of total income.

Outlook

Demand for ARB's products remains strong globally, although the company is concerned that logistical and supply chain constraints coupled with labour shortages and a global shortage of new vehicles are all increasing operational costs and disrupting the timely fulfilment of sales. It regards product development as a key element in helping it maintain a competitive edge and has opened a new engineering centre at its Melbourne headquarters. A strategic partnership with Ford Australia provides it with early access to Ford vehicle designs and the opportunity to market a complete range of accessories as new vehicles are released. It is also actively working on a full suite of premium aftermarket products for the new Ford Bronco in the US. Anticipating continuing growth in the American market, it has opened its third US distribution centre in Texas. It is also building a new 30 000-square-metre factory near its existing Thai operations in order to boost production capacity, with completion expected at the end of 2022. Domestically it continues its rollout of new ARB-brand retail stores. At June 2022 ARB had no debt and more than $52 million in cash holdings.

Year to 30 June	2021	2022
Revenues ($mn)	623.1	694.5
EBIT ($mn)	151.9	167.7
EBIT margin (%)	24.4	24.1
Gross margin (%)	43.8	45.3
Profit before tax ($mn)	150.0	165.7
Profit after tax ($mn)	112.9	122.0
Earnings per share (c)	139.96	149.40
Cash flow per share (c)	169.11	180.00
Dividend (c)	68	71
Percentage franked	100	100
Net tangible assets per share ($)	4.70	5.62
Interest cover (times)	82.0	84.0
Return on equity (%)	26.3	23.4
Debt-to-equity ratio (%)	~	~
Current ratio	3.0	3.6

Aristocrat Leisure Limited

ASX code: ALL www.aristocrat.com

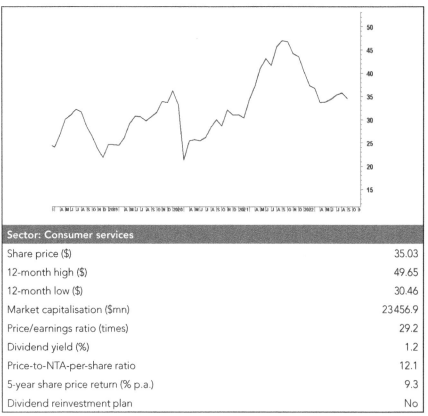

Sector: Consumer services	
Share price ($)	35.03
12-month high ($)	49.65
12-month low ($)	30.46
Market capitalisation ($mn)	23456.9
Price/earnings ratio (times)	29.2
Dividend yield (%)	1.2
Price-to-NTA-per-share ratio	12.1
5-year share price return (% p.a.)	9.3
Dividend reinvestment plan	No

Sydney-based Aristocrat, founded in 1953, is Australia's leading developer and manufacturer of electronic machines for the gaming industry, and it is also among the world's largest. It is licensed by more than 320 gaming jurisdictions worldwide. Its products and services include gaming machines, interactive video terminal systems, electronic tables, gaming machine support services and casino management systems. It is bringing a large selection of its games to online and mobile devices and is also actively developing its own online gaming business.

Latest business results (March 2022, half year)

Aristocrat continued to enjoy a strong recovery following the difficulties of the September 2020 year, when COVID-19 led to the closure of many of its clients' casino operations. On a constant-currency basis, revenues rose 20 per cent, with the after-tax profit up 42 per cent. The best result came from the company's gaming activities, particularly in North America, where sales surged 28 per cent, thanks especially to continuing strong demand for the 'Cash Express: Luxury Line' and 'Buffalo Link' products. The smaller Australian and international markets also recorded growth. The Pixel United business—formerly known as Aristocrat Digital, and supplying digital products to mobile devices—achieved single-digit growth. Pixel United has grown strongly in recent years to represent nearly half of total company turnover, although profit margins remain below those for gaming.

Outlook

Aristocrat enjoys a strong position in the global gaming industry, with high market shares in many regions. Nevertheless, this remains a competitive business, and the company is highly dependent on a continuing stream of attractive new and enhanced products. To develop these it must recruit and retain large numbers of highly skilled creative specialists and technology experts, and this has been one of its key challenges. Consequently, its design and development budget remains high at around 11 per cent to 12 per cent of annual revenues. Its Pixel United digital operation continues to grow, thanks especially to three popular games — 'RAID: Shadow Legends', 'Lightning Link' and 'Cashman Casino' — that together generate more than half of the revenues for this business. The company is also keen to develop its online gaming operations—known as real money gaming (RMG)—and has created a new business unit for this purpose. However, early in 2022 it failed in its takeover attempt for British RMG giant Playtech. With much of its income coming from outside Australia, Aristocrat's earnings are heavily influenced by currency rate trends.

Year to 30 September	2020	2021
Revenues ($mn)	4139.1	4736.6
EBIT ($mn)	618.5	1148.7
EBIT margin (%)	14.9	24.3
Profit before tax ($mn)	475.7	1016.8
Profit after tax ($mn)	357.1	765.6
Earnings per share (c)	55.98	120.11
Cash flow per share (c)	126.45	178.85
Dividend (c)	10	41
Percentage franked	100	100
Interest cover (times)	4.3	8.7
Return on equity (%)	13.4	21.8
Half year to 31 March	2021	2022
Revenues ($mn)	2229.7	2745.4
Profit before tax ($mn)	480.9	598.0
Profit after tax ($mn)	362.2	513.0
Earnings per share (c)	56.79	77.40
Dividend (c)	15	26
Percentage franked	100	100
Net tangible assets per share ($)	~	2.89
Debt-to-equity ratio (%)	48.9	~
Current ratio	2.6	3.8

ASX Limited

ASX code: ASX www.asx.com.au

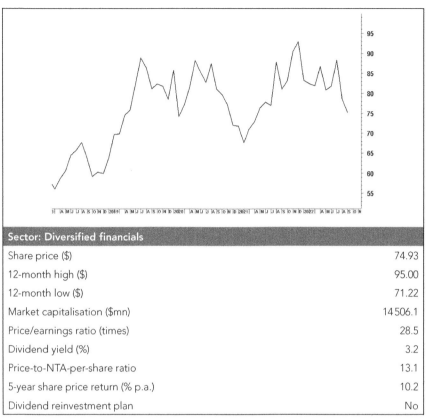

Sector: Diversified financials	
Share price ($)	74.93
12-month high ($)	95.00
12-month low ($)	71.22
Market capitalisation ($mn)	14 506.1
Price/earnings ratio (times)	28.5
Dividend yield (%)	3.2
Price-to-NTA-per-share ratio	13.1
5-year share price return (% p.a.)	10.2
Dividend reinvestment plan	No

ASX (Australian Securities Exchange) was formed in 1987 through the amalgamation of six independent stock exchanges that formerly operated in the state capital cities. Each of those exchanges had a history of share trading dating back to the 19th century. Though originally a mutual organisation of stockbrokers, in 1998 ASX became a listed company, with its shares traded on its own market. It expanded in 2006 when it merged with the Sydney Futures Exchange. Today it provides primary, secondary and derivative market services, along with clearing, settlement and compliance services. It is also a provider of a range of comprehensive market data and technical services.

Latest business results (June 2022, full year)

Revenues were up again and profits rebounded after their decline of the previous year. ASX has restructured its operations into four broad new divisions. The strongest result came from the Listings division, with revenues up 16.9 per cent. There was good growth in annual listing revenues and 217 new listings during the year, up from 176 in the previous year. The Technology and Data division achieved an 8.8 per cent increase in revenues, thanks especially to growing demand for equities and futures market data. Bustling equity-related market trading during the year — a daily average of $6.7 billion in trades, up 15.4 per cent — offset a small decline in futures revenues and saw the Markets division boost revenues by 4.1 per cent. The largest division, Securities and Payments, posted a 3.9 per cent rise, with solid performances from issuer services, cash market clearing and cash market settlement.

Outlook

ASX's profits are highly geared to levels of market activity. Nevertheless, such is the diverse variety of instruments available to investors nowadays that even market weakness does not necessarily lead to a decline in trading volumes. The company also enjoys a high degree of protection in its operations, with little effective competition for many of its businesses. It is constructing a major new platform using distributed ledger technology — sometimes referred to as blockchain — to replace its CHESS equities clearing and settlement system, with $216 million spent as of June 2022. It believes this project will transform Australia's post-trade equities environment and stimulate innovation across the market. However, the project has been subject to a long series of delays, and is not now expected to go live before late 2024. ASX expects its expenses to represent as much as 12 per cent of revenues in the June 2023 year, compared with 7.5 per cent in 2022.

Year to 30 June	2021	2022
Revenues ($mn)	962.3	1041.8
Securities & payments (%)	30	29
Markets (%)	30	29
Technology & data (%)	21	21
Listings (%)	19	21
EBIT ($mn)	641.2	689.2
EBIT margin (%)	66.6	66.2
Profit before tax ($mn)	687.9	730.3
Profit after tax ($mn)	480.9	508.5
Earnings per share (c)	248.41	262.68
Cash flow per share (c)	277.08	289.75
Dividend (c)	223.6	236.4
Percentage franked	100	100
Net tangible assets per share ($)	5.71	5.73
Interest cover (times)	~	~
Return on equity (%)	12.9	13.5
Debt-to-equity ratio (%)	~	~
Current ratio	1.1	1.1

AUB Group Limited

ASX code: AUB   www.aubgroup.com.au

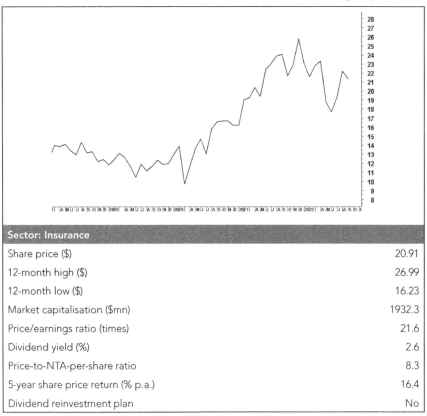

Sector: Insurance	
Share price ($)	20.91
12-month high ($)	26.99
12-month low ($)	16.23
Market capitalisation ($mn)	1932.3
Price/earnings ratio (times)	21.6
Dividend yield (%)	2.6
Price-to-NTA-per-share ratio	8.3
5-year share price return (% p.a.)	16.4
Dividend reinvestment plan	No

Sydney-based AUB Group, formerly known as Austbrokers Holdings, was established in 1985. It manages a network of insurance businesses throughout Australia and New Zealand. Its principal business is insurance broking, and it typically holds an equity stake of at least 50 per cent in each business, usually in partnership with the original owners. It also manages an underwriting agency business, which operates agencies in many specialised areas of the insurance business. In May 2022 it announced the acquisition of Lloyd's wholesale broker Tysers.

Latest business results (June 2022, full year)

AUB enjoyed further gains in revenues and underlying profits. The core Australian broking operation was responsible for 60 per cent of company turnover. It reported a further double-digit rise in profits, thanks to a growing number of clients, an increase in commercial insurance premiums, the company's continuing cost-reduction program and two acquisitions. By contrast, New Zealand broking, representing about 12 per cent of company turnover, experienced its second consecutive profit decline, due to heavy technology costs that are intended to transform business with a new operating platform. Excluding these expenses, NZ operations recorded a modest rise in profits. The underwriting business saw a sharp rise in profits, thanks to a full year's contribution from the 360 Underwriting Solutions acquisition and some strong organic growth.

Outlook

AUB has achieved success with its model of buying a stake in an insurance broking house but, in most cases, continuing to operate it with the original owners. This has allowed the businesses to preserve their local identity and management while benefiting from the support of a large group. The company is able to help its members develop their businesses through growth initiatives, including the addition of new products, and sometimes through appropriate bolt-on acquisitions. Since entering the New Zealand market it has become that country's largest broking management group. The company regards its acquisition of British broking house Tysers as transformational. The purchase price is $880 million, with potential deferred additional payments of up to $176 million, based on the achievement of revenue targets. Tysers is a leading specialist international insurance broker and the sixth-largest wholesale broker in the Lloyd's marketplace. AUB regards the acquisition as helping with its strategy of providing support for clients with international placement needs and allowing it to design and deliver new products for its network. AUB's early forecast is for underlying after-tax profit in the June 2023 year of $86 million to $91 million, with an additional benefit from Tysers.

Year to 30 June	2021	2022
Revenues ($mn)	313.3	332.5
EBIT ($mn)	105.8	115.7
EBIT margin (%)	33.8	34.8
Profit before tax ($mn)	94.4	106.1
Profit after tax ($mn)	65.3	74.0
Earnings per share (c)	87.93	96.70
Cash flow per share (c)	121.77	127.47
Dividend (c)	55	55
Percentage franked	100	100
Net tangible assets per share ($)	0.12	2.51
Interest cover (times)	20.4	25.9
Return on equity (%)	14.4	11.1
Debt-to-equity ratio (%)	22.7	~
Current ratio	1.2	1.5

Aurizon Holdings Limited

ASX code: AZJ   www.aurizon.com.au

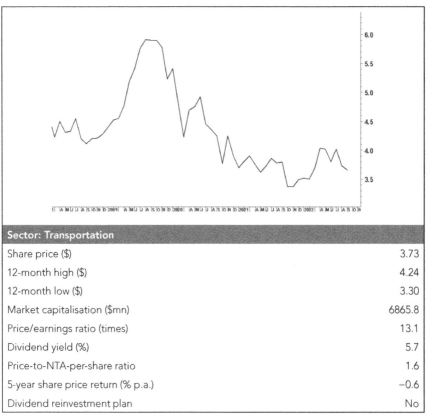

Sector: Transportation	
Share price ($)	3.73
12-month high ($)	4.24
12-month low ($)	3.30
Market capitalisation ($mn)	6865.8
Price/earnings ratio (times)	13.1
Dividend yield (%)	5.7
Price-to-NTA-per-share ratio	1.6
5-year share price return (% p.a.)	−0.6
Dividend reinvestment plan	No

Brisbane-based rail freight business Aurizon was formally established in 2004 when coal and bulk freight operations of the state-owned Queensland Rail were separated into a new entity, QR National. It was privatised in 2010 and later renamed as Aurizon. Today it operates under three broad segments. Its Coal division connects mines in Queensland and New South Wales with domestic customers and coal export terminals, and is responsible for carrying about half of Australia's export coal volume. The Network division manages the company's 2670-kilometre Central Queensland Coal Network. The Bulk division provides integrated supply chain services, including rail and road transportation, port services and material handling, for mining, metal, industrial and agricultural customers. In July 2022 Aurizon completed the acquisition of freight haulage group One Rail Australia.

Latest business results (June 2022, full year)

Revenues edged up but underlying profits slipped a little, and would have been down further but for some asset sales. The largest division, Coal, achieved a small increase in profits, with productivity gains offsetting a reduction in volumes. However, the Network division saw EBIT down 10 per cent, hit by lower fees, while the Bulk division suffered from the conclusion of some important contracts and weather-related disruptions, despite revenue growth. Though representing only around a quarter of total turnover, the Network division generates more than half of company profit. By contrast, the Bulk division contributes only about 10 per cent.

Outlook

With its heavy reliance on the fossil fuel business, Aurizon has been struggling to achieve growth, while recognising that moves globally towards reducing carbon emissions threaten its long-term future. It therefore regards the $2.35 billion One Rail acquisition as transformational. This new business includes operation of the 2200-kilometre railway from Tarcoola in South Australia to Darwin in the Northern Territory, with exposure to some 250 mining projects which are producing non-coal commodities, including copper, zinc, lithium, nickel and rare earths. Consequently, the company believes that by 2030 it can double profits for its Bulk division, while reducing its exposure to coal-related operations. In the short term Aurizon is seeing an increase in coal volumes following the Russian invasion of Ukraine. It is also enjoying a rise in its grain transport activities, thanks to record harvests. The company's early forecast is for EBITDA of between $1.47 billion and $1.55 billion in June 2023, compared with $1.47 billion in June 2022. This includes an 11-month contribution from the One Rail acquisition.

Year to 30 June	2021	2022
Revenues ($mn)	3019.3	3075.3
Coal (%)	53	51
Network (%)	25	26
Bulk (%)	20	22
EBIT ($mn)	903.1	875.3
EBIT margin (%)	29.9	28.5
Profit before tax ($mn)	757.8	750.3
Profit after tax ($mn)	533.2	524.9
Earnings per share (c)	28.54	28.52
Cash flow per share (c)	59.53	60.70
Dividend (c)	28.8	21.4
Percentage franked	70	98
Net tangible assets per share ($)	2.20	2.28
Interest cover (times)	6.2	7.0
Return on equity (%)	12.4	12.1
Debt-to-equity ratio (%)	84.0	69.1
Current ratio	1.1	0.9

Australia and New Zealand Banking Group Limited

ASX code: ANZ
www.anz.com.au

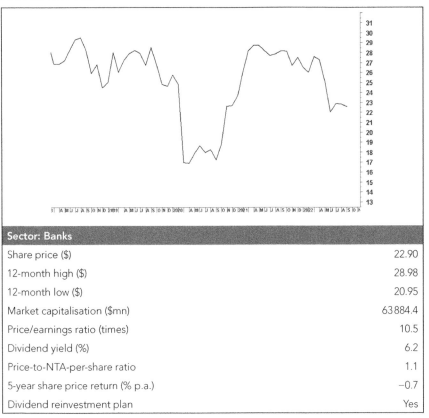

Sector: Banks	
Share price ($)	22.90
12-month high ($)	28.98
12-month low ($)	20.95
Market capitalisation ($mn)	63 884.4
Price/earnings ratio (times)	10.5
Dividend yield (%)	6.2
Price-to-NTA-per-share ratio	1.1
5-year share price return (% p.a.)	−0.7
Dividend reinvestment plan	Yes

Melbourne-based ANZ has its roots in the establishment of the Bank of Australasia in London in 1835. It is today one of the country's four banking giants and one of the largest companies. It is a market leader in New Zealand banking, and it is also active throughout Asia and the Pacific region. It has announced its intention to buy the banking business of Queensland-based Suncorp.

Latest business results (March 2022, half year)

Profits edged up, with rising costs partially restraining growth in retail and commercial banking. The Australia Retail and Commercial division, representing more than 55 per cent of total bank earnings, posted an 11 per cent rise in profits compared with the March 2021 half. This came despite competitive pressures, particularly in the home loans market, which helped drive a contraction in the net interest margin from 1.65 per cent in September 2021 to 1.58 per cent. Home loan balances were generally flat for the period. The New Zealand division recorded a 2 per cent rise in profits.

Interest rates had already been rising in New Zealand, helping stabilise margins. By contrast, the Institutional division saw profits slump by 23 per cent, with markets-related business especially weak.

Outlook

ANZ is set to grow with the $4.9 billion acquisition of the banking business of Suncorp, which was announced in July 2022. The deal requires regulatory approval, and completion of the process is not expected until the second half of 2023. The acquisition will add $47 billion in home loans to ANZ's portfolio, along with $45 billion in deposits and $11 billion in commercial loans. It will also provide annual cost synergies of some $260 million, along with 1.2 million new customers. Meanwhile, with interest rates rising, the bank expects only subdued growth in its home loans activities. It believes that most borrowers—both home owners and businesses—are in a position to manage higher rates. In addition, it expects rising interest rates to help stabilise profit margins. The bank continues to invest in digital technology to reduce the processing time for home loan applications. This includes its new retail banking platform, ANZ Plus, which is designed to provide smoother customer transactions and boost the personal banking business. Inflationary pressures mean the bank expects its operations to be affected by higher costs, and it has conceded that it will not be able to meet previously announced cost-reduction targets, although it continues its push to boost productivity.

Year to 30 September	2020	2021
Operating income ($mn)	17752.0	17447.0
Net interest income ($mn)	14049.0	14161.0
Operating expenses ($mn)	9383.0	9051.0
Profit before tax ($mn)	5631.0	8963.0
Profit after tax ($mn)	3758.0	6198.0
Earnings per share (c)	132.75	218.35
Dividend (c)	60	142
Percentage franked	100	100
Non-interest income to total income (%)	20.9	18.8
Cost-to-income ratio (%)	52.9	51.9
Return on equity (%)	6.2	10.0
Return on assets (%)	0.4	0.6
Half year to 31 March	2021	2022
Operating income ($mn)	8423.0	8948.0
Profit before tax ($mn)	4432.0	4441.0
Profit after tax ($mn)	2990.0	3113.0
Earnings per share (c)	105.36	110.85
Dividend (c)	70	72
Percentage franked	100	100
Net tangible assets per share ($)	20.61	20.68

Australian Ethical Investment Limited

ASX code: AEF

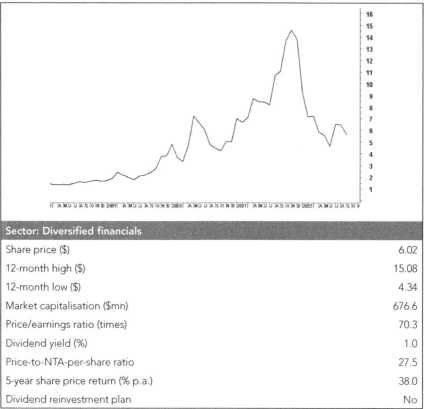

Sector: Diversified financials	
Share price ($)	6.02
12-month high ($)	15.08
12-month low ($)	4.34
Market capitalisation ($mn)	676.6
Price/earnings ratio (times)	70.3
Dividend yield (%)	1.0
Price-to-NTA-per-share ratio	27.5
5-year share price return (% p.a.)	38.0
Dividend reinvestment plan	No

Australian Ethical, based in Sydney, was founded in 1986. It is a wealth management company that specialises in investments in corporations that meet a set of ethical criteria. It operates a range of wholesale and retail funds, including superannuation, incorporating Australian and international shares, emerging companies and fixed interest. It has launched its first exchange-traded fund. The company donates up to 10 per cent of its profits to charities and activist groups through its Australian Ethical Foundation.

Latest business results (June 2022, full year)

Volatile global markets hit the company's operations, and while revenues rose, profits were down. Net inflows of $0.94 billion fell 8 per cent from the previous year, though this was still a solid result in a year when many fund managers were experiencing net outflows. In an increasingly competitive market, superannuation inflows rose 22 per cent. The company received performance fees of $0.4 million — down from $2.9 million in the previous year — relating to its Emerging Companies Fund. It also incurred a significant increase in its expenses, including a 35 per cent rise in staff costs to $25 million and an 84 per cent jump in marketing expenses to $9 million. During the year it reduced the fees for some of its products. Funds under management of $6.2 billion at June 2022 were up 2 per cent from a year earlier.

Outlook

Australian Ethical is a small company but is a leader in a fast-growing trend towards ethical investment. In a growing marketplace, with many major financial institutions launching their own ESG (environmental, social and governance) funds, Australian Ethical has attracted attention because of its perceived independence. The company's pledge is that it seeks out positive investments that support its three pillars of people, planet and animals. Its Ethical Charter gives details of the criteria it uses for its investments, and it provides a public list of the companies in which it is prepared to invest. It has adopted an aggressive growth strategy which in the short term will boost expenses and limit profit growth. Following discussions with the Christian Super superannuation fund, some 30 000 members of Christian Super, representing funds under management of around $1.96 billion, will transfer to Australian Ethical early in 2023. Nevertheless, despite its strong position, Australian Ethical remains heavily exposed to volatile financial markets, and its businesses could be hurt in any sustained downturn. At June 2022 the company had no debt and more than $27 million in cash holdings.

Year to 30 June	2021	2022
Revenues ($mn)	58.7	70.8
EBIT ($mn)	15.5	13.7
EBIT margin (%)	26.4	19.4
Profit before tax ($mn)	15.5	13.8
Profit after tax ($mn)	11.1	9.5
Earnings per share (c)	10.00	8.57
Cash flow per share (c)	11.06	9.65
Dividend (c)	7	6
Percentage franked	100	100
Net tangible assets per share ($)	0.21	0.22
Interest cover (times)	15 497.0	~
Return on equity (%)	49.1	38.9
Debt-to-equity ratio (%)	~	~
Current ratio	2.4	1.9

Baby Bunting Group Limited

ASX code: BBN   www.babybunting.com.au

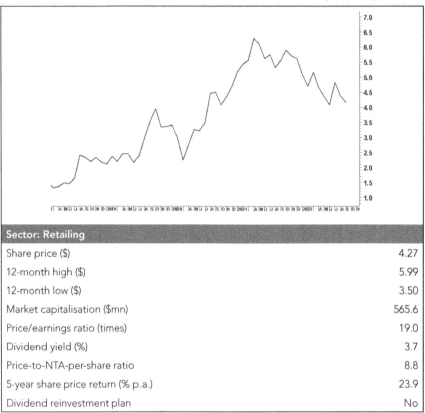

Sector: Retailing	
Share price ($)	4.27
12-month high ($)	5.99
12-month low ($)	3.50
Market capitalisation ($mn)	565.6
Price/earnings ratio (times)	19.0
Dividend yield (%)	3.7
Price-to-NTA-per-share ratio	8.8
5-year share price return (% p.a.)	23.9
Dividend reinvestment plan	No

Melbourne retailer Baby Bunting started in 1979 with the opening of a store in the suburb of Balwyn. It has since grown into a nationwide chain of stores specialising in some 6000 lines of baby and nursery products, including prams, car seats, carriers, furniture, nursery items, safety goods, babywear, manchester, toys, feeding products and maternity wear.

Latest business results (June 2022, full year)

Sales and underlying profits rose in another solid result. On a same-store basis, sales rose 5 per cent, and the company also opened four new stores. There was an 18.3 per cent rise in sales of Baby Bunting exclusive products and private label brands, which contributed to an increase in profit margins. The result was also helped by the first full year of the new national distribution centre, boosting efficiencies. Online sales grew by 24.2 per cent to comprise 22.2 per cent of total turnover. The company said sales would have been higher but for delays in obtaining supplies of certain products. At the end of June 2022 Baby Bunting operated 64 stores nationwide.

Outlook

Baby Bunting occupies a strong position in the $3.5 billion Australian baby goods retail market. With the demise of some competitors, it is now the only specialist baby goods retailer with a national presence, and its major rivals are stores such as Kmart, Target and Big W. It has numerous strategies for growth. It plans to open six new stores in the June 2023 year, with an eventual target of around 110 throughout Australia. Private label and exclusive products—generally providing higher profit margins than other goods—now comprise 45.3 per cent of sales, up from 41.4 per cent a year earlier, and the company's long-term goal is to raise this to 50 per cent. It sells its private label products under three brands, 4baby, Bilbi and JENGO. It also continues to invest in developing its online operations. In addition, it is expanding into the services sphere, with initial offerings that include car seat and breast pump rentals, along with car seat installations and repairs. A new loyalty program has attracted 1.4 million members, with members spending more per transaction than non-members. In July 2020 Baby Bunting began online sales to New Zealand customers, and in August 2022 it opened its first store in that country. It plans a New Zealand network of at least 10 stores. However, the company also faces challenges, including inflationary pressures, supply chain disruptions and staff recruitment and retention demands.

Year to 26 June*	2021	2022
Revenues ($mn)	468.4	507.3
EBIT ($mn)	42.3	49.3
EBIT margin (%)	9.0	9.7
Gross margin (%)	37.1	38.6
Profit before tax ($mn)	36.6	42.3
Profit after tax ($mn)	26.0	29.6
Earnings per share (c)	20.20	22.53
Cash flow per share (c)	41.96	46.73
Dividend (c)	14.1	15.6
Percentage franked	100	100
Net tangible assets per share ($)	0.46	0.48
Interest cover (times)	7.5	7.1
Return on equity (%)	26.1	26.8
Debt-to-equity ratio (%)	~	0.6
Current ratio	1.2	1.3

*27 June 2021

Bapcor Limited

ASX code: BAP   www.bapcor.com.au

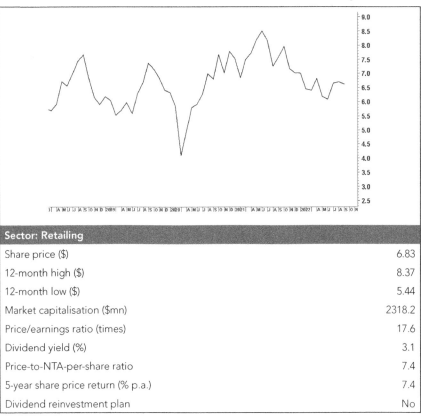

Sector: Retailing	
Share price ($)	6.83
12-month high ($)	8.37
12-month low ($)	5.44
Market capitalisation ($mn)	2318.2
Price/earnings ratio (times)	17.6
Dividend yield (%)	3.1
Price-to-NTA-per-share ratio	7.4
5-year share price return (% p.a.)	7.4
Dividend reinvestment plan	No

Melbourne company Bapcor started in 1971 as Burson Auto Parts, supplying a range of automotive products to workshops and service stations. It grew steadily, organically and by acquisition, opening stores throughout Australia, and taking its present name in 2016. It now services the automotive aftermarket under numerous brands, including Autobarn, Midas, Autopro and ABS. It has extensive operations in Australia and New Zealand, and in 2018 it opened its first stores in Thailand, in partnership with a local auto specialist company. In 2021 it acquired an equity stake in Singapore automotive parts distributor Tye Soon. Bapcor operates from more than 1100 locations across Australia, New Zealand and Thailand.

Latest business results (June 2022, full year)

Sales and profits edged up as Bapcor expanded its network of stores, offsetting the impact of some first-half lockdowns, staff shortages and supply chain disruptions. The largest division, Specialist Wholesale, comprises a range of small outlets that focus on sourcing replacement parts for the wholesale automotive aftermarket. It achieved revenue growth of 10 per cent, with profits up 16 per cent, following the acquisition of a series of truck and trailer parts businesses. The Trade division, comprising the Burson Auto Parts and the Precision Automotive Equipment business units, benefited from modest same-store sales growth, with profits slightly higher. The Retail division experienced a decline in same-store sales, with profits flat, due especially to first-half COVID lockdowns. New Zealand operations too were affected by the pandemic, with revenues and profits just a little higher.

Outlook

Bapcor is a leader in the supply of a huge range of auto parts to more than 30 000 auto workshop customers, and this business is expected to continue to grow as the population increases and as the average age of cars in Australia slowly rises. It plans a steady rollout of new stores and is also seeking to grow by acquisition. It sees significant growth potential in Thailand, although the impact of COVID means it has so far opened just six stores there. It has taken a 25 per cent equity stake in Singapore automotive parts distributor Tye Soon, which has operations in Singapore, Malaysia, Thailand and South Korea. Bapcor views this investment as an opportunity to develop a network of Asian businesses. It regards inventory availability as a key competitive advantage, and is investing in state-of-the-art centralised distribution centres in several locations. It has opened its first in Victoria, replacing 13 smaller regional centres, with significant cost benefits. A second centre is under construction in Queensland.

Year to 30 June	2021	2022
Revenues ($mn)	1761.7	1841.9
Specialist wholesale (%)	36	36
Trade (%)	35	35
Retail (%)	20	20
Bapcor New Zealand (%)	9	9
EBIT ($mn)	200.9	205.6
EBIT margin (%)	11.4	11.2
Gross margin (%)	46.1	46.7
Profit before tax ($mn)	186.0	186.5
Profit after tax ($mn)	130.1	131.6
Earnings per share (c)	38.33	38.77
Cash flow per share (c)	63.49	64.93
Dividend (c)	20	21.5
Percentage franked	100	100
Net tangible assets per share ($)	0.82	0.92
Interest cover (times)	13.4	10.7
Return on equity (%)	12.9	12.3
Debt-to-equity ratio (%)	15.8	24.4
Current ratio	1.9	2.4

Beach Energy Limited

ASX code: BPT   www.beachenergy.com.au

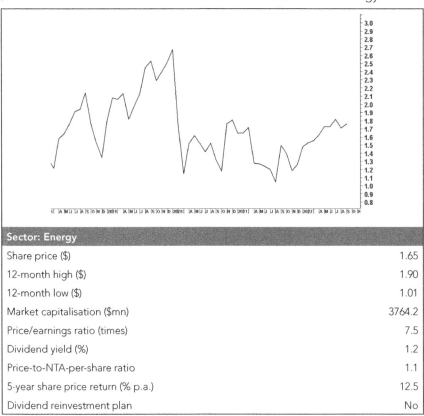

Sector: Energy	
Share price ($)	1.65
12-month high ($)	1.90
12-month low ($)	1.01
Market capitalisation ($mn)	3764.2
Price/earnings ratio (times)	7.5
Dividend yield (%)	1.2
Price-to-NTA-per-share ratio	1.1
5-year share price return (% p.a.)	12.5
Dividend reinvestment plan	No

Adelaide-based Beach Energy, with a history dating back to 1961, is a major oil and gas producer, and a key supplier of gas to eastern states. Its operations are concentrated on five production hubs — the Cooper/Eromanga Basin region of South Australia and Queensland, the Bass Basin in the Bass Strait, the Otway Basin of Victoria and South Australia, the Perth Basin and the Taranaki Basin in New Zealand. It also maintains an active exploration and development program in other areas of Australia and New Zealand. Seven Group Holdings owns more than 30 per cent of Beach's equity.

Latest business results (June 2022, full year)

Higher oil and gas prices offset reduced production, and revenues and profits were up, reversing two years of declines. Total production of 21.8 million barrels of oil equivalent (boe) fell from 25.6 million barrels in the previous year, due mainly to natural field decline. The average realised oil price of $140 per barrel was up sharply from $78.10, with the average realised gas/ethane price up 10 per cent. Having substantially reduced its debt levels, Beach at June 2022 held a net cash position of $167 million.

Outlook

Beach is working to boost its output, with a production target of 28 million boe in the June 2024 year. However, it expects little growth for June 2023, forecasting production of 20 million boe to 22.5 million boe, with capital spending of $800 million to $1 billion, compared with $872 million in the June 2022 year. Unit field operating costs are forecast to rise from $11.74 per boe to $12 to $13 per boe. In July 2022 Beach completed a major seven-well drilling project in the Otway Basin, delivering one new gas discovery and six development wells, and these are being connected to the Otway Gas Plant. It is also planning its next nearshore and offshore Otway exploration programs. It is preparing to drill the Yolla West infield well in the Bass Basin and the Kupe development well in the Taranaki Basin. It also has ongoing oil and gas exploration, appraisal and development drilling in the Cooper Basin. Thanks to its work in the Perth Basin, the company expects to enter the global liquefied natural gas (LNG) market in 2023, as LNG exports begin from the Waitsia Gas Project, which is operated by Mitsui E&P Australia. In August 2022 Beach announced that it had entered into a five-year LNG sales contract with BP. It also plans a new Perth Basin gas exploration program.

Year to 30 June	2021	2022
Revenues ($mn)	1562.0	1771.4
EBIT ($mn)	523.5	730.1
EBIT margin (%)	33.5	41.2
Gross margin (%)	38.1	43.8
Profit before tax ($mn)	518.0	716.6
Profit after tax ($mn)	363.0	504.0
Earnings per share (c)	15.92	22.11
Cash flow per share (c)	34.74	38.60
Dividend (c)	2	2
Percentage franked	100	100
Net tangible assets per share ($)	1.32	1.52
Interest cover (times)	95.2	54.1
Return on equity (%)	12.3	15.2
Debt-to-equity ratio (%)	1.5	~
Current ratio	1.7	1.4

Beacon Lighting Group Limited

ASX code: BLX　　　　　　　　　　　www.beaconlighting.com.au

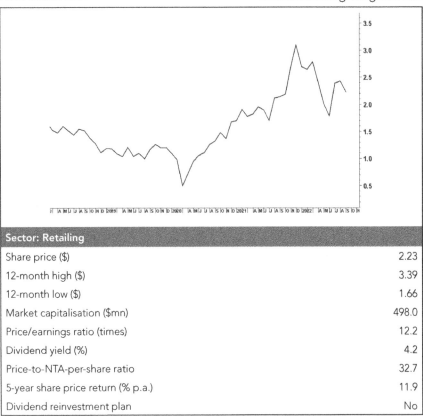

Sector: Retailing	
Share price ($)	2.23
12-month high ($)	3.39
12-month low ($)	1.66
Market capitalisation ($mn)	498.0
Price/earnings ratio (times)	12.2
Dividend yield (%)	4.2
Price-to-NTA-per-share ratio	32.7
5-year share price return (% p.a.)	11.9
Dividend reinvestment plan	No

Melbourne-based lighting specialist Beacon dates back to the launch of the first Beacon Lighting store in 1967. It steadily expanded throughout Australia, and today has 119 stores — two of them franchised — supplying a wide range of lighting fixtures and light globes, as well as ceiling fans. Its Beacon Commercial division supplies many commercial projects, including volume residential developments, apartment complexes, aged care facilities, hotels and retail fit-outs. It also operates sales offices in Hong Kong, Germany and the US, with a support office in China.

Latest business results (June 2022, full year)

Beacon overcame COVID lockdowns early in the year, and then supply chain disruptions, to post a rise in its sales and profits. There was like-for-like sales growth of 0.3 per cent at its stores, with a solid second half offsetting a first-half decline. Victoria and Western Australia were the best-performing states. Online sales grew by 31.3 per cent to $34.1 million. Beacon International sales increased by 27.9 per cent to $15.7 million and Beacon Commercial sales grew by 15.8 per cent. During the year the company opened five new stores.

Outlook

Beacon's business is closely linked to trends in the housing market, which recently has been strong, although it has been starting to show some signs of impending weakness. It plans to continue opening new stores and introducing new products, and has developed a variety of further schemes for long-term growth. Its key strategy is an emphasis on developing its commercial business, estimating the trade market in Australia for its products as worth $2.1 billion annually. It is opening its stores at 7:30 am and has launched a dedicated trade marketing program, with the development of trade-specific products and the introduction of a trade desk and a specialist trade consultant at each store. Sales to members of the Beacon Trade Club loyalty program rose by 24 per cent in the June 2022 year. Another strategy is the promotion of online business, and it has been upgrading its websites in anticipation of continuing strong demand. It is also working to boost exports. It is now selling ceiling fans to consumers in the US, and has launched a sales channel on Tmall.com in China. Its Connected Light Solutions business supplies outdoor lighting for a variety of urban applications and saw 23.8 per cent growth in the June 2022 year. Masson for Light works with architects to supply designer lights for prestige construction projects, and enjoyed 32.4 per cent growth.

Year to 26 June*	2021	2022
Revenues ($mn)	289.3	304.8
EBIT ($mn)	59.3	63.6
EBIT margin (%)	20.5	20.9
Gross margin (%)	68.4	69.1
Profit before tax ($mn)	53.8	58.0
Profit after tax ($mn)	37.6	40.7
Earnings per share (c)	16.93	18.24
Cash flow per share (c)	28.83	31.18
Dividend (c)	8.8	9.3
Percentage franked	100	100
Net tangible assets per share ($)	~	0.07
Interest cover (times)	10.7	11.4
Return on equity (%)	37.8	33.1
Debt-to-equity ratio (%)	~	~
Current ratio	1.4	1.5

*27 June 2021

BHP Group Limited

www.bhp.com

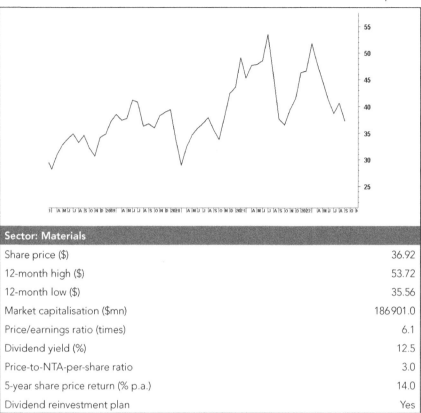

Sector: Materials	
Share price ($)	36.92
12-month high ($)	53.72
12-month low ($)	35.56
Market capitalisation ($mn)	186901.0
Price/earnings ratio (times)	6.1
Dividend yield (%)	12.5
Price-to-NTA-per-share ratio	3.0
5-year share price return (% p.a.)	14.0
Dividend reinvestment plan	Yes

Melbourne-based resources giant BHP was founded as Broken Hill Proprietary in 1885. In 2001 it merged with another resources major, Billiton, which dated back to 1851. Today it segments its operations into five broad product areas — iron ore, copper, coal, nickel and potash — with activities in many countries. It has sold its oil and gas interests to Woodside Petroleum. In August 2022 it announced a takeover bid for South Australian copper miner Oz Minerals.

Latest business results (June 2022, full year)

Surging coal prices generated a substantial boost in revenues and profits, easily offsetting a modest decline in BHP's mainstay iron ore business. Coal revenues trebled, with underlying EBIT, which had been in the red in the June 2021 year, soaring to US$8.7 billion. Copper revenues rose 7 per cent, thanks to higher prices, but profits fell as costs rose. Lower prices sent iron ore revenues down 11 per cent, with EBIT falling 20 per cent. Nevertheless, the company's low production costs for iron ore meant that it still contributed 56 per cent of BHP's total EBIT. The company's oil and gas operations, following their sale, have been treated as a discontinued business, and are not included in the figures in this book. The previous year's figures have been restated to exclude this business. Note that BHP reports its results in US dollars. The Australian dollar figures in this book — converted at prevailing exchange rates — are for guidance only.

Outlook

BHP is restructuring its operations in order to gain greater exposure to what it believes are mega-trends of decarbonisation and electrification, with an exploration program that is focused on copper and nickel. It is boosting copper production at its Escondida and Spence projects in Chile, and its takeover bid for Oz Minerals is also intended to enhance its copper exposure. It forecasts long-term escalating demand for nickel from the electric vehicle industry, and is exploring ways to increase the scale of its Nickel West project in Western Australia. It also expects over the medium term to increase its Western Australian iron ore production. It is spending US$5.7 billion for its Jansen potash project in Canada, with initial production expected from 2027, in order to meet global fertiliser demand that the company believes could double from present levels by the 2040s. It has sold its interests in two coal businesses, Cerrejón and BHP Mitsui Coal, and will cease mining at its New South Wales Energy Coal project by 2030.

Year to 30 June	2021	2022
Revenues ($mn)	74 896.1	89 175.3
Iron ore (%)	61	47
Copper (%)	28	26
Coal (%)	9	24
EBIT ($mn)	33 572.4	46 720.5
EBIT margin (%)	44.8	52.4
Profit before tax ($mn)	31 963.2	45 393.2
Profit after tax ($mn)	17 994.7	30 684.9
Earnings per share (c)	355.84	606.30
Cash flow per share (c)	488.12	760.12
Dividend (c)	396.05	463.14
Percentage franked	100	100
Net tangible assets per share ($)	13.14	12.48
Interest cover (times)	20.9	35.2
Return on equity (%)	26.1	46.0
Debt-to-equity ratio (%)	10.3	~
Current ratio	1.6	1.7

BlueScope Steel Limited

ASX code: BSL   www.bluescope.com

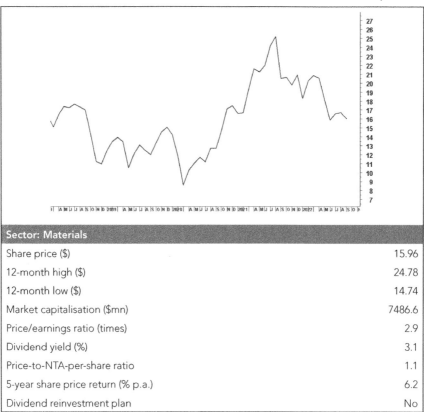

Sector: Materials	
Share price ($)	15.96
12-month high ($)	24.78
12-month low ($)	14.74
Market capitalisation ($mn)	7486.6
Price/earnings ratio (times)	2.9
Dividend yield (%)	3.1
Price-to-NTA-per-share ratio	1.1
5-year share price return (% p.a.)	6.2
Dividend reinvestment plan	No

Melbourne-based BlueScope Steel, originally a division of BHP, was established as an independent company in 2002. It is a major international producer of steel products for a wide variety of industrial applications. It is one of the world's largest manufacturers of painted and coated steel products, including Colorbond roofing materials. The company is structured into five businesses. Australian Steel Products operates the country's largest steelworks at Port Kembla, with a focus on the building and construction industry. North Star BlueScope Steel is a leading American producer of hot rolled coil. Building Products Asia and North America comprises metal coating, painting and roll-forming businesses. Buildings and Coated Products North America services low-rise non-residential customers. The New Zealand and Pacific Islands division operates production facilities in New Zealand, Fiji, New Caledonia and Vanuatu.

Latest business results (June 2022, full year)

Higher global steel prices, strong demand and US dollar strength easily offset rising costs to help generate a superb result for BlueScope, with profits more than doubling from the previous year. The core Australian Steel Products division benefited from a buoyant domestic building and construction environment, with higher value products particularly in demand. The North Star business was a beneficiary of strong US construction demand, with most other sectors also returning to pre-COVID levels, and an 89 per cent rise in revenues delivered a 180 per cent increase in profits. Though just 23 per cent of BlueScope's turnover, North Star contributed 47 per cent of company EBIT. Higher sales prices pushed revenues and profits higher for the New Zealand and Pacific Islands division, despite reduced demand.

Outlook

BlueScope occupies a solid position within the Australian economy, and to a lesser extent within the economies of the US and Asia. Its fortunes will be greatly affected by economic trends in these regions. It is also influenced by global steel prices, currency rate trends and raw material prices. It is planning some major expansions to its operations, particularly in the US, where it benefits from energy costs substantially below those in Australia. It is especially optimistic about the growth potential of its North Star steel mill in the US and is considering a new hot strip mill with a production capacity of 500 000 tonnes per annum. In June 2022 it completed the $717 million acquisition of America's second-largest metal coil painting operation. It has appointed a renowned international urban design firm to devise a masterplan for 200 hectares of surplus land adjacent to the Port Kembla Steelworks.

Year to 30 June	2021	2022
Revenues ($mn)	12 872.9	19 029.9
Australian steel products (%)	43	42
North Star BlueScope Steel (%)	18	23
Building products Asia & North America (%)	24	22
Buildings & coated products North America (%)	8	8
New Zealand & Pacific Islands (%)	7	5
EBIT ($mn)	1723.8	3787.2
EBIT margin (%)	13.4	19.9
Profit before tax ($mn)	1662.1	3729.2
Profit after tax ($mn)	1166.3	2701.1
Earnings per share (c)	231.60	549.36
Cash flow per share (c)	328.24	661.12
Dividend (c)	31	50
Percentage franked	0	0
Net tangible assets per share ($)	11.37	14.83
Interest cover (times)	27.9	65.3
Return on equity (%)	16.5	31.0
Debt-to-equity ratio (%)	~	~
Current ratio	1.9	1.7

Breville Group Limited

ASX code: BRG　　　　　　　　　www.brevillegroup.com

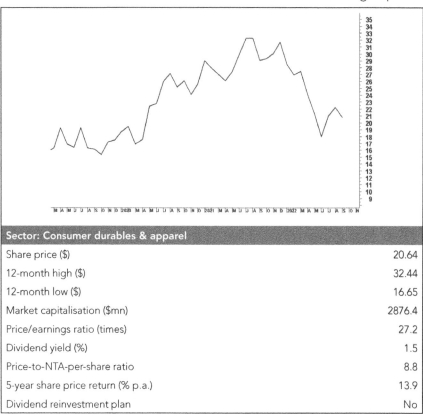

Sector: Consumer durables & apparel	
Share price ($)	20.64
12-month high ($)	32.44
12-month low ($)	16.65
Market capitalisation ($mn)	2876.4
Price/earnings ratio (times)	27.2
Dividend yield (%)	1.5
Price-to-NTA-per-share ratio	8.8
5-year share price return (% p.a.)	13.9
Dividend reinvestment plan	No

Sydney-based Breville Group traces its origins to the production of the first Breville radio in 1932. It later moved into the home appliance business and was subsequently acquired by Housewares International. In 2008 Housewares changed its name to Breville Group, and today the company is a leading designer and distributor of kitchen home appliances under various brands, including Breville, Sage, Baratza, Polyscience and Kambrook. Breville sells its products in some 80 countries, and international business is responsible for around 80 per cent of company turnover. Premier Investments hold 28 per cent of Breville's equity. In July 2022 the company acquired the Italian premium coffee-making equipment manufacturer Lelit.

Latest business results (June 2022, full year)

Breville enjoyed another solid year of double-digit sales and profit expansion, though with a slowing of growth in the second half as demand fell in Europe. Breville segments its operations into two broad divisions, Global Product and Distribution. The former, responsible for the sale of products designed and developed by Breville, again generated more than 80 per cent of company turnover, with revenues up 20 per cent — 18 per cent on a constant currency basis — and gross profit rising by 18 per cent. Booming sales in the US more than offset the second-half slowdown in Europe. The Distribution division sells products designed and developed by third parties, including Nespresso coffee equipment. It achieved sales growth of 18 per cent, with gross profit up 12.5 per cent.

Outlook

Breville has been achieving great success with its strategy of developing its own lines of premium home appliances for the North American, European and Australia/New Zealand markets. North America alone now represents half of company revenues and Europe has passed Australia/New Zealand as the second-largest region. The company continues steadily to enter new markets. During 2022 it launched sales in Poland and also made its first direct entry into Asia with the start of business in South Korea. The company is boosting its product development budget and is realising particular success with new coffee machines, sous vide cookers and air fryer products. It regards coffee in particular as offering great potential, and its $169 million acquisition of Lelit follows the purchase in 2020 of coffee grinder manufacturer Baratza. Lelit produces premium espresso machines for both home and café use, and the acquisition makes Breville a force in the international specialty coffee equipment sector. However, it faces challenges of rising costs, supply chain problems and a possible slowdown in consumer spending.

Year to 30 June	2021	2022
Revenues ($mn)	1187.7	1418.4
EBIT ($mn)	134.2	153.8
EBIT margin (%)	11.3	10.8
Gross margin (%)	34.8	34.3
Profit before tax ($mn)	127.4	147.8
Profit after tax ($mn)	91.0	105.7
Earnings per share (c)	65.76	75.89
Cash flow per share (c)	85.18	97.77
Dividend (c)	26.5	30
Percentage franked	100	100
Net tangible assets per share ($)	1.84	2.36
Interest cover (times)	19.8	25.9
Return on equity (%)	19.7	18.9
Debt-to-equity ratio (%)	~	0.7
Current ratio	2.2	2.5

Brickworks Limited

ASX code: BKW   investors.brickworks.com.au

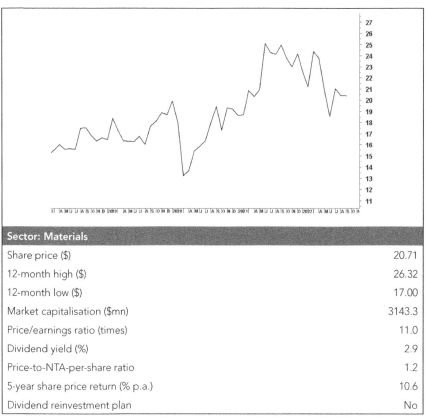

Sector: Materials	
Share price ($)	20.71
12-month high ($)	26.32
12-month low ($)	17.00
Market capitalisation ($mn)	3143.3
Price/earnings ratio (times)	11.0
Dividend yield (%)	2.9
Price-to-NTA-per-share ratio	1.2
5-year share price return (% p.a.)	10.6
Dividend reinvestment plan	No

Sydney-based Brickworks, founded in 1934, is one of Australia's largest manufacturers of building products used especially in the home construction sector. Its brands include Austral Bricks, Austral Masonry, Austral Precast, Bristile Roofing, Bowral Bricks, Nubrik, GB Masonry and UrbanStone. Since 2018 it has been building up a portfolio of American brick-making assets, and it is now also a leading producer of bricks in the north-east United States. In Australia it manages an extensive land portfolio, based on surplus and redundant building product sites, and it operates an industrial property trust in a joint venture with Goodman. In a cross-shareholding arrangement, it owns 26 per cent of the equity of Washington H. Soul Pattinson, while Soul Pattinson owns 44 per cent of the equity in Brickworks.

Latest business results (January 2022, half year)

Its property and investment activities combined to generate a powerful result, with an additional boost from domestic construction material operations. In fact, the Property division contributed more than three-quarters of company earnings for the period, including a significant revaluation profit. The division also posted a large development profit, thanks in part to the completion of work on a major 200 000-square-metre Sydney warehouse for Amazon, the largest warehouse ever built in Australia. The

Investments division—essentially the shareholding in Washington H. Soul Pattinson—also realised a strong surge in profits. The Building Products Australia division saw EBIT rise 66 per cent, with a particularly strong result from Austral Bricks and very strong demand in Queensland. The company was able to boost margins, with price increases and improved production efficiencies more than offsetting supply chain difficulties and inflationary pressures. North American brick sales continued to grow, but profits were down, hit by pandemic-related interruptions to operations and rising costs. Brickworks also reported a large, significant profit—not included in the figures in these pages—related mainly to the merger during the period of Washington H. Soul Pattinson with Milton Corporation.

Outlook

Domestic building material demand remains strong, although the company has noted signs of a looming slowdown, with rising interest rates, a decline in building approvals and lower levels of immigration. Profits for American brick-making operations remain low, but Brickworks is confident it can deliver long-term earnings growth through its strategies of rationalisation, plant upgrades and premium product positioning. However, with property and investments together currently generating more than 90 per cent of EBIT, it is these businesses that will likely have the most near-term impact on profit trends for the company.

Year to 31 July	2020	2021
Revenues ($mn)	949.9	890.3
EBIT ($mn)	205.8	386.2
EBIT margin (%)	21.7	43.4
Gross margin (%)	28.7	28.7
Profit before tax ($mn)	179.8	364.4
Profit after tax ($mn)	146.3	285.2
Earnings per share (c)	97.59	188.77
Cash flow per share (c)	147.55	235.34
Dividend (c)	59	61
Percentage franked	100	100
Interest cover (times)	7.9	17.7
Return on equity (%)	6.4	11.7
Half year to 31 January	2021	2022
Revenues ($mn)	431.7	535.0
Profit before tax ($mn)	116.6	440.5
Profit after tax ($mn)	89.6	330.5
Earnings per share (c)	59.79	217.85
Dividend (c)	21	22
Percentage franked	100	100
Net tangible assets per share ($)	13.84	16.75
Debt-to-equity ratio (%)	20.0	20.9
Current ratio	2.2	2.3

Carsales.com Limited

ASX code: CAR   shareholder.carsales.com.au

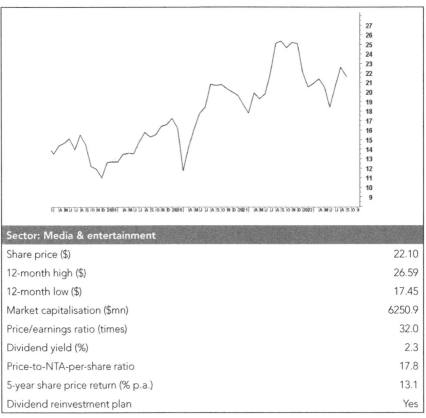

Sector: Media & entertainment	
Share price ($)	22.10
12-month high ($)	26.59
12-month low ($)	17.45
Market capitalisation ($mn)	6250.9
Price/earnings ratio (times)	32.0
Dividend yield (%)	2.3
Price-to-NTA-per-share ratio	17.8
5-year share price return (% p.a.)	13.1
Dividend reinvestment plan	Yes

Carsales.com was founded in Melbourne in 1997 and has grown to become the market leader in online automotive advertising. It also operates specialist websites for the sale of a variety of other goods, including boats, motorcycles, trucks, construction equipment, farm machinery, caravans and tyres. It has expanded abroad, with interests in automotive businesses in the US, Asia and Latin America, and overseas business now represents more than a third of total turnover. A smaller division provides a diverse range of data services for customers, including software as a service, research and reporting, valuations, appraisals, website development and photography services. It has acquired the US online marketplace Trader Interactive.

Latest business results (June 2022, full year)

Revenues and underlying profits grew, with a solid domestic performance, thanks to an upbeat used car market, and a notable contribution from the new Trader Interactive acquisition. The core Australian online advertising services business benefited as car buyers increasingly turned to second-hand models, due to shortages of new vehicles. A new reporting segment called Australia — carsales investments, and incorporating online tyre wholesale and retail businesses and inspection services, saw revenues up strongly, thanks to an acquisition, but was in the red. The company's international operations achieved double-digit growth in sales and profits, thanks to the 2021 acquisition of a 49 per cent stake in Trader Interactive and good performances from investments in South Korea and Brazil.

Outlook

Carsales.com operates domestically in a largely mature market in which it has a dominant market share. It believes underlying market conditions remain solid, and it continues to tweak its products in order to achieve growth. It expects the increased penetration of premium products to contribute to stronger revenues and profits in the June 2023 year. It also expects continuing strong progress in its Korean Encar business, which is that country's leader in automotive classifieds. Its largest investment in Latin America is in Brazil's Webmotors, whose operations were hurt by the COVID pandemic. This business is now recovering and Carsales expects growth to accelerate. In 2021 Carsales acquired a 49 per cent holding in Trader Interactive for $800 million, and in mid-2022 it announced the planned $1.17 billion acquisition of the remaining 51 per cent. Trader Interactive is an American leader in the provision of digital markets for commercial and recreational vehicles and industrial equipment, and Carsales.com believes it can use its own technology to build on these businesses. With the acquisition completed, international operations will represent nearly half of total company turnover.

Year to 30 June	2021	2022
Revenues ($mn)	427.2	509.1
Australia — online advertising services (%)	63	60
Asia (%)	20	19
Australia — carsales investments (%)	6	11
Australia — data, research & services (%)	9	9
EBIT ($mn)	226.6	273.1
EBIT margin (%)	53.0	53.6
Profit before tax ($mn)	212.7	259.5
Profit after tax ($mn)	152.8	194.8
Earnings per share (c)	61.53	68.96
Cash flow per share (c)	77.72	85.49
Dividend (c)	47.5	50
Percentage franked	100	100
Net tangible assets per share ($)	1.01	1.24
Interest cover (times)	12.1	15.8
Return on equity (%)	24.9	20.0
Debt-to-equity ratio (%)	~	52.5
Current ratio	4.2	1.7

Clinuvel Pharmaceuticals Limited

ASX code: CUV   www.clinuvel.com

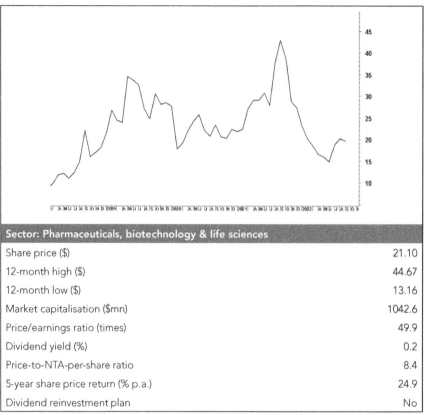

Sector: Pharmaceuticals, biotechnology & life sciences	
Share price ($)	21.10
12-month high ($)	44.67
12-month low ($)	13.16
Market capitalisation ($mn)	1042.6
Price/earnings ratio (times)	49.9
Dividend yield (%)	0.2
Price-to-NTA-per-share ratio	8.4
5-year share price return (% p.a.)	24.9
Dividend reinvestment plan	No

Melbourne-based biopharmaceutical company Clinuvel dates back to 1987, when scientists devised technologies for the protection of skin using human hormones. Today it is a global company with a focus on developing drugs for the treatment of various skin disorders. Its lead therapy afamelanotide — known as Scenesse — has been shown to be effective in treating severe phototoxicity — intolerance of light — in many severely affected patients. It has been approved by regulators for commercial distribution in Europe, the US, Israel and Australia. The company is also developing other drugs. Clinuvel operates from offices in Australia, Switzerland, Ireland, the UK, Singapore and the US.

Latest business results (June 2022, full year)

Revenues and profits generally rose, thanks to fast-growing demand for Scenesse in the markets where it has been approved. However, the after-tax profit fell, due to a substantially higher tax bill, the result of a large deferred tax expense charge. Expenses grew by 44 per cent, with the wage bill and the cost of materials rising and a big jump in share-based payments.

Outlook

Scenesse reduces the severity of phototoxic skin reactions in patients with a rare light intolerance condition known as erythropoietic protoporphyria. Such patients can experience severe pain from sun exposure, as well as swelling and scarring of exposed areas of the body such as the face and hands, with hospitalisation and powerful pain killers sometimes necessary. Scenesse is the first drug developed for this condition. Following regulatory approval it was launched in Europe in 2016 and in the US in 2020, and the company is actively seeking to have it approved in other countries. Clinuvel is also involved in a series of drug trials. It has launched tests in the US to determine whether Scenesse can be used to treat vitiligo, a skin disorder where patches of skin become pale or white. Its DNA repair program is aimed particularly at developing treatments for patients with the hereditary disorder xeroderma pigmentosum, which involves extreme sensitivity to sunlight. It is also working on the development of a range of over-the-counter skin protection products, based on Scenesse. In 2020 it announced the development of a new drug, Prénumbra, a liquid formulation of Scenesse, and has begun studies on using this drug in the treatment of arterial ischaemic stroke. It is developing a third drug, Neuracthel, which it believes could have applications in the treatment of neurological, endocrinological and degenerative diseases. At June 2022 Clinuvel had no debt and more than $120 million in cash holdings.

Year to 30 June	2021	2022
Revenues ($mn)	48.0	65.7
EBIT ($mn)	25.4	34.1
EBIT margin (%)	52.9	51.9
Profit before tax ($mn)	25.7	34.3
Profit after tax ($mn)	24.7	20.9
Earnings per share (c)	50.05	42.25
Cash flow per share (c)	51.79	43.79
Dividend (c)	2.5	4
Percentage franked	0	100
Net tangible assets per share ($)	1.97	2.51
Interest cover (times)	~	~
Return on equity (%)	29.0	18.6
Debt-to-equity ratio (%)	~	~
Current ratio	11.8	10.2

Clover Corporation Limited

ASX code: CLV

www.clovercorp.com.au

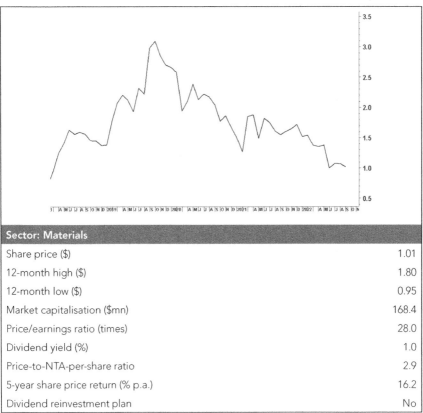

Sector: Materials	
Share price ($)	1.01
12-month high ($)	1.80
12-month low ($)	0.95
Market capitalisation ($mn)	168.4
Price/earnings ratio (times)	28.0
Dividend yield (%)	1.0
Price-to-NTA-per-share ratio	2.9
5-year share price return (% p.a.)	16.2
Dividend reinvestment plan	No

Melbourne-based Clover, founded in 1988 as a family-owned company, develops value-added nutrients for use in foods or as nutritional supplements. Its key product is docosahexaenoic acid, a form of omega 3. It sells this under the Nu-Mega and Ocean Gold range of tuna oils. It also markets nutritional oil powders, based on technology developed by the Commonwealth Scientific and Industrial Research Organisation (CSIRO). In addition, the company has developed technology that allows nutritional oils to be added to infant formula, foods and beverages. Overseas customers account for around two-thirds of company sales.

Latest business results (January 2022, half year)

Sales revenues edged up but profits were down. However, the company attributed this to one-off expenses associated with legal action to protect its intellectual property and delays in opening its joint venture Melody Dairies spray drying facility in New Zealand. Without these costs its profit would have been in line with the January 2021 period. The important Asian market, representing more than 40 per cent of total company turnover, achieved double-digit growth in sales. Exports to the Americas also grew. But the Australia/New Zealand and Europe segments both experienced weaker demand. Much domestic demand represents sales to Chinese buyers—including students and tourists—who purchase infant formula for resale to customers in China. However, the pandemic has led to a precipitous decline in both tourist and international student numbers, while at the same time the Chinese market has become more competitive.

Outlook

Clover believes its business has bottomed, and it expects a steady recovery. With travel restrictions starting to ease it has been hiring additional sales staff, with the aim of seeking out new business opportunities overseas. It has also been placing new products on trial with target customers with the aim of expanding markets it already serves in the medical foods, general food and drinks, and nutraceuticals segments. The relocation of Clover's R&D facilities to larger premises in Brisbane will help accelerate the introduction of new products. It sees infant formula as providing particularly strong growth potential for its microencapsulated powders, and has been developing relationships with leading manufacturers across Europe and China. It has achieved some initial trial orders from China, and expects the Chinese market to expand considerably when the licensing process is completed in 2023. In March 2022 Clover announced the settlement of its intellectual property legal action, and expects to receive more than $1.4 million in damages and legal costs.

Year to 31 July	2020	2021
Revenues ($mn)	88.3	60.5
EBIT ($mn)	18.2	8.6
EBIT margin (%)	20.7	14.2
Profit before tax ($mn)	17.7	8.2
Profit after tax ($mn)	12.5	6.0
Earnings per share (c)	7.51	3.61
Cash flow per share (c)	7.92	4.04
Dividend (c)	2.5	1
Percentage franked	100	100
Interest cover (times)	31.1	21.4
Return on equity (%)	24.3	10.4
Half year to 31 January	2021	2022
Revenues ($mn)	29.4	29.7
Profit before tax ($mn)	3.3	2.8
Profit after tax ($mn)	2.5	2.0
Earnings per share (c)	1.51	1.21
Dividend (c)	0.5	0.5
Percentage franked	100	100
Net tangible assets per share ($)	0.32	0.34
Debt-to-equity ratio (%)	7.1	7.0
Current ratio	8.0	6.9

Cochlear Limited

ASX code: COH

www.cochlear.com

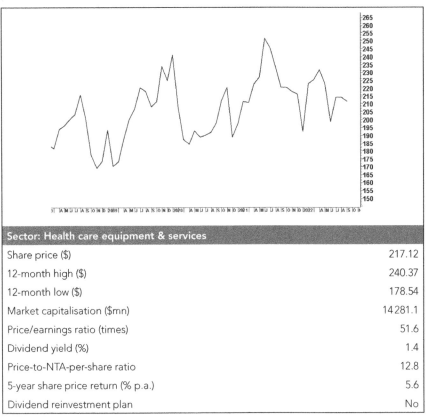

Sector: Health care equipment & services

Share price ($)	217.12
12-month high ($)	240.37
12-month low ($)	178.54
Market capitalisation ($mn)	14 281.1
Price/earnings ratio (times)	51.6
Dividend yield (%)	1.4
Price-to-NTA-per-share ratio	12.8
5-year share price return (% p.a.)	5.6
Dividend reinvestment plan	No

Sydney-based Cochlear, founded in 1981, has around 60 per cent of the world market for cochlear bionic-ear implants, which are intended to assist the communication ability of people suffering from severe hearing impediments. It also sells the Baha bone-anchored hearing implant, as well as a range of acoustic products. With manufacturing facilities and technology centres in Australia, Sweden, Belgium, China and the US, it has sales in over 180 countries, and overseas business accounts for more than 90 per cent of revenues and profits. It has announced the acquisition of Danish hearing implant manufacturer Oticon Medical.

Latest business results (June 2022, full year)

Sales and profits rose again, having crashed two years earlier when the COVID-19 pandemic halted elective surgery in many countries. Cochlear implant sales rose 5 per cent to 38 182 units, with revenues up 3 per cent, and some notably strong growth in China and the Middle East. Services revenues rose 15 per cent, especially for sound processor upgrades, as a result of the reopening of some clinics after COVID lockdowns. Acoustics revenues jumped 28 per cent, thanks to new products and a recovery from COVID-related surgery delays. A 15 per cent increase in operating expenses included a substantial investment in cloud computing operations. Research and development costs rose 8 per cent to $211 million.

Outlook

Cochlear continues to launch new products at an impressive rate, with a high level of research and development, and this is helping it maintain its market leadership. It sees great potential for its newly launched Nucleus 8 sound processor. A particular recent marketing focus has been adults and seniors in developed markets, which it regards as its biggest opportunity, given the large and growing market size and a current penetration rate of only about 3 per cent. The company points to research suggesting that good hearing is an important contributor to healthy ageing. Another key target is children in emerging markets. It is investing as much as $150 million over four to five years on a cloud-based transformation program aimed at boosting efficiency, and this will constrain profit growth. Its $170 million acquisition of Oticon Medical, a major international manufacturer of hearing implants, will provide Cochlear with greater scale in its operations. It is expected to add $75 million to $80 million to annual revenues, although Oticon is currently running at a loss. Cochlear's early June 2023 forecast is for strong growth in sales and an after-tax profit of $290 million to $305 million.

Year to 30 June	2021	2022
Revenues ($mn)	1497.6	1648.3
Cochlear implants (%)	60	57
Services (%)	29	31
Acoustics (%)	11	12
EBIT ($mn)	326.3	382.7
EBIT margin (%)	21.8	23.2
Gross margin (%)	72.0	74.6
Profit before tax ($mn)	317.9	376.5
Profit after tax ($mn)	234.0	277.0
Earnings per share (c)	356.23	421.16
Cash flow per share (c)	472.54	532.15
Dividend (c)	255	300
Percentage franked	0	19
Net tangible assets per share ($)	17.15	16.94
Interest cover (times)	38.8	61.7
Return on equity (%)	15.1	16.4
Debt-to-equity ratio (%)	~	~
Current ratio	3.1	2.5

Codan Limited

ASX code: CDA www.codan.com.au

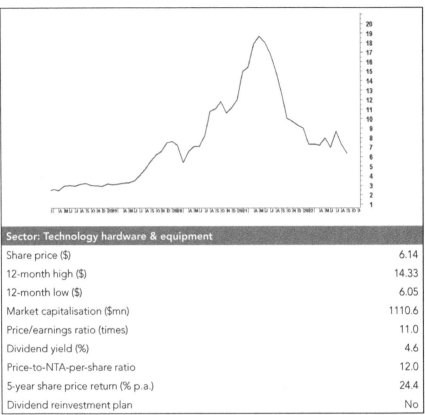

Sector: Technology hardware & equipment	
Share price ($)	6.14
12-month high ($)	14.33
12-month low ($)	6.05
Market capitalisation ($mn)	1110.6
Price/earnings ratio (times)	11.0
Dividend yield (%)	4.6
Price-to-NTA-per-share ratio	12.0
5-year share price return (% p.a.)	24.4
Dividend reinvestment plan	No

Adelaide electronics company Codan was founded in 1959. It is a leading world manufacturer of metal-detecting products, including metal detectors for hobbyists, gold detectors for small-scale miners and landmine detectors for humanitarian applications. A second division produces high-frequency communication radios for military and humanitarian use. Codan sells to more than 150 countries, and overseas sales represent more than 90 per cent of company revenues. In 2021 it acquired two American communication technology companies, Domo Tactical Communications (DTC) and Zetron, and the British company Broadcast Wireless Systems.

Latest business results (June 2022, full year)

Its 2021 acquisitions helped Codan to a solid rise in revenues, and there was also modest profit expansion. Its metal detection business has in recent years powered some impressive growth, but this year sales fell 20 per cent, with profits down 15 per cent. In part this reflected a decision by Codan to pass on rising costs to customers, constraining demand. Sales to artisan gold miners in Africa fell. Recreational sales generally held firm, despite rising prices, some stock shortages and the cessation of sales into Russia. Communications division sales soared 153 per cent, thanks to the acquisitions, with profits more than trebling. There was strong demand for DTC products in military markets, including Codan's largest-ever order, worth $38 million. Zetron too secured some large contracts. Nevertheless, despite surging demand for Codan's communications products, the metal detection business remained more profitable, contributing about 70 per cent of total company profit.

Outlook

Codan is a significant force in two niche high-tech product areas. Its high-margin metal detectors dominate the African artisanal gold mining market, and it is also a significant force in recreational markets. It expects weakness to continue during much of 2022, but with a recovery coming in 2023 as it introduces new products and enters new markets. The Communications division held an order book of $149 million at June 2022, a 23 per cent increase from June 2021, and the company forecasts strong growth during the year. The acquisition of DTC transitions the company from offering customers a traditional voice-only platform for its tactical communications products to now including data and video. This has opened new markets for Codan, including law enforcement, intelligence, drones and broadcasting, though, given the rise in instability in the world, the company expects good growth from military customers. Zetron provides a full suite of integrated emergency response technologies and Codan expects significant cost synergies following the full integration of this business into its operations.

Year to 30 June	2021	2022
Revenues ($mn)	437.0	506.1
Metal detection (%)	75	52
Communications (%)	22	48
EBIT ($mn)	139.6	137.4
EBIT margin (%)	31.7	26.8
Gross margin (%)	55.6	56.6
Profit before tax ($mn)	138.7	135.7
Profit after tax ($mn)	97.3	100.7
Earnings per share (c)	53.92	55.71
Cash flow per share (c)	64.47	69.31
Dividend (c)	27	28
Percentage franked	100	100
Net tangible assets per share ($)	0.25	0.51
Interest cover (times)	389.6	129.4
Return on equity (%)	35.3	30.0
Debt-to-equity ratio (%)	0.5	8.0
Current ratio	1.1	1.7

Collins Foods Limited

ASX code: CKF www.collinsfoods.com

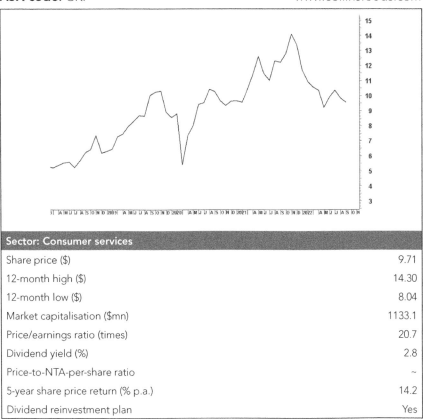

Sector: Consumer services	
Share price ($)	9.71
12-month high ($)	14.30
12-month low ($)	8.04
Market capitalisation ($mn)	1133.1
Price/earnings ratio (times)	20.7
Dividend yield (%)	2.8
Price-to-NTA-per-share ratio	~
5-year share price return (% p.a.)	14.2
Dividend reinvestment plan	Yes

Collins Foods, based in Brisbane, dates back to 1968 when it obtained the KFC fried chicken franchise for Queensland. Today it owns and operates KFC outlets across Australia, and is the country's largest KFC franchisee. It also owns KFC stores in Germany and the Netherlands. It has closed its Sizzler restaurant business in Australia, though continues to operate as a franchisor of Sizzler restaurants in Thailand and Japan. It has launched the Taco Bell Mexican restaurant brand in Australia.

Latest business results (May 2022, full year)

Collins achieved another year of rising sales and profits, thanks especially to strong growth in Europe and continuing solid demand in Australia. Revenues in Europe jumped 41 per cent to $190 million, with same-store growth of 16.8 per cent. Business in the previous year had been quite severely hurt by lockdowns. There was also a contribution from 15 restaurants acquired during the year in the Netherlands, and from the opening of three new restaurants in that country. Australia recorded same-store growth of 1.4 per cent — compared with 12.9 per cent in the preceding year — with an additional contribution from 10 new restaurants opened during the year. The launch of four new restaurants helped generate revenue growth of 27.5 per cent for Taco Bell, but same-store sales actually fell, and this business remained in the red. The small Sizzler Asia franchise business made a profit. At the end of the period the company operated 261 KFC restaurants in Australia, with a further 45 in the Netherlands and 17 in Germany. It also ran 20 Taco Bell restaurants in Australia. It operated as franchisor for 66 Sizzler restaurants in Asia.

Outlook

Having weathered significant disruptions from the COVID-19 pandemic, Collins now faces supply chain shortages and inflationary pressures. It has been raising menu prices in response, but expects some short-term margin pressure. Nevertheless, it believes the longer-term outlook is positive and plans a steady rollout of new restaurants. It continues to experience strong same-store growth in Europe and plans two to five new restaurants there in the May 2023 year. It has become the largest KFC franchisee in the Netherlands and expects to launch as many as 130 new restaurants in that country over the next 10 years. It also plans to open as many as 12 new Australian KFC restaurants in the May 2023 year, along with nine to 12 Taco Bell outlets. It has begun drone delivery trials in Brisbane.

Year to 1 May*	2021	2022
Revenues ($mn)	1065.9	1184.5
KFC restaurants Australia (%)	84	81
KFC restaurants Europe (%)	13	16
Taco Bell restaurants (%)	3	3
EBIT ($mn)	90.3	110.9
EBIT margin (%)	8.5	9.4
Gross margin (%)	52.4	52.3
Profit before tax ($mn)	60.9	80.7
Profit after tax ($mn)	37.3	54.8
Earnings per share (c)	31.97	46.96
Cash flow per share (c)	104.09	126.73
Dividend (c)	23	27
Percentage franked	100	100
Net tangible assets per share ($)	~	~
Interest cover (times)	3.1	3.7
Return on equity (%)	10.3	14.5
Debt-to-equity ratio (%)	48.4	44.2
Current ratio	0.8	0.7

*2 May 2021

Commonwealth Bank of Australia

ASX code: CBA   www.commbank.com.au

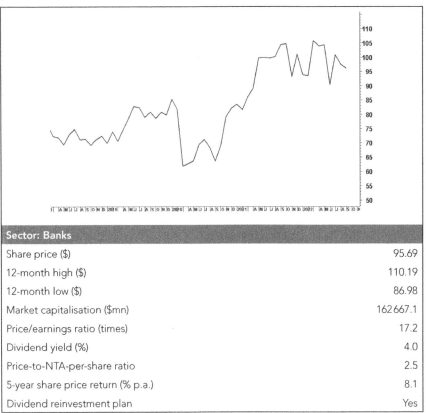

Sector: Banks	
Share price ($)	95.69
12-month high ($)	110.19
12-month low ($)	86.98
Market capitalisation ($mn)	162667.1
Price/earnings ratio (times)	17.2
Dividend yield (%)	4.0
Price-to-NTA-per-share ratio	2.5
5-year share price return (% p.a.)	8.1
Dividend reinvestment plan	Yes

The Commonwealth Bank, based in Sydney, was founded in 1911. It is today one of Australia's largest banks, and one of the country's top providers of home loans, personal loans and credit cards, as well as the largest holder of deposits. Commonwealth Securities is a prominent online stockbroker. It has significant interests in New Zealand through ASB Bank. It owns Bankwest in Western Australia.

Latest business results (June 2022, full year)

In a good result, the cash profit rose for a second successive year, after three straight years of decline. The core Retail Banking Services division enjoyed a 5 per cent rise in profits, thanks in particular to continuing strong home lending and deposit volumes, partly offset by a lower home loan interest margin. This business was also hurt by inflationary pressures. The Business Banking division achieved a 6 per cent rise in profits, with higher levels of business lending and deposit volumes, again partly offset by a lower interest margin. The smaller Institutional Banking and Markets division saw a 13 per cent profit increase, with an improved net interest margin and a reduced loan impairment expense offsetting lower deposits income. New Zealand profits rose 9 per cent. Productivity benefits helped offset the pressures of rising inflation, and the bank also benefited from a decrease in its loan impairment expense.

Outlook

Commonwealth Bank occupies a powerful position in the domestic economy as well as in the local banking industry. Thanks to a large branch network, offering many cross-selling opportunities, it has pricing power that has generally enabled it to maintain a cost advantage over some of its rivals. It is optimistic about the medium-term and long-term outlook for the economy. However, it has expressed wariness that rising interest rates and higher inflation will lead to short-term challenges. These include a slowdown in new mortgages and business lending, with high levels of competition in the mortgage market another adverse influence. It continues to work at reducing costs — in two years it has reduced the number of its branches from 1100 to 807 — though it could struggle in an environment of rising inflation. It is also working to boost its business banking arm, with 200 000 new business transaction accounts and 15 per cent growth in business deposits in the June 2022 year, although it continues to lag the market leader, National Australia Bank. It is also rolling out a range of new products that are designed to compete with smaller fintech companies.

Year to 30 June	2021	2022
Operating income ($mn)	24 104.0	24 935.0
Net interest income ($mn)	19 302.0	19 473.0
Operating expenses ($mn)	11 485.0	11 816.0
Profit before tax ($mn)	12 243.0	13 618.0
Profit after tax ($mn)	8653.0	9595.0
Earnings per share (c)	488.59	557.20
Dividend (c)	350	385
Percentage franked	100	100
Non-interest income to total income (%)	19.9	21.9
Net tangible assets per share ($)	40.49	38.79
Cost-to-income ratio (%)	47.6	47.4
Return on equity (%)	11.5	12.7
Return on assets (%)	0.8	0.8

Computershare Limited

ASX code: CPU   www.computershare.com

Sector: Software & services	
Share price ($)	24.51
12-month high ($)	26.56
12-month low ($)	16.12
Market capitalisation ($mn)	14 942.3
Price/earnings ratio (times)	47.4
Dividend yield (%)	2.2
Price-to-NTA-per-share ratio	~
5-year share price return (% p.a.)	11.9
Dividend reinvestment plan	Yes

Melbourne-based Computershare, established in 1978, is one of the world's leading financial services and technology providers for the global securities industry, offering services to listed companies, investors, employees, exchanges and other financial institutions. These offerings include share registration, employee equity plans, corporate governance, class action administration and other specialised financial, governance and stakeholder communication services. It manages more than 75 million customer records for more than 40 000 clients across all major financial markets, with significant market shares in many countries. More than 85 per cent of revenues comes from abroad, including around 55 per cent from the US. In November 2021 Computershare completed the US$750 million acquisition of Wells Fargo Corporate Trust Services, now renamed as Computershare Corporate Trust.

Latest business results (June 2022, full year)

Client fee income growth offset transaction revenue weakness, to help deliver a solid result. The company also benefited from stringent cost controls, which helped it manage the impact of inflation, as well as from rising interest rates. A significant further benefit came from the addition of Computershare Corporate Trust. The company's largest operating segment, issuer services, actually saw a decline in revenues and profits, due in particular to some large one-time deals in the previous year that were not repeated in the June 2022 year. Nevertheless, this business, representing 38 per cent of total turnover, generated about half of the company's profits. The second-largest operating segment, mortgage and property rental services, experienced a substantial jump in profits, though from a low base, and this remains a low-margin business for the company. Note that Computershare reports its results in US dollars. The Australian dollar figures in this book—converted at prevailing exchange rates—are for guidance only.

Outlook

Computershare is a beneficiary of robust worldwide equity markets, and can suffer in periods of volatility. It is also hurt by rising inflation. Nevertheless, it continues to gain market share in its issuer services and employee share plan operations, and it is working to turn around its underperforming mortgage services business. It holds a considerable amount of clients' funds in various forms, and is a notable beneficiary of rising interest rates. It also has a high percentage of recurring revenue. It sees particular potential for Computershare Corporate Trust, which it says is already exceeding expectations. With the benefits of rising interest rates and a full year's contribution from Computershare Corporate Trust, the company believes it can achieve a 55 per cent jump in EPS in the June 2023 year.

Year to 30 June	2021	2022
Revenues ($mn)	3001.5	3509.7
Issuer services (%)	43	38
Mortgage & property rental services (%)	26	23
Employee share plans & voucher services (%)	14	13
Computershare Corporate Trust (%)	0	13
Communication services & utilities (%)	7	7
EBIT ($mn)	426.6	502.7
EBIT margin (%)	14.2	14.3
Profit before tax ($mn)	355.4	423.9
Profit after tax ($mn)	248.7	311.9
Earnings per share (c)	44.44	51.66
Cash flow per share (c)	100.71	113.83
Dividend (c)	46	54
Percentage franked	80	18
Net tangible assets per share ($)	~	~
Interest cover (times)	6.0	6.4
Return on equity (%)	9.3	10.0
Debt-to-equity ratio (%)	39.2	63.9
Current ratio	1.7	1.6

Credit Corp Group Limited

ASX code: CCP www.creditcorpgroup.com.au

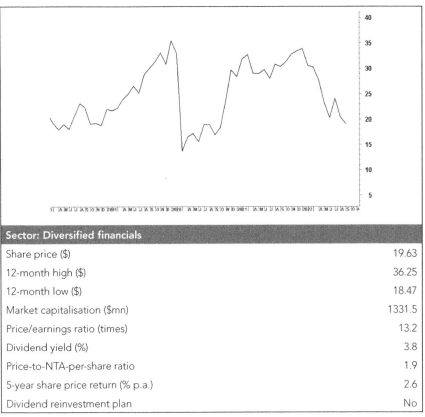

Sector: Diversified financials	
Share price ($)	19.63
12-month high ($)	36.25
12-month low ($)	18.47
Market capitalisation ($mn)	1331.5
Price/earnings ratio (times)	13.2
Dividend yield (%)	3.8
Price-to-NTA-per-share ratio	1.9
5-year share price return (% p.a.)	2.6
Dividend reinvestment plan	No

Sydney-based Credit Corp was formed in 1992, although it has its origins in companies that started in the early 1970s. It engages in debt collection activity, through the acquisition of defaulted consumer debt for companies in numerous industries, notably the banking, finance, telecommunications and utility sectors. It has operations in Australia, New Zealand and the United States. It maintains an agency collection service, under the brands National Credit Management and Baycorp, for clients who wish to outsource debt collections without actually selling the debt. It also operates a consumer lending business.

Latest business results (June 2022, full year)

Continuing growth in the US and a good recovery in consumer lending helped deliver a solid result, although it included a $4.5 million COVID-related payment from the US government, and the company reported that its underlying after-tax profit was $96.2 million. Its core business — representing around 56 per cent of turnover — is its Australia/New Zealand debt collection operation, and profits were virtually flat, on a 5 per cent rise in revenues. However, US debt collection activities continued to grow strongly, to represent more than 20 per cent of total turnover, with revenues and profits posting double-digit rises. Consumer lending was also strong, with robust demand for the Wallet Wizard business and a relaunch of the company's auto-lending product, and revenues and profits posted double-digit gains. At June 2022 Credit Corp's loan book of $251 million was up from $184 million a year earlier.

Outlook

Credit Corp's main business effectively involves buying consumer debt at a discount to its face value, then seeking to recover an amount in excess of the purchase price. Often this recovery takes the form of phased payments over an extended period, and Credit Corp thus has substantial recurring income. Setting an appropriate price for the acquisition of parcels of debt is one of the keys to success, and Credit Corp has acquired considerable expertise in this. It is achieving particular success with its sustained drive into the American market, and expects earnings there eventually to be similar to those for its Australian and New Zealand operations. However, it concedes that US labour shortages have been impeding recent growth. Consumer lending also shows solid potential, with a move into the US market and the planned launch of new products in the June 2023 year. Nevertheless, the company's early forecast is that weakness in domestic debt-collection operations will lead to a June 2023 after-tax profit of $90 million to $97 million.

Year to 30 June	2021	2022
Revenues ($mn)	374.8	411.2
EBIT ($mn)	131.7	148.2
EBIT margin (%)	35.2	36.0
Profit before tax ($mn)	125.9	143.0
Profit after tax ($mn)	88.1	100.7
Earnings per share (c)	130.92	148.89
Cash flow per share (c)	147.02	164.43
Dividend (c)	72	74
Percentage franked	100	100
Net tangible assets per share ($)	9.57	10.51
Interest cover (times)	22.7	28.8
Return on equity (%)	14.0	14.3
Debt-to-equity ratio (%)	~	13.4
Current ratio	5.6	6.2

CSL Limited

ASX code: CSL

www.csl.com

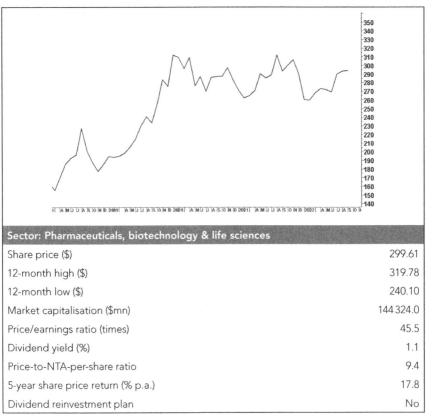

Sector: Pharmaceuticals, biotechnology & life sciences	
Share price ($)	299.61
12-month high ($)	319.78
12-month low ($)	240.10
Market capitalisation ($mn)	144 324.0
Price/earnings ratio (times)	45.5
Dividend yield (%)	1.1
Price-to-NTA-per-share ratio	9.4
5-year share price return (% p.a.)	17.8
Dividend reinvestment plan	No

Melbourne-based CSL, formerly the state-owned Commonwealth Serum Laboratories, was founded in 1916. It has grown organically and through acquisition to become a major global biotechnology company, with operations in numerous countries — with particular strength in the US, Australia, Germany, the UK, China and Switzerland — and more than 90 per cent of revenues derive from outside Australia. Its principal business now, through its CSL Behring division, is the provision of plasma-derived coagulation therapies for the treatment of a range of medical conditions. CSL Plasma, a subdivision of CSL Behring, is a major global collector of human blood plasma. The Seqirus division is one of the world's largest influenza vaccine companies and a producer of other prescription medicines and pharmaceutical products. CSL enjoys high margins and high market shares for many of its products. In August 2022 it acquired Swiss biotech company Vifor Pharma.

Latest business results (June 2022, full year)

Revenues rose but profits edged down in a difficult trading environment for CSL. The COVID pandemic sparked a sharp decline in blood donations in the June 2021 year, and due to long manufacturing lead times this led to constrained sales of the company's core plasma therapies in the June 2022 year. Though blood plasma collections have since recovered strongly, costs have risen, and the company has reported that it has fallen two years behind projected growth in plasma collections. Among non-plasma products, the recombinant haemophilia B product Idelvion saw sales up 20 per cent and the peri-operative bleeding product Kcentra enjoyed an 18 per cent rise in sales. The CSL Seqirus division benefited from strong demand for influenza vaccines. Note that CSL reports its results in US dollars. The figures in this book have been converted to Australian dollars based on prevailing exchange rates.

Outlook

CSL remains a powerhouse biotechnology company, with an impressive research and development capability and a solid pipeline of potential new products. It expects the strong recovery in plasma collections to continue, though with higher costs also remaining. In addition, it expects continuing strong influenza vaccine demand. It sees great potential for its $16.7 billion Vifor Pharma acquisition, one of the largest-ever acquisitions by an Australian company. Vifor boasts a world-leading iron replacement platform for treatment of diseases such as iron deficiency anaemia and through its extensive dialysis portfolio has built a strong presence in renal diseases. The company's early forecast, excluding Vifor, is for a June 2023 after-tax profit of US$2.4 billion to US$2.5 billion, up from US$2.3 billion in June 2022.

Year to 30 June	2021	2022
Revenues ($mn)	13 130.9	13 885.3
EBIT ($mn)	4118.4	4010.1
EBIT margin (%)	31.4	28.9
Gross margin (%)	55.2	52.4
Profit before tax ($mn)	3898.8	3807.7
Profit after tax ($mn)	3125.0	3088.6
Earnings per share (c)	686.84	658.90
Cash flow per share (c)	830.08	803.64
Dividend (c)	293.93	318.12
Percentage franked	5	5
Net tangible assets per share ($)	13.51	32.03
Interest cover (times)	18.8	19.8
Return on equity (%)	30.3	19.1
Debt-to-equity ratio (%)	47.7	~
Current ratio	2.4	2.3

CSR Limited

ASX code: CSR   www.csr.com.au

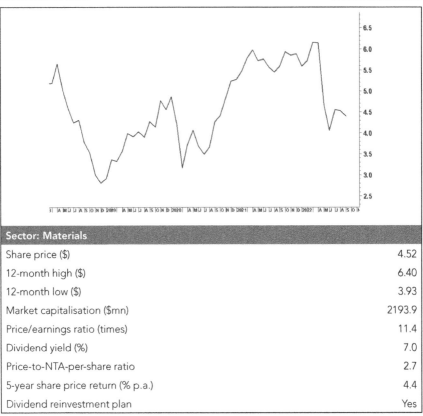

Sector: Materials	
Share price ($)	4.52
12-month high ($)	6.40
12-month low ($)	3.93
Market capitalisation ($mn)	2193.9
Price/earnings ratio (times)	11.4
Dividend yield (%)	7.0
Price-to-NTA-per-share ratio	2.7
5-year share price return (% p.a.)	4.4
Dividend reinvestment plan	Yes

Sydney-based CSR, founded in 1855 as a sugar refiner, is now a leading manufacturer of building products for residential and commercial construction, with distribution throughout Australia and New Zealand. Its brands include Gyprock plasterboard, Bradford insulation products, Monier roof tiles, Hebel concrete products and PGH bricks and pavers. It is also a joint venture partner in Australia's second-largest aluminium smelter at Tomago. In addition, it operates a residential and industrial property development business, based on former industrial sites.

Latest business results (March 2022, full year)

A strong housing market, a recovery in aluminium pricing and continuing buoyant property sales combined to deliver an excellent result. The Building Products division achieved a 24 per cent jump in profits, with structural and organisational improvements generating higher margins. There was particular strength from Gyprock, the company's largest business, as well as from the masonry and insulation businesses of PGH Bricks, Bradford Insulation and Monier Roofing. CSR's Aluminium division delivered EBIT of $39.7 million, up from $23.4 million a year earlier, thanks to a

20 per cent increase in average aluminium prices, partially offset by rising production costs. The property business benefited from continuing strong sales at the Horsley Park industrial development in Sydney, along with the sale of land at Sydney's Badgerys Creek, contributing EBIT of $46.9 million, down from $54.2 million.

Outlook

Inflationary pressures and rising interest rates could put a dent in the detached housing market but the company sees demand continuing to rise at least into 2023. It is also experiencing a modest recovery in both the apartment and commercial markets, after an extended slowdown over several years. It has been able to raise prices on many products to meet higher costs, and expects it will be able to continue doing so. It will also continue to benefit from improved profit margins. With a network of over 170 manufacturing and distribution sites, it believes it has the flexibility to boost production to meet growing demand. It is making a significant expansion of its PGH bricks operation in Queensland. Its Aluminium division has locked in prices with an extensive hedging program that extends to 2027, although it remains vulnerable to rising energy costs. Property will also continue to make a solid contribution. CSR owns almost 1400 hectares of land across Australia at some 50 property sites, including more than 1000 hectares in urban areas, and it expects property to generate EBIT of around $52 million in March 2023.

Year to 31 March	2021	2022
Revenues ($mn)	2122.4	2311.6
Building products (%)	72	70
Aluminium (%)	28	30
EBIT ($mn)	237.9	291.4
EBIT margin (%)	11.2	12.6
Gross margin (%)	28.5	30.3
Profit before tax ($mn)	231.8	281.9
Profit after tax ($mn)	160.4	192.6
Earnings per share (c)	33.07	39.74
Cash flow per share (c)	52.90	57.99
Dividend (c)	23	31.5
Percentage franked	100	100
Net tangible assets per share ($)	2.16	1.69
Interest cover (times)	20.3	20.1
Return on equity (%)	14.7	19.1
Debt-to-equity ratio (%)	~	~
Current ratio	1.7	1.3

Data#3 Limited

ASX code: DTL   www.data3.com

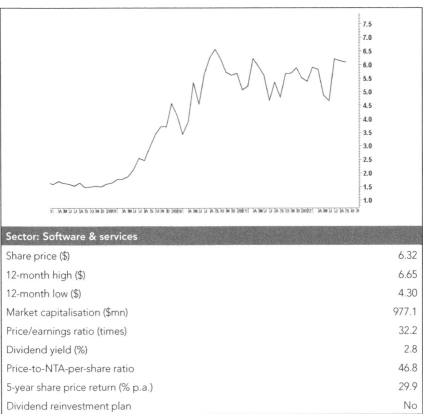

Sector: Software & services	
Share price ($)	6.32
12-month high ($)	6.65
12-month low ($)	4.30
Market capitalisation ($mn)	977.1
Price/earnings ratio (times)	32.2
Dividend yield (%)	2.8
Price-to-NTA-per-share ratio	46.8
5-year share price return (% p.a.)	29.9
Dividend reinvestment plan	No

Brisbane-based IT consultant Data#3 was formed in 1984 from the merger of computer software consultancy Powell, Clark and Associates with IBM typewriter dealer Albrand Typewriters and Office Machines. Today it operates from offices around Australia and in Fiji, providing information and communication technology services to a wide range of businesses that include banking and finance, mining, tourism and leisure, legal, health care, manufacturing, distribution, government and utilities.

Latest business results (June 2022, full year)

Data#3 achieved a fourth straight year of higher sales and profits in a good result, as customer demand largely returned to a normal pattern after the disruptions caused by COVID. However, supply constraints continued, and the company reported a significant backlog of unmet orders at the end of the financial year. It said pre-tax profit would have been about $6 million higher but for these constraints. There was particularly strong growth in public cloud revenues, up 33 per cent to $1040 million. Data#3 divides its activities into three broad segments. The first of these, software solutions, involves managing clients' software investments. New contracts won during the year helped boost revenues by 14.8 per cent to $1434 million. A second segment, infrastructure solutions, helps clients maximise returns from infrastructure investments in servers, storage, networks and devices. This business was hit by significant supply chain delays, and revenues fell 5.7 per cent to $440 million. A third, much smaller business segment is services, and this enjoyed a strong year, with particularly strong demand for the company's Microsoft Azure Managed Services work.

Outlook

A key competitive advantage for Data#3 is the strength of its partnerships with major vendors, the most important of these being Microsoft, Cisco, HP and Dell. It says it achieved significant market share growth for each of these during the June 2022 year. It is increasingly placing its focus on smaller contracts that reduce risk and enhance profitability. It is also working to boost its exposure to higher-margin services business. With cyber-security its customers' major priority, this is another important focus for the company. It expects supply constraints caused by the global shortage of computer chips to continue for at least a further 12 months, though it believes its strong relationships with customers and suppliers will help it lessen the problem. It is also working to confront the issue of a tight labour market and difficulties in hiring well-qualified professionals. At June 2022 Data#3 had no debt and cash holdings of nearly $150 million, and it continues to seek out expansion opportunities.

Year to 30 June	2021	2022
Revenues ($mn)	1955.2	2192.4
EBIT ($mn)	37.7	45.2
EBIT margin (%)	1.9	2.1
Profit before tax ($mn)	36.9	44.1
Profit after tax ($mn)	25.4	30.3
Earnings per share (c)	16.51	19.61
Cash flow per share (c)	20.43	23.61
Dividend (c)	15	17.9
Percentage franked	100	100
Net tangible assets per share ($)	0.10	0.13
Interest cover (times)	52.2	41.0
Return on equity (%)	46.8	51.3
Debt-to-equity ratio (%)	~	~
Current ratio	1.1	1.1

Elders Limited

ASX code: ELD

www.elders.com.au

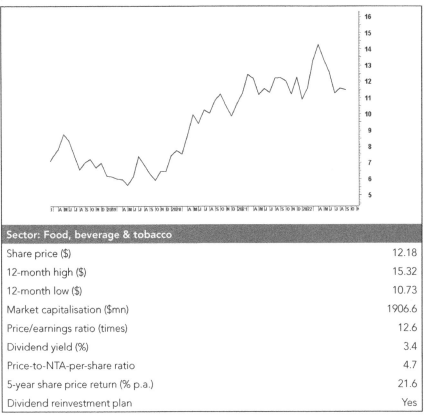

Sector: Food, beverage & tobacco

Share price ($)	12.18
12-month high ($)	15.32
12-month low ($)	10.73
Market capitalisation ($mn)	1906.6
Price/earnings ratio (times)	12.6
Dividend yield (%)	3.4
Price-to-NTA-per-share ratio	4.7
5-year share price return (% p.a.)	21.6
Dividend reinvestment plan	Yes

Adelaide-based agribusiness giant Elders dates back to 1839, when Scotsman Alexander Elder established a store in South Australia. It has grown and undergone many transformations, until today it is a leader in a range of businesses serving rural Australia. It is a prominent supplier of agricultural products, including seeds, fertilisers, chemicals and animal health products. It is a leading agent for the sale of wool, grain and livestock. It is also a major provider of financial and real estate services to the rural sector. An operation in China imports, processes and distributes Australian meat.

Latest business results (March 2022, half year)

Elders reported another excellent result, with strength once again in all key product lines and regions. Elders groups its business into three broad divisions. The main one of these, Branch Network, representing three-quarters of total turnover, incorporates agricultural retail products, agency services, and real estate and financial services. It reported a 40 per cent jump in sales, with profits surging by more than 50 per cent, thanks to buoyant sales of fertiliser and crop protection chemicals and historically high livestock prices. The Wholesale Products division, which supplies rural merchandise to retailers throughout Australia, represents 15 per cent of turnover, and it too achieved excellent growth, as customers concerned about possible supply chain disruptions brought forward their spending. A third, smaller division, Feed and Processing Services, includes two feedlots and the company's Chinese activities. It saw a big jump in profits, though from a low base, with solid growth in demand from domestic and export customers at the Killara feedlot.

Outlook

Elders is heavily geared to the rural economy, and the near-term outlook is for further buoyancy, with continuing strong demand for fertilisers, crop protection products and animal feed. As one of Australia's agribusiness leaders, Elders expects to continue to benefit, and it has developed an ambitious eight-point plan aimed at winning market shares across all its products and services, along with higher profits and moves into new product lines. Its 2019 acquisition of Australian Independent Rural Retailers has significantly boosted its wholesaling operation. The company is also optimistic about the outlook for its high-margin agency services, and believes the strong rural economy will continue to drive high levels of demand for rural properties, boosting its real estate business, despite rising interest rates. Elders is seeking to grow through acquisition, in order to expand its client base and increase its product offerings, and it has said that it has a solid pipeline of potential bolt-on acquisitions.

Year to 30 September	2020	2021
Revenues ($mn)	2092.6	2548.9
EBIT ($mn)	120.6	166.5
EBIT margin (%)	5.8	6.5
Gross margin (%)	20.6	20.3
Profit before tax ($mn)	111.3	157.7
Profit after tax ($mn)	107.7	151.1
Earnings per share (c)	69.89	96.67
Cash flow per share (c)	97.01	122.85
Dividend (c)	22	42
Percentage franked	100	20
Interest cover (times)	33.6	32.4
Return on equity (%)	18.5	20.9
Half year to 31 March	2021	2022
Revenues ($mn)	1100.5	1514.8
Profit before tax ($mn)	69.3	129.4
Profit after tax ($mn)	68.2	91.2
Earnings per share (c)	43.70	58.30
Dividend (c)	20	28
Percentage franked	20	30
Net tangible assets per share ($)	1.92	2.58
Debt-to-equity ratio (%)	23.5	32.1
Current ratio	1.2	1.3

Enero Group Limited

ASX code: EGG

www.enero.com

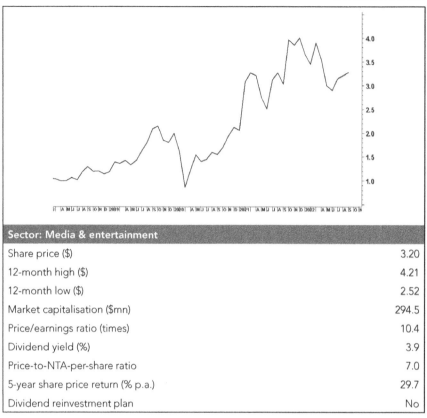

Sector: Media & entertainment	
Share price ($)	3.20
12-month high ($)	4.21
12-month low ($)	2.52
Market capitalisation ($mn)	294.5
Price/earnings ratio (times)	10.4
Dividend yield (%)	3.9
Price-to-NTA-per-share ratio	7.0
5-year share price return (% p.a.)	29.7
Dividend reinvestment plan	No

Sydney marketing and communications services specialist Enero, formerly known as Photon Group, was founded in 2000. It has expanded greatly through a flurry of acquisitions, mergers and divestments, and today divides its activities into three broad segments — creative and content, integrated communications and PR, and digital, data, analytics and technology. Its brands include Hotwire, BMF, CPR, OB Media and Orchard. It operates from three key locations — Australia, America and the UK — with offices in 13 cities and business in many countries. Nearly two-thirds of company income comes from overseas operations.

Latest business results (June 2022, full year)

Revenues and profits rose by double-digit amounts in a good result for Enero, with strength across all key geographic markets. Solid support came from the company's exposure to the fast-growing technology, healthcare and consumer sectors. Profit margins increased as the company worked to constrain rising costs, aided by a good performance from the high-margin OB Media, which functions as a digital platform, connecting publishers with the world's largest search engines. During the year this business delivered more than 285 million consumers to advertiser websites, 120 per cent higher than in the previous year. Most of the good result came from the company's American operations, with net revenues up 47 per cent and profits jumping 59 per cent. By contrast, Australian and European operations recorded just modest growth. In addition, American profit margins were greatly superior to those elsewhere.

Outlook

Enero occupies strong positions in niche areas of the marketing, PR, communications and advertising sectors. It expects its recent strong growth to continue during the June 2023 year, thanks to both organic expansion and the benefit of new acquisitions, although rising costs present a challenge. More than a third of its revenues derive from clients in the technology sector, predominantly in high-growth areas such as cloud computing and cyber-security. Another specialty is providing communications and marketing services to the healthcare industry. Its BMF creative agency has delivered a series of health campaigns for the federal government and its Orchard digital agency is also active in this growth sector. It sees great potential in its July 2022 acquisition for at least $48 million of the American business-to-business sales and marketing agency ROI DNA. This company will become part of Enero's Hotwire global PR and communications agency, delivering a significant portfolio of technology clients. Also in July 2022 Enero acquired for at least $4.7 million the Singapore-based business-to-business technology marketing agency GetIT, which will help the Hotwire business expand in Asia.

Year to 30 June	2021	2022
Revenues ($mn)	402.5	522.1
Creative technology & data (%)	67	73
Brand transformation (%)	33	27
EBIT ($mn)	42.8	59.3
EBIT margin (%)	10.6	11.4
Gross margin (%)	39.9	37.4
Profit before tax ($mn)	41.4	58.3
Profit after tax ($mn)	22.8	27.1
Earnings per share (c)	26.35	30.88
Cash flow per share (c)	34.54	38.79
Dividend (c)	14.9	12.5
Percentage franked	100	100
Net tangible assets per share ($)	0.16	0.46
Interest cover (times)	31.5	61.1
Return on equity (%)	18.2	19.7
Debt-to-equity ratio (%)	~	~
Current ratio	1.2	1.8

Fiducian Group Limited

ASX code: FID   www.fiducian.com.au

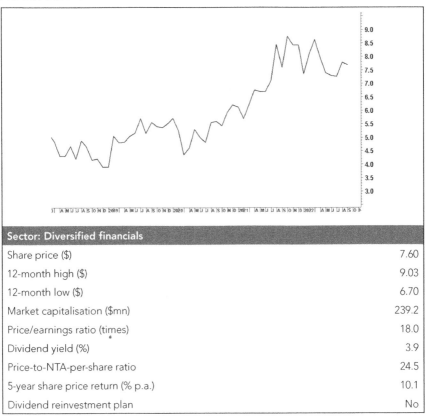

Sector: Diversified financials	
Share price ($)	7.60
12-month high ($)	9.03
12-month low ($)	6.70
Market capitalisation ($mn)	239.2
Price/earnings ratio (times)	18.0
Dividend yield (%)	3.9
Price-to-NTA-per-share ratio	24.5
5-year share price return (% p.a.)	10.1
Dividend reinvestment plan	No

Sydney financial services company Fiducian Group was founded in 1996 by executive chairman Indy Singh, who owns more than a third of the company equity. Initially it specialised in the provision of masterfund, client administration and financial planning services to financial advisory groups. It has since expanded and is now a holding company with five divisions — Fiducian Portfolio Services is in charge of trustee and superannuation services; Fiducian Investment Management Services operates the company's managed funds; Fiducian Services is the administration service provider for all the company's products; Fiducian Financial Services manages the company's financial planning businesses; and Fiducian Business Services provides accounting and business services.

Latest business results (June 2022, full year)

Revenues and underlying profits rose once more in a challenging financial environment. For reporting purposes the company divides its operations into broad segments. The largest of these is funds management, which enjoyed a solid increase in revenues and profits, thanks to the company's success in selecting strongly performing funds to offer to its clients. The financial planning business also achieved higher revenues and profits, helped by the acquisition in February 2022 of the financial planning business of the People's Choice Credit Union of South Australia. Thanks to the acquisition, funds under advice rose from $3.7 billion in June 2021 to $4.4 billion, offsetting declines during the year in financial markets. A third segment, platform administration, offers portfolio wrap administration services to financial planners, and this business too reported a rise in revenues and profits. At June 2022 the total funds under management, advice and administration of $10.9 billion was up by 5 per cent from a year earlier.

Outlook

Fiducian managed 47 financial planning offices across Australia at June 2022, both company-owned and franchised, with a total of 86 authorised representatives. It is continually seeking new offices to join the group, and it has also been achieving solid organic growth. At the same time, Fiducian itself has been named as a possible takeover target for a larger financial institution. The funds management business offers a suite of funds from various asset managers, and the company believes that its method of choosing managers with differing investment styles offers the ability to deliver above-average returns with greater diversification and reduced risk. Fiducian management have stated that their long-term goal is to deliver consistent double-digit earnings growth. However, the company is vulnerable to any major downturn in financial markets. At June 2022 it had no debt and cash holdings of more than $17 million.

Year to 30 June	2021	2022
Revenues ($mn)	58.6	69.3
Funds management (%)	39	39
Financial planning (%)	33	34
Platform administration (%)	28	27
EBIT ($mn)	16.7	18.8
EBIT margin (%)	28.5	27.2
Profit before tax ($mn)	16.9	19.1
Profit after tax ($mn)	12.2	13.3
Earnings per share (c)	38.73	42.31
Cash flow per share (c)	50.27	55.31
Dividend (c)	26.9	29.7
Percentage franked	100	100
Net tangible assets per share ($)	0.58	0.31
Interest cover (times)	~	~
Return on equity (%)	30.1	29.3
Debt-to-equity ratio (%)	~	~
Current ratio	2.9	1.7

Fortescue Metals Group Limited

ASX code: FMG

www.fmgl.com.au

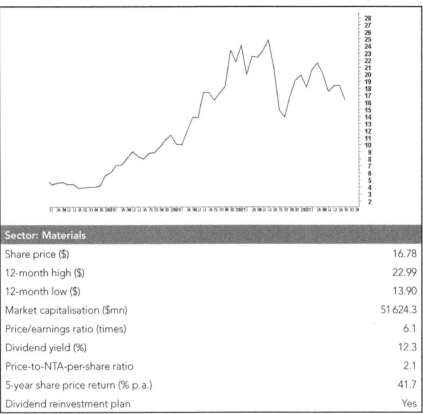

Sector: Materials	
Share price ($)	16.78
12-month high ($)	22.99
12-month low ($)	13.90
Market capitalisation ($mn)	51 624.3
Price/earnings ratio (times)	6.1
Dividend yield (%)	12.3
Price-to-NTA-per-share ratio	2.1
5-year share price return (% p.a.)	41.7
Dividend reinvestment plan	Yes

Perth-based Fortescue was founded in 2003. It has been responsible for discovering and developing some of the largest iron ore mines in the world and is today one of the world's largest iron ore producers, with operations at the Chichester Hub, the Solomon Hub and the Western Hub, all in the Pilbara region. It operates its own heavy-haul railway between its mines and Port Hedland. Its Iron Bridge Magnetite Project is under development and it is engaged in exploration work at sites in Western Australia, New South Wales and South Australia, with other ventures in South America. Nearly 90 per cent of its iron ore sales are to China.

Latest business results (June 2022, full year)

A falling iron ore price sent revenues and profits down, a reversal of the previous year when higher prices saw profits more than double. Sales of 189 million tonnes were up 4 per cent from the previous year, but the average price received of US$100 per tonne was 26 per cent lower. Average production costs of US$15.91 per tonne were up 14 per cent, due especially to an increase in diesel prices and other consumables and a rising wages bill. Note that Fortescue reports its results in US dollars. The

Australian dollar figures in this book — converted at prevailing exchange rates — are for guidance only.

Outlook

Its heavy debt burden brought Fortescue near to collapse in 2012, and since then it has been devoting enormous efforts into making itself more financially stable. In 2012 its basic production costs were as high as US$50 a tonne, but they have since fallen substantially and are now among the lowest in the world. Its US$3.6 billion Iron Bridge Magnetite Project is expected to produce 22 million tonnes of iron ore annually, starting from the March 2023 quarter. The company has launched Fortescue Future Industries, a global green energy business, with a particular focus on green hydrogen. In March 2022 Fortescue acquired for £164 million Williams Advanced Engineering of the UK, with plans to develop high-performance battery systems for its mining haul fleet. Then in June 2022 Fortescue announced a partnership with German–Swiss equipment manufacturer Liebherr to develop a fleet of zero-emission haul trucks. Nevertheless, Fortescue's near-term fortunes are tied intimately to the price of iron ore, which can be volatile and is greatly influenced by the state of the Chinese economy. Fortescue forecasts iron ore shipments during the June 2023 year of 187 million tonnes to 192 million tonnes.

Year to 30 June	2021	2022
Revenues ($mn)	29 321.1	23 821.9
EBIT ($mn)	19 540.7	12 304.1
EBIT margin (%)	66.6	51.7
Gross margin (%)	69.5	56.0
Profit before tax ($mn)	19 371.1	12 117.8
Profit after tax ($mn)	13 546.1	8489.0
Earnings per share (c)	440.22	275.92
Cash flow per share (c)	498.64	343.95
Dividend (c)	358	207
Percentage franked	100	100
Net tangible assets per share ($)	7.68	8.05
Interest cover (times)	115.2	66.0
Return on equity (%)	63.3	34.8
Debt-to-equity ratio (%)	~	5.1
Current ratio	2.3	2.9

Globe International Limited

ASX code: GLB   www.globecorporate.com

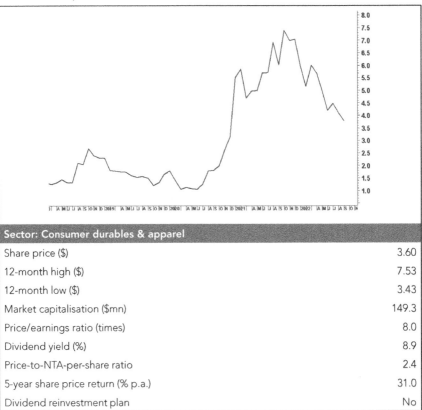

Sector: Consumer durables & apparel	
Share price ($)	3.60
12-month high ($)	7.53
12-month low ($)	3.43
Market capitalisation ($mn)	149.3
Price/earnings ratio (times)	8.0
Dividend yield (%)	8.9
Price-to-NTA-per-share ratio	2.4
5-year share price return (% p.a.)	31.0
Dividend reinvestment plan	No

Melbourne-based Globe, formerly called Hardcore Enterprises, was founded in 1985 by three brothers, two of them skateboard champions. It is a producer of skateboards, bicycles, roller skates and specialist footwear and apparel. Its brands include Globe, Salty Crew, FXD, Impala Skate, Dot Boards and Milkbar Bikes. It also distributes a range of third-party brands. Its products are sold in more than 100 countries, and it operates from offices in Melbourne, Los Angeles, Newport Beach, San Diego, Hossegor (France) and Shenzhen. It manages Globe and Salty Crew stores in Australia, Indonesia, Hong Kong and France.

Latest business results (June 2022, full year)

Sales edged up 3 per cent, but profits plummeted as the company was hit by a combination of a higher cost base, major shipping delays, rising inflation, higher interest rates and a softening of demand for the company's non-apparel range. Solid demand for the company's apparel and footwear brands was largely offset by declining sales of hardgoods brands, although the company reported that hardgoods were still trading profitably and at levels that were significantly higher than before the pandemic. North American sales were strong, up 13 per cent, or 9 per cent in local currency terms, but EBIT crashed 59 per cent. The more established Australasia segment saw sales slip 3 per cent, hurt by extended COVID-related lockdowns in the first half, and EBIT fell 13 per cent. European revenues were down 5 per cent, with profits plunging 76 per cent. Though representing 44 per cent of sales, Australasian business contributed about 70 per cent of profit.

Outlook

Globe has reported that it experienced a change in consumer behaviour in the March–June 2022 quarter, as rising interest rates and inflationary pressure started to affect discretionary spending. It expected that this would lead to downward pressure on its sales during the June 2023 year. Nevertheless, it planned to continue to look for opportunities to grow. The company was also working to find ways to reduce the impact of rising costs on its operations. The company plans to acquire a property near its Australian headquarters to provide additional warehouse and retail space. It will also carry out a fit-out of its new North American headquarters. Having experienced a slowdown in non-apparel demand during the June 2022 year, Globe at June 2022 was holding inventory of $66.5 million, up 38 per cent from a year earlier, and it was faced with the challenge of clearing the excess in a manner that preserved its brand image.

Year to 30 June	2021	2022
Revenues ($mn)	266.5	274.5
Australasia (%)	46	44
North America (%)	38	41
Europe (%)	16	15
EBIT ($mn)	46.7	27.5
EBIT margin (%)	17.5	10.0
Profit before tax ($mn)	46.4	26.4
Profit after tax ($mn)	33.3	18.6
Earnings per share (c)	80.24	44.96
Cash flow per share (c)	88.18	52.84
Dividend (c)	32	32
Percentage franked	100	100
Net tangible assets per share ($)	1.42	1.47
Interest cover (times)	23 350.0	51.7
Return on equity (%)	57.9	25.5
Debt-to-equity ratio (%)	~	1.2
Current ratio	2.1	2.2

Grange Resources Limited

ASX code: GRR   www.grangeresources.com.au

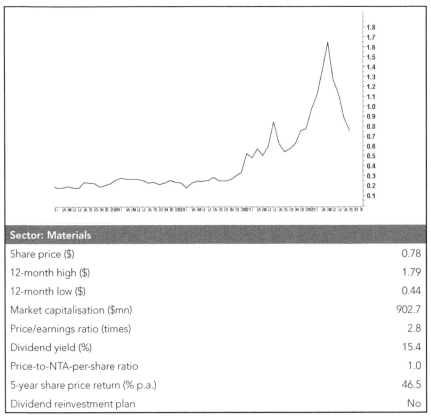

Sector: Materials	
Share price ($)	0.78
12-month high ($)	1.79
12-month low ($)	0.44
Market capitalisation ($mn)	902.7
Price/earnings ratio (times)	2.8
Dividend yield (%)	15.4
Price-to-NTA-per-share ratio	1.0
5-year share price return (% p.a.)	46.5
Dividend reinvestment plan	No

Based in Burnie, Tasmania, Grange Resources is an iron ore producer. It dates back to the 1980s when it was a Western Australian gold–copper miner with the name Sabminco. It is today involved in three major projects — the Savage River magnetite iron ore mine and the Port Latta pellet plant and port facility, both in Tasmania, and a 70 per cent share in the Southdown Magnetite Project in Western Australia's Great Southern region.

Latest business results (June 2022, half year)

A weakened iron ore price and rising costs sent revenues and profits down. The company produced 1.27 million tonnes of iron ore products, mainly iron ore pellets, the same as in the June 2021 period. It received an average price of $241.59 per tonne, down from $339.21. Production expenses of $113.66 per tonne were up from $100.23, due especially to higher energy costs, although the company also reported that it experienced increased levels of absenteeism from its staff due to COVID. About 60 per cent of the iron ore was shipped to China and around 36 per cent to Korea. The company also received $11.3 million in property development revenues, up from $1 million in the June 2021 period.

Outlook

Grange's fortunes are quite dependent on movements in the iron ore market, which in turn have become fairly reliant on Chinese political and economic trends. The company's business involves the mining of magnetite from its Savage River mine and then refining it at the Port Latta plant into an iron ore concentrate that can be used for steel production. It estimates that Savage River has a mine life that will extend into the 2030s, and it is involved in studies to determine how best to maximise efficient and effective future mining operations. Port Latta can produce more than 2 million tonnes annually of iron ore pellets and Grange plans to boost this. The company holds long-term supply contracts for 1 million tonnes of its annual production, and the remainder is sold via a spot sales tendering and contracting process. It is carrying out a feasibility study regarding its Southdown Magnetite Project in Western Australia, with a view to initiating mining operations. It expects the study to be completed late in 2022 and is seeking strategic investors to join it in the development of the mine. After losing money, it has ended its joint venture to develop luxury apartments in Melbourne. At June 2022 Grange had no debt and cash holdings of nearly $300 million.

Year to 31 December	2020	2021
Revenues ($mn)	526.3	781.7
EBIT ($mn)	224.6	439.0
EBIT margin (%)	42.7	56.2
Gross margin (%)	43.9	56.9
Profit before tax ($mn)	208.9	460.9
Profit after tax ($mn)	204.2	322.3
Earnings per share (c)	17.64	27.84
Cash flow per share (c)	22.76	34.99
Dividend (c)	3	12
Percentage franked	100	100
Interest cover (times)	14.3	~
Return on equity (%)	32.8	40.7
Half year to 30 June	2021	2022
Revenues ($mn)	450.6	341.1
Profit before tax ($mn)	294.0	191.9
Profit after tax ($mn)	205.3	132.2
Earnings per share (c)	17.79	11.42
Dividend (c)	2	2
Percentage franked	100	100
Net tangible assets per share ($)	0.76	0.74
Debt-to-equity ratio (%)	~	~
Current ratio	4.9	5.1

GUD Holdings Limited

ASX code: GUD   www.gud.com.au

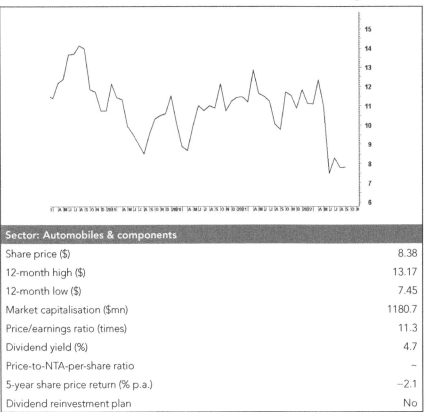

Sector: Automobiles & components	
Share price ($)	8.38
12-month high ($)	13.17
12-month low ($)	7.45
Market capitalisation ($mn)	1180.7
Price/earnings ratio (times)	11.3
Dividend yield (%)	4.7
Price-to-NTA-per-share ratio	~
5-year share price return (% p.a.)	−2.1
Dividend reinvestment plan	No

GUD, based in Melbourne and founded in 1940, is a manufacturer and distributor of a diversified range of auto and industrial products. Its main automotive brands include Ryco, Wesfil, Goss, Brown and Watson International (BWI) — incorporating the Narva and Projecta brands — Griffiths Equipment, Innovative Mechatronic Group (IMG), AA Gaskets and Disc Brakes Australia. The company also manufactures and distributes Davey water pumps and water treatment products. In 2021 it acquired auto accessories specialist AutoPacific Group (APG).

Latest business results (June 2022, full year)

A robust car parts business and the AutoPacific acquisition generated another solid rise in underlying revenues and profits for GUD. Sales for the core Automotive division surged 29.8 per cent, largely due to acquisitions made during the year, but with 6.5 per cent organic growth also contributing, and most of the company's products reporting good growth. There was a six-month contribution from AutoPacific, although this came in below expectations, with supply constraints for new vehicles hurting demand. The low-margin Davey water products operation benefited from restructuring moves and achieved 11.9 per cent sales growth, though with profits edging down. A large impairment charge of Davey's intangible assets meant that on a statutory basis GUD saw overall profits decline.

Outlook

Having divested itself of a series of businesses, GUD is now focused on the steadily growing Australian automotive aftermarket sector. It believes its $744.6 million AutoPacific acquisition will provide a new pillar for growth. AutoPacific is a leader in the manufacture of towing and trailering accessories, with facilities in Australia, New Zealand and Thailand. However, in the short term its business has been hurt by disruptions in the market for new cars. Other acquisitions made during the June 2022 year included Automotive Clutch Services and specialist lighting products business Vision X. GUD is now seeking to boost its exposure to the electric vehicle sector, with a view to becoming a leader in the electric vehicle aftermarket in Australia and New Zealand. Already around 69 per cent of its automotive sales are unrelated to the combustion engine. Much of the demand for GUD's products is from vehicles more than five years old, and it expects the average age of Australian cars to rise from 10.4 years in 2020 to 10.9 years by 2025. It continues to broaden the product ranges for its various brands and it is also seeking to expand exports. It continues to restructure its Davey division and expects an improved performance for this business in the June 2023 year.

Year to 30 June	2021	2022
Revenues ($mn)	557.0	835.5
Automotive (%)	80	69
APG (%)	0	16
Davey (%)	20	15
EBIT ($mn)	101.2	147.8
EBIT margin (%)	18.2	17.7
Gross margin (%)	44.3	40.2
Profit before tax ($mn)	90.8	129.8
Profit after tax ($mn)	64.0	88.9
Earnings per share (c)	70.35	74.43
Cash flow per share (c)	90.77	97.20
Dividend (c)	57	39
Percentage franked	100	100
Net tangible assets per share ($)	~	~
Interest cover (times)	9.7	8.2
Return on equity (%)	19.3	14.4
Debt-to-equity ratio (%)	37.7	55.1
Current ratio	2.7	2.2

GWA Group Limited

ASX code: GWA   www.gwagroup.com.au

Sector: Capital goods	
Share price ($)	1.98
12-month high ($)	2.86
12-month low ($)	1.76
Market capitalisation ($mn)	525.1
Price/earnings ratio (times)	11.1
Dividend yield (%)	7.6
Price-to-NTA-per-share ratio	~
5-year share price return (% p.a.)	1.6
Dividend reinvestment plan	No

Brisbane-based GWA is a prominent designer, importer and distributor of residential and commercial bathroom and kitchen products, marketed under brands that include Caroma, Dorf, Fowler, Methven, Stylus and Clark. About 11 per cent of its sales are in New Zealand, with 8 per cent to other countries, primarily the United Kingdom.

Latest business results (June 2022, full year)

Underlying profits rose after two straight years of decline, with revenues also higher. Australian sales were up by 6.5 per cent, with a particularly solid second half performance and a noteworthy strengthening of commercial renovation demand. Sales to the builder segment also rose. Residential renovation demand remained strong, although tempered by project delays due to labour and material shortages. The commercial new build and multi-residential sectors continued to be weak. Two price rises during the year helped mitigate rising costs. New Zealand business was hit by COVID-related lockdowns and staff absences, and sales fell 16.6 per cent. Other international sales rose 3.7 per cent, with a strong performance in the United Kingdom offsetting a decline in China. At the end of the financial year the company closed its loss-making Chinese sales operations, incurring expenses of $4.9 million.

Outlook

After a long series of restructurings GWA is now almost completely exposed to a bathroom and kitchen fixtures market that in Australia is worth up to $1.4 billion annually. It claims market shares as high as 50 per cent for some of its products, with an overall share of about 23 per cent. It has targeted three sectors — renovations and replacements (currently about 61 per cent of the company's Australian revenues), commercial construction (21 per cent) and detached housing (14 per cent) — and is developing new, high-margin products specifically for these markets. It sees demand remaining strong for renovation work, with the commercial segment also firm, especially in such areas as care facilities. New home demand could ease as interest rates rise, but the company notes that there can be a 15-month time lag between building approval and construction completion, when bathroom and kitchen products are installed. The company continues to work to lessen the impact of raw material and component shortages as well as shipping and other supply chain disruptions. This has included stocking up on inventory to ensure products are always available for customers. With costs continuing to rise, the company effected a further 5 per cent increase in its prices from July 2022 and has indicated it is prepared to make further rises if necessary.

Year to 30 June	2021	2022
Revenues ($mn)	405.7	418.7
EBIT ($mn)	68.5	74.8
EBIT margin (%)	16.9	17.9
Gross margin (%)	40.4	38.6
Profit before tax ($mn)	60.4	67.6
Profit after tax ($mn)	42.3	47.3
Earnings per share (c)	16.03	17.84
Cash flow per share (c)	23.76	25.39
Dividend (c)	12.5	15
Percentage franked	100	100
Net tangible assets per share ($)	~	~
Interest cover (times)	8.5	10.3
Return on equity (%)	14.7	15.8
Debt-to-equity ratio (%)	34.9	45.1
Current ratio	1.7	2.0

Hansen Technologies Limited

ASX code: HSN   www.hansencx.com

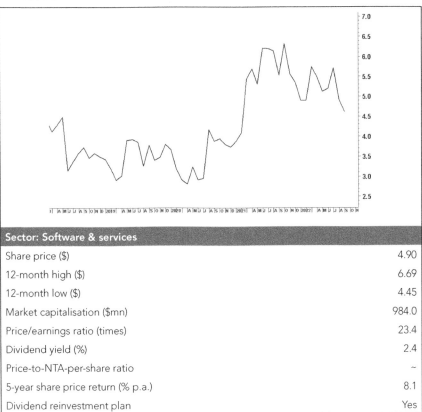

Sector: Software & services	
Share price ($)	4.90
12-month high ($)	6.69
12-month low ($)	4.45
Market capitalisation ($mn)	984.0
Price/earnings ratio (times)	23.4
Dividend yield (%)	2.4
Price-to-NTA-per-share ratio	~
5-year share price return (% p.a.)	8.1
Dividend reinvestment plan	Yes

Melbourne company Hansen Technologies dates back to an IT business launched in 1971. It later moved into the development of billing software systems and is today a significant global provider of these services, specialising in the electricity, gas, water, pay television and telecommunications sectors. Hansen has offices around the world, and services some 600 customers across 16 product lines in over 80 countries.

Latest business results (June 2022, full year)

Revenues and profits, which rose sharply in the previous year, this time fell back as the company's costs grew. However, Hansen noted that a one-time licence pre-payment from German client Telefonica boosted the June 2021 revenue figure by $21 million. Also, in the previous year the company had benefited from some notable new contract wins and expanded contracts with existing customers. Company expenses were affected by rising staff costs — which had fallen in the previous year — and increased hardware and software expenditure. Also higher were travel expenses, as easing COVID restrictions enabled more corporate travel. During the year the company signed a major US$24.6 million contract with American power company Exelon Corporation.

Outlook

Though a small company, Hansen has developed a high reputation for its services. Its billing software enables its customers to create, sell and deliver new products and services, as well as manage and analyse customer data and control critical revenue management and customer support processes. Once it does business with a customer it stands to benefit further from a long-term stream of recurring revenue. Hansen's particular strategy is growth by acquisition, and with the billing services industry still fragmented and largely regionalised, it expects further attractive acquisition opportunities to present themselves. In particular, it is aiming at assets that own intellectual property and with recurring revenue streams that will help Hansen move into new regions or market segments. It has a dedicated mergers and acquisitions team that has developed a proactive relationship with many brokers and bankers around the world, and has the ability to move quickly if it finds the right opportunities. However, it made no new acquisitions during the June 2022 year. To help reduce costs it has been making a significant investment in development centres in Vietnam and India. It sees the rapid pace of regulatory change in many countries as a particular tailwind that creates growing demand for its services. Nevertheless, it faces the challenge of securing and retaining talented professionals in a tight IT employment market, and it expects some margin pressure from cost inflation.

Year to 30 June	2021	2022
Revenues ($mn)	307.7	296.5
EBIT ($mn)	74.8	54.6
EBIT margin (%)	24.3	18.4
Profit before tax ($mn)	70.1	51.0
Profit after tax ($mn)	57.3	41.9
Earnings per share (c)	28.81	20.91
Cash flow per share (c)	49.36	41.91
Dividend (c)	10	12
Percentage franked	38	42
Net tangible assets per share ($)	~	~
Interest cover (times)	16.2	15.3
Return on equity (%)	21.2	13.9
Debt-to-equity ratio (%)	22.7	9.0
Current ratio	0.7	1.8

Harvey Norman Holdings Limited

ASX code: HVN   www.harveynormanholdings.com.au

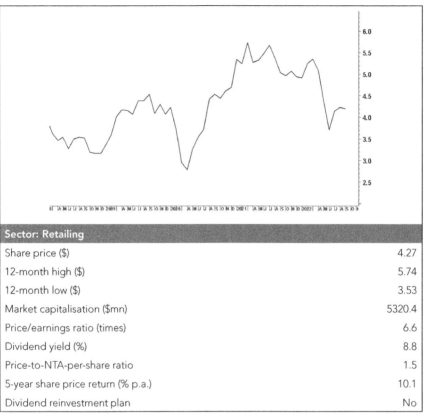

Sector: Retailing	
Share price ($)	4.27
12-month high ($)	5.74
12-month low ($)	3.53
Market capitalisation ($mn)	5320.4
Price/earnings ratio (times)	6.6
Dividend yield (%)	8.8
Price-to-NTA-per-share ratio	1.5
5-year share price return (% p.a.)	10.1
Dividend reinvestment plan	No

Sydney-based Harvey Norman, established in 1982, operates a chain of 304 retail stores specialising in electrical and electronic goods, home appliances, furniture, flooring, carpets and manchester items, throughout Australia, New Zealand, Ireland, Northern Ireland, Singapore, Malaysia, Slovenia and Croatia, under the Harvey Norman, Domayne and Joyce Mayne banners. The 195 Australian stores are independently held as part of a franchise operation, from which Harvey Norman receives income for advisory and advertising services. It also receives a considerable amount of income from its own stores, from its $3.7 billion property portfolio and from the provision of finance to franchisees and customers.

Latest business results (June 2022, full year)

A second-half recovery was insufficient to offset first-half weakness, due especially to COVID-related lockdowns and store closures, and profits edged down. Total store sales — franchise and company-owned — fell 2 per cent to $9.56 billion. However, sales of $2.88 billion by the company's own stores were up 1.5 per cent, although total profits for the company's own stores were down. Franchise income received by Harvey Norman fell 3.6 per cent to $1.19 billion. The property business reported a 26 per cent rise in pre-tax profit, although this was largely the result of property revaluations. The company said that excluding the impact of property revaluations its total after-tax profit was $673.6 million.

Outlook

Harvey Norman is highly exposed to economic conditions and faces a myriad of challenges, including rising costs, higher interest rates, shipment delays, staffing shortages, falling house prices and a possible slowdown in consumer spending. It has high fixed costs, so even a modest decline in sales can translate to a larger fall in earnings. However, the company has pointed to a low jobless rate and high levels of household savings as reasons for optimism about future demand. In addition, it benefits from continuing technological innovation that induces customers to upgrade to large-screen and smart TVs and to obtain the latest mobile phone and accessories. Other growth categories include drones, scooters, gaming hardware and software, air purifiers and home security systems. The company aims to expand in the emerging economies of South-East Asia and Eastern Europe. During the June 2023 year it plans to open five new stores: two in Malaysia, with one each in New Zealand, Croatia and Ireland. It also expects two new franchised stores in Australia. For the June 2024 year it plans six new overseas stores, including its first two in Hungary.

Year to 30 June	2021	2022
Revenues ($mn)	4438.6	4505.7
Retail (%)	63	63
Franchising operations (%)	27	26
Property (%)	9	11
EBIT ($mn)	1233.0	1193.0
EBIT margin (%)	27.8	26.5
Gross margin (%)	33.6	33.4
Profit before tax ($mn)	1182.5	1140.4
Profit after tax ($mn)	841.4	811.5
Earnings per share (c)	67.53	65.13
Cash flow per share (c)	74.54	72.40
Dividend (c)	35	37.5
Percentage franked	100	100
Net tangible assets per share ($)	2.55	2.83
Interest cover (times)	27.3	26.4
Return on equity (%)	23.0	20.0
Debt-to-equity ratio (%)	7.6	10.5
Current ratio	1.5	1.9

Healius Limited

ASX code: HLS
www.healius.com.au

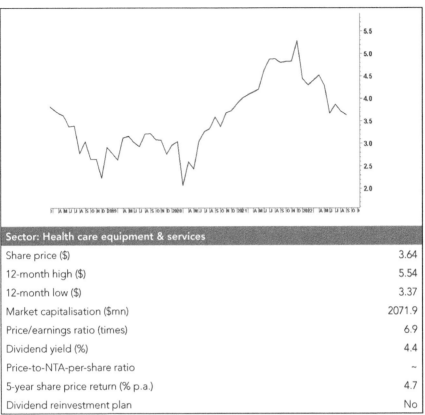

Sector: Health care equipment & services	
Share price ($)	3.64
12-month high ($)	5.54
12-month low ($)	3.37
Market capitalisation ($mn)	2071.9
Price/earnings ratio (times)	6.9
Dividend yield (%)	4.4
Price-to-NTA-per-share ratio	~
5-year share price return (% p.a.)	4.7
Dividend reinvestment plan	No

Sydney-based Healius, formerly known as Primary Health Care, has its origins in the Perth pathology provider Western Diagnostic Pathology, established in 1985. It has grown through a series of acquisitions and divestments, and today is one of Australia's leading providers of pathology services. Its other businesses are imaging and day hospital services. Its many brands include Dorevitch Pathology, Western Diagnostic Pathology, Lumus Imaging and Montserrat Day Hospitals. In February 2022 it acquired the Agilex bioanalytical laboratory business. It has sold its Adora Fertility operation.

Latest business results (June 2022, full year)

Revenues and profits surged, as the company's pathology laboratories played a leading role in Australia's COVID testing regime. By contrast, other businesses were generally weak, hit by lockdowns, elective surgery restrictions and isolation requirements. Growth was particularly strong in the first half, when COVID testing demand was high. However, non-COVID testing declined slightly. The Lumus Imaging division experienced reduced business, in line with the nationwide trend, with revenues and profits lower. The very small Day Hospitals division was also weak.

Outlook

Healius believes that, as COVID testing demand continues to ease, its various activities could, in the short term, benefit from backlogs that have developed during the period of the pandemic. However, it expects that business will likely then over the medium term return to their normal trend patterns. In the case of its core pathology business, this means an annual growth rate of around 5 per cent to 6 per cent, based on an expanding and ageing population. It believes a set of tailwinds will benefit its business, including the increasing importance of diagnostic tests in reducing downstream healthcare costs, innovations in diagnostic testing and the expansion of digital health. Consequently, it has developed a set of strategies designed to cut costs and stimulate growth. It sees the $301 million Agilex acquisition as providing an entry to the fast-growing global bioanalytical laboratory services market. It has signed an agreement with US Alzheimer's disease research group C_2N Diagnostics to bring to Australia that company's blood test for memory and dementia care. It continues to streamline its businesses in order to focus on pathology and imaging. It has divested itself of its fertility interests and several of its day hospitals, and plans to sell its remaining hospitals. At the same time it is seeking further acquisitions in pathology and imaging. Since launching its Sustainable Improvement Program in 2019 it has cut its annualised cost base by $58 million, with further savings still to come.

Year to 30 June	2021	2022
Revenues ($mn)	1913.1	2337.7
Pathology (%)	76	81
Imaging (%)	21	17
Day hospitals (%)	3	2
EBIT ($mn)	266.5	492.3
EBIT margin (%)	13.9	21.1
Profit before tax ($mn)	178.9	441.8
Profit after tax ($mn)	148.4	309.3
Earnings per share (c)	23.95	53.00
Cash flow per share (c)	63.86	100.72
Dividend (c)	13.25	16
Percentage franked	100	100
Net tangible assets per share ($)	~	~
Interest cover (times)	3.0	9.7
Return on equity (%)	7.8	16.4
Debt-to-equity ratio (%)	10.1	27.3
Current ratio	0.5	0.6

IDP Education Limited

ASX code: IEL   www.idp.com

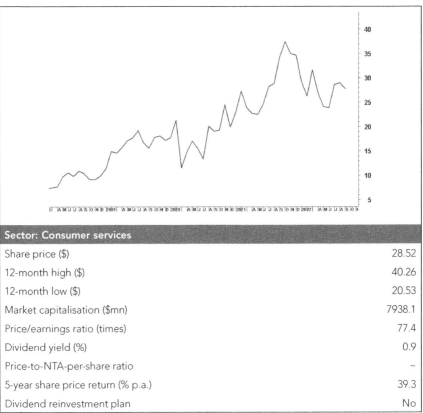

Sector: Consumer services	
Share price ($)	28.52
12-month high ($)	40.26
12-month low ($)	20.53
Market capitalisation ($mn)	7938.1
Price/earnings ratio (times)	77.4
Dividend yield (%)	0.9
Price-to-NTA-per-share ratio	~
5-year share price return (% p.a.)	39.3
Dividend reinvestment plan	No

Melbourne-based IDP Education dates back to 1969 and the launch of the Australian Asian Universities Cooperation Scheme, aimed at helping Asian students study in Australia. In 1981 it changed its name to the International Development Program (IDP), and opened a series of offices throughout Asia. It has since expanded through acquisition and organic growth, and today helps students from around the world find placements in higher education programs in English-speaking countries. It also works with University of Cambridge ESOL Examinations and the British Council to administer worldwide testing for the International English Language Testing System (IELTS). About 25 per cent of IDP's equity is held by 38 Australian universities.

Latest business results (June 2022, full year)

Revenues and profits came racing back, having crashed in the previous year when pandemic-related lockdowns and travel restrictions severely hurt business. Though some travel disruptions continued, particularly in the first half, the company saw the majority of restrictions lifted during the year. Nearly two-thirds of the company's turnover now derives from its English-language testing services, and it reported that this business returned to near full capacity in July 2021, followed in August by the

£130 million acquisition of the British Council's English language testing business in India. Altogether the company administered 1.9 million tests, up 67 per cent from the previous year. The company's other main business, student placement services, saw revenues up 50 per cent, with placements in the UK, US and Canada rebounding in the first half, and in Australia in the second half, as travel restrictions eased. A very small business involves English-language teaching at nine schools in Cambodia and Vietnam, with revenues flat for the year.

Outlook

IDP is investing heavily in transforming itself into a company with significant digital capabilities. It has helped develop a new English language testing platform that supports the delivery of the IELTS online. Its student placement operation now includes a technology platform that delivers a range of digital services to students. In December 2021 it launched its FastLane app that allows students to get an indicative placement offer from an institution instantly, and by August 2022 this had been accepted by 65 universities and was on the phones of more than 900 000 students. The company's strategy is to expand its physical network and complement this with digital platforms, and it believes this is already helping it gain market share. Its acquisition of the British Council's English language testing business in India significantly expands IDP's position in that key market.

Year to 30 June	2021	2022
Revenues ($mn)	528.7	793.3
Asia (%)	60	74
Rest of world (%)	31	21
Australasia (%)	9	5
EBIT ($mn)	64.1	158.9
EBIT margin (%)	12.1	20.0
Profit before tax ($mn)	58.9	152.1
Profit after tax ($mn)	39.7	102.6
Earnings per share (c)	14.26	36.86
Cash flow per share (c)	27.76	50.60
Dividend (c)	8	27
Percentage franked	0	12
Net tangible assets per share ($)	0.72	~
Interest cover (times)	~	110.0
Return on equity (%)	10.3	24.3
Debt-to-equity ratio (%)	~	~
Current ratio	2.5	1.6

IGO Limited

ASX code: IGO   www.igo.com.au

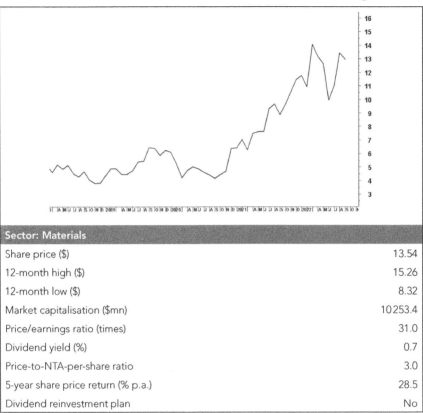

Sector: Materials	
Share price ($)	13.54
12-month high ($)	15.26
12-month low ($)	8.32
Market capitalisation ($mn)	10 253.4
Price/earnings ratio (times)	31.0
Dividend yield (%)	0.7
Price-to-NTA-per-share ratio	3.0
5-year share price return (% p.a.)	28.5
Dividend reinvestment plan	No

Perth company IGO, formerly known as Independence Group, was established in 2000 to explore for gold and nickel. Today it has operations at a number of sites in Western Australia. It mines for nickel, copper and cobalt at its Nova development. It also holds a 49 per cent stake in Tianqi Lithium Energy Australia, which itself has a 51 per cent holding of the Greenbushes Lithium Mine and 100 per cent ownership of the Kwinana Lithium Hydroxide Refinery. In June 2022 IGO acquired nickel miner Western Areas, delivering to it the Forrestania and Cosmos projects. In addition, the company maintains an extensive exploration program.

Latest business results (June 2022, full year)

Rising metals prices and IGO's investment in Tianqi Lithium Energy Australia powered the company to a sharp rise in revenues and profits. During the year its Nova mine produced 26 675 tonnes of nickel, 11 483 tonnes of copper and 982 tonnes of cobalt. Despite rising inflation, the company was able to keep its nickel production costs at a low $1.95 per pound. Its revenues figure for the year primarily reflected Nova production, and rose 34 per cent from June 2021, thanks to significant growth in average nickel, copper and cobalt prices. The company's after-tax profit figure was boosted by $176.7 million due to an initial contribution from the Tianqi Lithium Energy Australia investment.

Outlook

The June 2022 year was a time of transition for IGO as it worked to transform itself into a major producer of commodities related to clean energy. Having sold its Tropicana Gold Mine for around $900 million it acquired its stake in Tianqi Lithium Energy Australia in a $1.4 billion deal with China's Tianqi Lithium at the start of the financial year. Late in June 2022 it acquired Western Areas for $1.3 billion. It is now positioned as a major producer of nickel and lithium. Its nickel production has expanded with the addition of the Forrestania project, though with a big jump in costs. It is developing the Odysseus underground nickel mine at its newly acquired Cosmos project, with initial nickel concentrate output forecast for mid 2023. It is also considering the development of a nickel processing operation to produce battery-grade nickel sulphate for the lithium-ion battery industry. Output is being boosted at the Greenbushes Lithium Mine, the world's largest hard rock lithium mine. The Kwinana Lithium Hydroxide Refinery produced its first battery-grade lithium hydroxide in May 2022, and will move to commercial production levels during the June 2023 year.

Year to 30 June	2021	2022
Revenues ($mn)	671.7	902.8
EBIT ($mn)	180.2	467.3
EBIT margin (%)	26.8	51.8
Profit before tax ($mn)	156.6	463.5
Profit after tax ($mn)	116.8	330.9
Earnings per share (c)	17.21	43.70
Cash flow per share (c)	43.09	66.89
Dividend (c)	10	10
Percentage franked	100	100
Net tangible assets per share ($)	4.19	4.46
Interest cover (times)	7.6	123.0
Return on equity (%)	4.6	10.0
Debt-to-equity ratio (%)	~	10.7
Current ratio	3.3	1.7

Iluka Resources Limited

ASX code: ILU · www.iluka.com

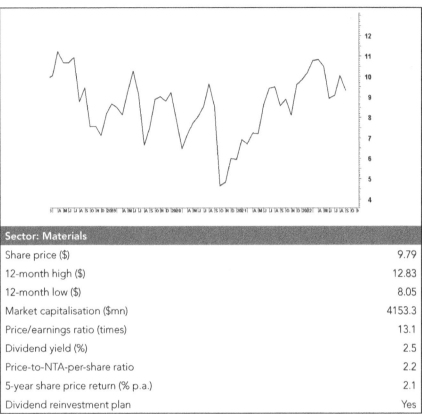

Sector: Materials	
Share price ($)	9.79
12-month high ($)	12.83
12-month low ($)	8.05
Market capitalisation ($mn)	4153.3
Price/earnings ratio (times)	13.1
Dividend yield (%)	2.5
Price-to-NTA-per-share ratio	2.2
5-year share price return (% p.a.)	2.1
Dividend reinvestment plan	Yes

Perth resources company Iluka started in 1954 as Westralian Sands, before merging in 1998 with the titanium mineral business of RGC and subsequently taking its present name. It is today a global leader in the mining and processing of mineral sands and rare earths. It has four operations in Western Australia: it manages the Cataby mine, a large ilmenite deposit with associated zircon and rutile; its Eneabba development involves the reclaiming and processing of a strategic stockpile high in monazite; its Narngulu mineral separation plant produces zircon, rutile and ilmenite products; and the Capel operation incorporates two synthetic rutile kilns. In South Australia it operates the world's largest zircon mine, Jacinth-Ambrosia, and it is involved in exploration and development work in other states. It holds a 20 per cent holding in ASX-listed Deterra Royalties, a company that receives royalties from certain BHP iron ore tenements. In August 2022 Iluka demerged its West African subsidiary Sierra Rutile into a separate company.

Latest business results (June 2022, half year)

Tight global supply for its products sent prices higher, boosting revenues and profits, despite a decline in volume sales. The result also benefited from the weaker dollar. The price of zircon for the company rose by an average of 40 per cent from the June 2021 half, with rutile up 23 per cent. These price rises easily offset escalating energy and labour costs. The company's Sierra Leone business recorded higher profits. However, this is now classified as a discontinued operation and is not included in the figures in this book.

Outlook

Rare earth minerals are a key component for a growing number of high-tech industries. They are essential for the creation of powerful magnets for wind turbines and electric vehicles. They are also needed in vehicle emission control units and in modern rechargeable batteries, as well as for many defence industry applications, including jet engines and drones. Consequently, they are in growing demand globally. However, with some 80 per cent of the world's supply now coming from China, countries in the West have been urging Australia, which has large-scale reserves of rare earths, to boost output. In April 2022 Iluka received a $1.2 billion loan from the government to build Australia's first rare earth refinery at its Eneabba operation, with production expected from 2025. It is also moving towards launching new mining projects at Balranald in New South Wales and Wimmera in Victoria. Following its demerger, Sierra Rutile now trades as a separate company on the ASX.

Year to 31 December	2020	2021
Revenues ($mn)	990.6	1559.4
EBIT ($mn)	238.3	481.1
EBIT margin (%)	24.1	30.9
Profit before tax ($mn)	204.6	466.5
Profit after tax ($mn)	151.2	314.8
Earnings per share (c)	35.79	74.55
Cash flow per share (c)	78.65	114.38
Dividend (c)	2	24
Percentage franked	100	100
Interest cover (times)	33.6	84.4
Return on equity (%)	15.1	21.8
Half year to 30 June	2021	2022
Revenues ($mn)	673.3	836.6
Profit before tax ($mn)	219.0	404.3
Profit after tax ($mn)	151.2	286.0
Earnings per share (c)	35.80	67.80
Dividend (c)	12	25
Percentage franked	100	100
Net tangible assets per share ($)	3.27	4.46
Debt-to-equity ratio (%)	~	~
Current ratio	3.4	3.0

IPH Limited

ASX code: IPH   www.iphltd.com.au

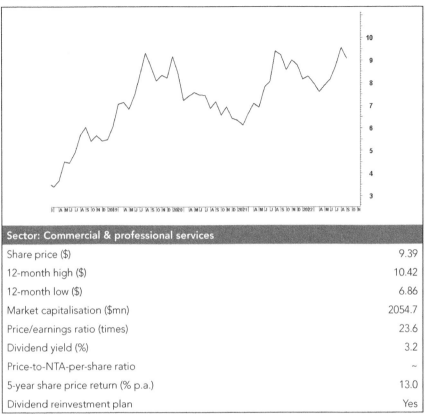

Sector: Commercial & professional services	
Share price ($)	9.39
12-month high ($)	10.42
12-month low ($)	6.86
Market capitalisation ($mn)	2054.7
Price/earnings ratio (times)	23.6
Dividend yield (%)	3.2
Price-to-NTA-per-share ratio	~
5-year share price return (% p.a.)	13.0
Dividend reinvestment plan	Yes

Sydney-based IPH, formed in 2014 but with roots that stretch back to 1887, is a holding company for a group of businesses offering a wide range of intellectual property services and products. These include the filing, prosecution, enforcement and management of patents, designs, trademarks and other intellectual property. IPH operates under various brands from offices in Australia, New Zealand, Singapore, Malaysia, China, Indonesia, Thailand and Hong Kong. In July 2022 it completed the sale of its data analytics software subsidiary Practice Insight. In August 2022 it announced the acquisition of leading Canadian intellectual property agency Smart & Biggar.

Latest business results (June 2022, full year)

Revenues and underlying profits bounced back, having edged down in the previous year due mainly to currency movements. This time the company benefited from dollar weakness, along with organic growth, especially in its Asian businesses. For reporting purposes the company segments its operations into Australian and New Zealand businesses, representing nearly three-quarters of total turnover, and Asian activities. A significantly reduced volume of intellectual property filings by a major

Australian client hurt domestic operations, with profits just edging up. However, continuing patent filing growth across most Asian jurisdictions, with particular strength again in China, generated double-digit rises in revenues and profits for the company's Asian segment.

Outlook

IPH has established itself as one of the leaders in Australia, New Zealand and South-East Asia in the intellectual property business. It has expanded steadily, through organic growth and acquisition. As it grows it achieves economies of scale that boost margins. It is achieving success with its strategy of leveraging its network of companies, and domestic subsidiaries are now among the foremost clients of its trademark and patent operations in Beijing and Hong Kong. It continues to seek out further acquisition opportunities. It regards its $387 million acquisition of Smart & Biggar as transformational for the company. Smart & Biggar occupies a leading place in Canada's intellectual property sector and is expected to boost IPH's EPS by 10 per cent in June 2023 as well as providing a platform for further growth into new jurisdictions. In December 2021 IPH integrated its Spruson & Ferguson Australia and its Shelston IP businesses, and after some short-term disruption this operation is achieving synergies and growth. In July 2021 it acquired Applied Marks, one of Australia's leading online automated trademark application platforms, and this has led to the creation of a new digital services function for the company that is generating growth and efficiencies.

Year to 30 June	2021	2022
Revenues ($mn)	359.7	385.1
EBIT ($mn)	108.5	120.7
EBIT margin (%)	30.2	31.3
Profit before tax ($mn)	102.6	116.0
Profit after tax ($mn)	76.2	86.7
Earnings per share (c)	35.26	39.74
Cash flow per share (c)	52.60	57.87
Dividend (c)	29.5	30.5
Percentage franked	45	45
Net tangible assets per share ($)	~	~
Interest cover (times)	18.3	25.9
Return on equity (%)	17.9	20.2
Debt-to-equity ratio (%)	10.5	7.0
Current ratio	2.7	2.8

IRESS Limited

ASX code: IRE   www.iress.com

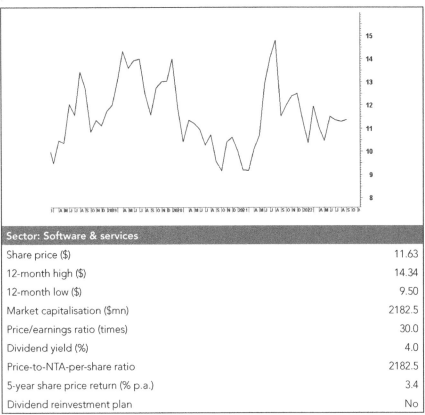

Sector: Software & services	
Share price ($)	11.63
12-month high ($)	14.34
12-month low ($)	9.50
Market capitalisation ($mn)	2182.5
Price/earnings ratio (times)	30.0
Dividend yield (%)	4.0
Price-to-NTA-per-share ratio	2182.5
5-year share price return (% p.a.)	3.4
Dividend reinvestment plan	No

Melbourne-based IRESS was founded in 1993. It produces the IRESS (Integrated Real-time Equity System) share market information system, used widely throughout the Australian investment community. Within the IRESS system it offers a portfolio of information and trading products with numerous applications for stockbrokers, fund managers and other financial professionals. It is also active in wealth management services, with its Xplan financial planning software. A third activity is the Mortgages division, which provides mortgage processing software, and a fourth business provides fund administration software to the superannuation industry. The company has expanded its operations to 17 offices in Australia, New Zealand, the United Kingdom, France, Canada, Singapore and South Africa, and its software is used by more than 10 000 businesses.

Latest business results (June 2022, half year)

Revenues were up but rising costs helped send profits down. However, the company reported that it had adjusted its June 2021 results due to one-off earn-out payments for two acquisitions, and on that basis the June 2022 underlying after-tax profit actually rose by 29 per cent. The company divides its operation into five segments.

The Asia Pacific segment represents 57 per cent of total turnover, and achieved modest sales growth across most products and regions, with an excellent 29 per cent jump in Asian revenues, thanks especially to the new QuantHouse Asia market data business. The United Kingdom and Europe segment is a further quarter of revenues, and business was mixed, with revenues up 3 per cent. A third segment, Mortgages, achieved a 20 per cent increase in sales, thanks to new clients and rising recurring subscription licence revenues.

Outlook

IRESS's businesses are strongly geared to levels of financial market activity, which can lead to volatility in its operations. It is also vulnerable to structural changes in the financial sector. Nevertheless, its products are widely used in Australia, and the company reports high levels of customer loyalty, with recurring revenues responsible for up to 90 per cent of total turnover. It benefits from the steady growth of superannuation assets, and targets 18 per cent growth annually for its superannuation products. The company calculates that it has an addressable market across its various financial sectors worth more than $5 billion, and it has announced an ambitious growth plan, with a target of achieving an after-tax profit of as much as $135 million in the June 2025 year. Much of this involves spending some $30 million on upgrading and integrating its various software platforms into a single, cloud-based technology platform.

Year to 31 December	2020	2021
Revenues ($mn)	542.6	595.9
EBIT ($mn)	86.1	101.9
EBIT margin (%)	15.9	17.1
Profit before tax ($mn)	78.1	92.9
Profit after tax ($mn)	59.1	73.8
Earnings per share (c)	32.28	38.77
Cash flow per share (c)	53.78	63.45
Dividend (c)	46	46
Percentage franked	38	38
Interest cover (times)	10.8	11.3
Return on equity (%)	11.6	13.1

Half year to 30 June	2021	2022
Revenues ($mn)	290.2	308.2
Profit before tax ($mn)	50.4	40.4
Profit after tax ($mn)	40.9	30.6
Earnings per share (c)	21.40	16.40
Dividend (c)	16	16
Percentage franked	80	25
Net tangible assets per share ($)	~	~
Debt-to-equity ratio (%)	31.6	62.9
Current ratio	1.3	1.5

JB Hi-Fi Limited

ASX code: JBH   investors.jbhifi.com.au

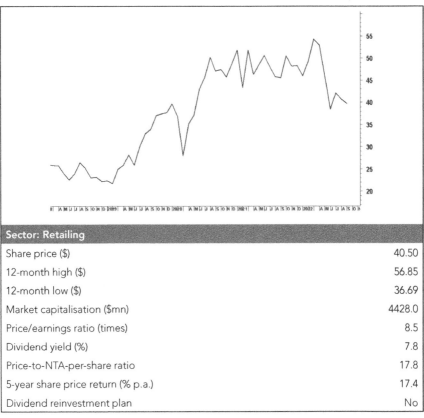

Sector: Retailing	
Share price ($)	40.50
12-month high ($)	56.85
12-month low ($)	36.69
Market capitalisation ($mn)	4428.0
Price/earnings ratio (times)	8.5
Dividend yield (%)	7.8
Price-to-NTA-per-share ratio	17.8
5-year share price return (% p.a.)	17.4
Dividend reinvestment plan	No

Melbourne-based JB Hi-Fi dates back to the opening in 1974 of a single recorded music store in the Melbourne suburb of East Keilor. It has since grown into a nationwide chain of home electronic and home appliance products outlets, and it has also expanded to New Zealand. In Australia it operates The Good Guys chain of home appliance stores. Its JB Hi-Fi Solutions division sells to the commercial, educational and insurance sectors. The company also maintains a growing online presence. At the end of June 2022 it operated 199 JB Hi-Fi and JB Hi-Fi Home stores in Australia, 14 JB Hi-Fi stores in New Zealand and 106 The Good Guys stores in Australia.

Latest business results (June 2022, full year)

Sales and profits rose again in a positive result, with a particularly good performance in the second half as COVID restrictions eased. At JB Hi-Fi Australia sales were up 4 per cent, with strong demand in the communications, visual, small appliance, smart home and accessories categories. By contrast, software sales continued to fall. The Good Guys posted a 2.7 per cent rise in sales, with a double-digit profit rise, driven by strong demand in the laundry, portable appliance, floorcare, dishwasher and visual categories. Profit margins at The Good Guys are nearly at the same level as those prevailing at JB Hi-Fi Australia. New Zealand saw sales just edge up for the year, but with underlying profits down, and profit margins remain substantially below those for the company's Australian operations. Online sales, which soared 78.1 per cent in the previous year, grew by a further 52.8 per cent, to represent 17.6 per cent of total turnover.

Outlook

JB Hi-Fi has a strong brand image throughout Australia and great customer loyalty. It has shown an impressive ability to contain costs. It continues to open new stores, though at a slower pace than in previous years. It is boosting floor space at its stores for growth categories such as mobile phones, gaming and connected technology. It is also working to strengthen its online operations. A strategic review of New Zealand operations is expected to lead to a restructuring aimed at boosting profit margins, along with the opening of new stores. The company's commercial business, JB Hi-Fi Solutions, is being separated into three new brands, JB Hi-Fi Business, JB Hi-Fi Education and The Good Guys Commercial. But the company faces challenges that include rising costs and interest rates, supply chain disruptions and a possible slowdown in consumer spending.

Year to 30 June	2021	2022
Revenues ($mn)	8916.1	9232.0
JB Australia (%)	67	67
The Good Guys (%)	30	30
JB New Zealand (%)	3	3
EBIT ($mn)	743.1	794.6
EBIT margin (%)	8.3	8.6
Gross margin (%)	22.2	22.5
Profit before tax ($mn)	720.0	775.3
Profit after tax ($mn)	506.1	544.9
Earnings per share (c)	440.85	479.24
Cash flow per share (c)	624.56	668.16
Dividend (c)	287	316
Percentage franked	100	100
Net tangible assets per share ($)	2.41	2.28
Interest cover (times)	32.2	41.2
Return on equity (%)	41.9	42.1
Debt-to-equity ratio (%)	~	~
Current ratio	1.1	1.1

Johns Lyng Group Limited

ASX code: JLG   www.johnslyng.com.au

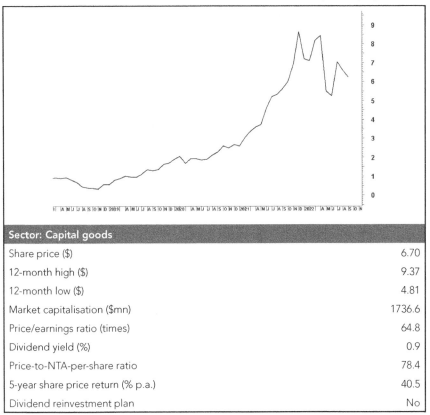

Sector: Capital goods	
Share price ($)	6.70
12-month high ($)	9.37
12-month low ($)	4.81
Market capitalisation ($mn)	1736.6
Price/earnings ratio (times)	64.8
Dividend yield (%)	0.9
Price-to-NTA-per-share ratio	78.4
5-year share price return (% p.a.)	40.5
Dividend reinvestment plan	No

Specialist Melbourne building company Johns Lyng Group was established in 1953 as Johns & Lyng Builders. It has a particular specialty in building and restoration work for insurance claims, with operations nationwide under various brands, and its clients include most of Australia's leading insurance companies. Its Johns Lyng Commercial Builders business is responsible for construction work across a wide variety of fields, including education, aged care, hospitality and retail. The company has grown substantially through acquisition, including in January 2022 the American specialist construction company Reconstruction Experts.

Latest business results (June 2022, full year)

A particularly strong result from its core Insurance Building and Restoration Services division, compounded by a string of acquisitions during the year, generated a substantial rise in revenues and profits. This division has a particular specialty in repair work related to major weather disasters, mainly storms and floods. In March 2022 the company was appointed major contractor for the $142 million governmental Property Assessment and Demolition Program for victims of NSW floods. Altogether the company recorded weather disaster revenues of nearly $165 million, which was 90 per cent higher than in the previous year. The small Commercial Building Services division, which is engaged in flooring work, emergency repairs, retail shop fitting, and heating and air conditioning services, also enjoyed double-digit growth in revenues and profits, partly due to COVID-related disruptions in the previous year. However, the Commercial Construction division was hit by sharply rising costs for its operations and fell into the red, despite expanding business.

Outlook

Johns Lyng has developed a high reputation for its insurance-related work and it continues to expand, with major new clients in recent years and market share gains. It sees particular potential in its strata management activities, with substantial cross-selling opportunities for its building work. Thanks to a series of acquisitions in this highly fragmented sector it now manages some 90 000 strata lots at around 3500 properties, and it expects this number will continue to grow as it rolls out its Strata Building Services division. Following the 2019 acquisition of the US-based fire and flood restoration business Steamatic, the company has been researching the American market. It now believes that the US can become a key pillar of long-term future growth, leading to the US$145 million acquisition of insurance repair services provider Reconstruction Experts. The company's early forecast for June 2023 is for revenues of at least $1 billion, with EBITDA of $105.3 million, which is 26 per cent higher than in June 2022.

Year to 30 June	2021	2022
Revenues ($mn)	568.4	895.0
Insurance building & restoration (%)	78	84
Commercial construction (%)	14	10
Commercial building services (%)	8	6
EBIT ($mn)	40.8	59.0
EBIT margin (%)	7.2	6.6
Gross margin (%)	21.0	22.0
Profit before tax ($mn)	39.1	56.9
Profit after tax ($mn)	18.6	25.1
Earnings per share (c)	8.30	10.34
Cash flow per share (c)	12.58	16.55
Dividend (c)	5	5.7
Percentage franked	100	100
Net tangible assets per share ($)	0.02	0.09
Interest cover (times)	46.6	49.7
Return on equity (%)	31.6	13.0
Debt-to-equity ratio (%)	~	~
Current ratio	1.1	1.2

Jumbo Interactive Limited

ASX code: JIN www.jumbointeractive.com

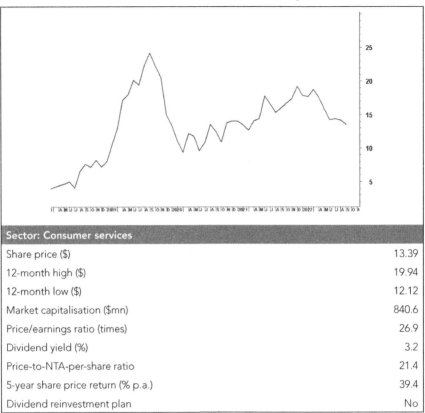

Sector: Consumer services	
Share price ($)	13.39
12-month high ($)	19.94
12-month low ($)	12.12
Market capitalisation ($mn)	840.6
Price/earnings ratio (times)	26.9
Dividend yield (%)	3.2
Price-to-NTA-per-share ratio	21.4
5-year share price return (% p.a.)	39.4
Dividend reinvestment plan	No

Jumbo Interactive was founded in Brisbane in 1995 as an internet service provider, but has since evolved into a major operator of internet services for lotteries. Its core business, Oz Lotteries, involves the provision of lottery services for The Lottery Corporation — which was formerly a part of Tabcorp — at its ozlotteries.com website. These lotteries include OzLotto, Powerball, Lotto Strike and Lucky Lotteries. It has introduced a Software-as-a-Service (SaaS) business, called Powered by Jumbo, that manages lotteries for charitable organisations and other institutions. It also runs a Managed Services division to provide lottery management services on an international basis. It has entered the British market with the acquisition of Gatherwell and the Canadian market with the acquisition of Stride Management. It has announced plans to acquire British lottery manager StarVale Group.

Latest business results (June 2022, full year)

Revenues and profits continued to rise. Large Powerball and OzLotto jackpots are an important stimulus to sales, and the result benefited from 43 jackpots worth at least $15 million, compared with 38 in the previous year. There was also a $120 million Powerball in February 2022, and lottery retailing revenues rose 21 per cent to

$91 million. The Powered by Jumbo SaaS business also continued to grow, benefiting from a strong relationship with Lotterywest in Western Australia and the start of operations with the first UK client, and revenues from external customers jumped 68 per cent. The Managed Services division recorded $4.8 million in revenues, up from $3.3 million in the previous year, most of this derived from the company's British subsidiary Gatherwell. There was a one-month contribution in Canada from the new Stride Management acquisition.

Outlook

Jumbo is a significant beneficiary of the Australian love of gambling. A new software platform and a vigorous marketing campaign have helped stimulate its recent growth. It is also enjoying success with new apps for mobile devices, and reports that these have succeeded in attracting a new demographic of younger customers. It sees great potential from its Stride Management and StarVale acquisitions, which together add approximately 1.6 million active players to its platforms, bringing the total to around 4 million. It has said that boosting the number of active players is one of its key growth strategies. StarVale, for which it is paying around $32 million, plus deferred consideration up to $8.5 million, manages lotteries for some 45 British charities and not-for-profit organisations. Jumbo is now seeking a strategic partnership for entry to the US market.

Year to 30 June	2021	2022
Revenues ($mn)	83.3	104.3
EBIT ($mn)	38.9	45.3
EBIT margin (%)	46.7	43.5
Profit before tax ($mn)	39.1	45.2
Profit after tax ($mn)	28.3	31.2
Earnings per share (c)	45.39	49.85
Cash flow per share (c)	58.58	63.83
Dividend (c)	36.5	42.5
Percentage franked	100	100
Net tangible assets per share ($)	0.67	0.63
Interest cover (times)	~	448.9
Return on equity (%)	34.5	35.0
Debt-to-equity ratio (%)	~	~
Current ratio	2.9	2.6

Lifestyle Communities Limited

ASX code: LIC   www.lifestylecommunities.com.au

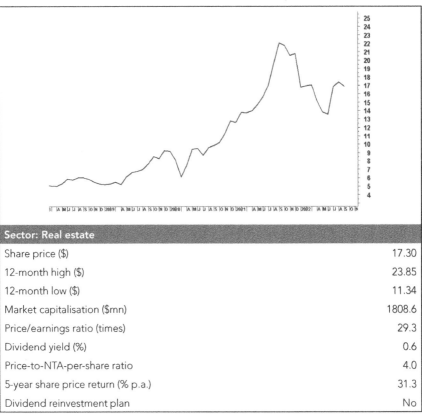

Sector: Real estate	
Share price ($)	17.30
12-month high ($)	23.85
12-month low ($)	11.34
Market capitalisation ($mn)	1808.6
Price/earnings ratio (times)	29.3
Dividend yield (%)	0.6
Price-to-NTA-per-share ratio	4.0
5-year share price return (% p.a.)	31.3
Dividend reinvestment plan	No

Melbourne company Lifestyle Communities, founded in 2003, develops and maintains residential and retirement communities throughout Victoria, in growth areas of Melbourne and in regional centres. These are aimed at over-50s and retirees. At June 2022 it had completed 19 communities and was managing 3193 homes with more than 4500 residents.

Latest business results (June 2022, full year)

Revenues and underlying profits rose strongly as the company bounced back from the depths of the COVID pandemic, which had necessitated the lockdown of many of its facilities and also led to a sharp slowing of business activity. The company settled 401 new homes, up from 255 in the previous year, noting that lockdowns for the first four months of the financial year were followed by a significant upswing in demand during the Christmas and New Year period. A growing number of homes under management meant that annuity income rose 25 per cent to $40.6 million. This included $29.7 million in site rental fees, up from $25 million a year earlier. It also included $10.9 million in deferred management fees, up from $7.3 million a year earlier, from the resale of 143 existing homes, up from 105. Note that on a statutory basis the company's profit figures also include non-cash property revaluations, which are not included in the figures in these pages. Thus, on a statutory basis the after-tax profit actually fell from $91.1 million in the June 2021 year to $88.9 million in June 2022.

Outlook

Lifestyle Communities operates on a model that differs from many retirement facilities, in that its residents own their homes but pay a rental charge to the company for the land, on a 90-year lease. It thus has a growing annuity-style income as its business expands. It promotes its communities to active seniors, and the average age of new residents is around 67, which is about 10 years younger than the average age for new residents of retirement homes generally in Australia. Its goal has been to buy two or three new sites each year, focused on Melbourne's growth corridors and on key Victorian regional centres. It is accelerating its activities during the June 2023 year with construction beginning on seven new projects. These, along with projects already in development, are expected to generate 1400 to 1700 new home settlements by June 2025. As the company expands its rental income will increase. In addition, the number of resales — sales of established homes — will also grow, boosting its deferred management fee income.

Year to 30 June	2021	2022
Revenues ($mn)	137.8	224.2
EBIT ($mn)	77.2	101.0
EBIT margin (%)	56.0	45.0
Gross margin (%)	20.8	20.8
Profit before tax ($mn)	75.8	99.6
Profit after tax ($mn)	36.4	61.4
Earnings per share (c)	34.88	59.00
Cash flow per share (c)	36.16	60.65
Dividend (c)	8	10.5
Percentage franked	100	100
Net tangible assets per share ($)	3.61	4.33
Interest cover (times)	55.4	71.4
Return on equity (%)	10.9	14.8
Debt-to-equity ratio (%)	49.6	53.6
Current ratio	1.9	0.8

Macquarie Group Limited

ASX code: MQG   www.macquarie.com.au

Sector: Diversified financials	
Share price ($)	178.38
12-month high ($)	217.32
12-month low ($)	157.03
Market capitalisation ($mn)	68435.1
Price/earnings ratio (times)	13.6
Dividend yield (%)	3.5
Price-to-NTA-per-share ratio	2.8
5-year share price return (% p.a.)	15.8
Dividend reinvestment plan	Yes

Sydney-based Macquarie Group was established in 1969 as Hill Samuel Australia, a subsidiary of a British merchant bank. It is now Australia's leading locally owned investment bank, with a wide spread of activities and boasting special expertise in specific industries that include finance, resources and commodities, energy, infrastructure and real estate. It operates in 33 markets around the world, and international business accounts for more than three-quarters of total company revenue.

Latest business results (March 2022, full year)

Macquarie enjoyed an excellent year, with strong gains for revenues and profits, including a particular boost from volatile energy markets. The largest of the bank's four broad operating segments, Commodities and Global Markets, enjoyed a 50 per cent jump in profits, just as it had in the previous year, as oil and gas customers in Europe and the US scrambled to secure supplies, especially following the Russian invasion of Ukraine. Profits for Macquarie Capital surged more than threefold, though from a low base, thanks to a wave of merger and acquisition activity, for which the bank acted as financial adviser. A third operating segment, Macquarie Asset Management, saw profits just edge up, with $27 billion raised in new equity, and assets under management up 38 per cent to $773.1 billion. The Banking and Financial Services segment, which provides banking and wealth management services to the Australian market, recorded a 30 per rise in profits, with the home loan portfolio up 34 per cent to $89.5 billion and the business banking portfolio up 13 per cent to $11.5 billion.

Outlook

At a time of global economic uncertainty, Macquarie is not prepared to make forecasts for the March 2023 year, although it is well able to profit from economic and market volatility. The bank is one of Europe's largest commodities traders and also owns a gas transmission network in Germany. However, it expects an easing of the extreme volatility in energy markets that characterised the latter months of the March 2022 year, even with the continuation of the Ukraine conflict. On the other hand, rising inflation around the world will benefit its asset management activities. For future growth it is placing a strong emphasis on building a portfolio of decarbonisation assets, through its Green Investment Group, with some 250 green energy projects in hand and profits growing strongly. It has become a leader in the wind and solar industries, and is expanding its involvement in emerging technologies, including utility-scale energy storage, hydrogen fuel and zero-emission transport.

Year to 31 March	2021	2022
Operating income ($mn)	12 774.0	17 324.0
Net interest income ($mn)	2195.0	2860.0
Operating expenses ($mn)	8867.0	10 785.0
Profit before tax ($mn)	3907.0	6539.0
Profit after tax ($mn)	3015.0	4706.0
Earnings per share (c)	871.54	1312.71
Dividend (c)	470	622
Percentage franked	40	40
Non-interest income to total income (%)	82.8	83.5
Net tangible assets per share ($)	53.91	64.59
Cost-to-income ratio (%)	69.4	62.3
Return on equity (%)	14.0	18.6
Return on assets (%)	1.2	1.5

Magellan Financial Group Limited

ASX code: MFG www.magellangroup.com.au

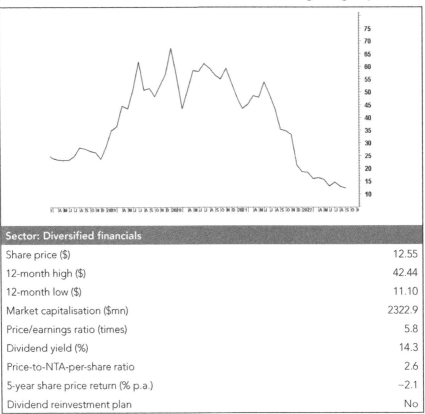

Sector: Diversified financials	
Share price ($)	12.55
12-month high ($)	42.44
12-month low ($)	11.10
Market capitalisation ($mn)	2322.9
Price/earnings ratio (times)	5.8
Dividend yield (%)	14.3
Price-to-NTA-per-share ratio	2.6
5-year share price return (% p.a.)	−2.1
Dividend reinvestment plan	No

Sydney-based Magellan is a specialist investment management company that evolved in 2006 from the ASX-listed Pengana Hedgefunds Limited. Its main business is Magellan Asset Management, which offers managed funds to retail and institutional investors, with particular specialties in global equities, global listed infrastructure, Australian equities — through Airlie Funds Management — and sustainable asset investments.

Latest business results (June 2022, full year)

Revenues and underlying profits fell in a bad year for Magellan as it suffered a series of client outflows from its funds, particularly during the second half. Consequently, funds under management crashed from $113.9 billion at June 2021 to $61.3 billion in June 2022. Management and services fees were down 7 per cent to $592.6 million, and performance fees fell for the third straight year, down 62 per cent to $11.5 million. At the same time, the company's costs were up, including a 25 per cent jump in employee expenses, and the cost-to-income ratio rose from 16.8 per cent to 21.3 per cent.

Outlook

Magellan has been through a torrid period, as the continuing underperformance of its main global funds sparked a chain of client withdrawals. It led to management upheavals, including the departure of its co-founder and chief investment officer Hamish Douglass. Now, under new management, it is seeking to rebuild. The company's flagship product, the Magellan Global Fund, has invested in some global technology stocks at a time when these have been out of favour, and the challenge for the company is to raise performance. The company recognises that its business is heavily dependent on the quality of its staff, and in March 2022 it announced a staff engagement and retention program, including a retention bonus plan and the issue of share options to employees who stay with the company. Nevertheless, it also remains very dependent on the state of financial markets, and it would suffer from any big sell-off in equities, or from a prolonged bear market. In addition, more than 80 per cent of funds under management are exposed to currency fluctuations. Through its Magellan Capital Partners division the company has made strategic investments in technology services provider FinClear Holdings and in the financial services firm Barrenjoey Capital Partners. It has sold its holding in restaurant chain Guzman y Gomez. In order to tap into a trend towards ethical investing, the company has opened its Magellan Sustainable Fund to retail investors. In July 2022 it decided to end its Magellan FuturePay product, which was aimed at providing investors with retirement income.

Year to 30 June	2021	2022
Revenues ($mn)	667.1	605.6
EBIT ($mn)	588.5	517.0
EBIT margin (%)	88.2	85.4
Profit before tax ($mn)	587.5	515.2
Profit after tax ($mn)	412.4	399.7
Earnings per share (c)	224.89	215.91
Cash flow per share (c)	228.75	219.77
Dividend (c)	211.2	179
Percentage franked	75	77
Net tangible assets per share ($)	4.71	4.89
Interest cover (times)	587.3	286.4
Return on equity (%)	40.5	39.6
Debt-to-equity ratio (%)	~	~
Current ratio	1.6	2.4

McMillan Shakespeare Limited

ASX code: MMS   www.mmsg.com.au

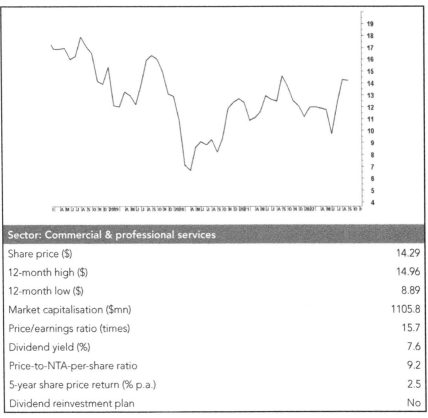

Sector: Commercial & professional services	
Share price ($)	14.29
12-month high ($)	14.96
12-month low ($)	8.89
Market capitalisation ($mn)	1105.8
Price/earnings ratio (times)	15.7
Dividend yield (%)	7.6
Price-to-NTA-per-share ratio	9.2
5-year share price return (% p.a.)	2.5
Dividend reinvestment plan	No

Melbourne-based McMillan Shakespeare, founded in 1988, is a specialist provider of salary packaging, vehicle leasing and finance services. It operates under three broad categories. The Asset Management Services division arranges financing and provides related management services for motor vehicles, commercial vehicles and equipment. The Group Remuneration Services division provides administrative services for salary packaging. It also arranges motor vehicle novated leases — three-way agreements between employer, employee and financier to lease a vehicle — as well as providing related ancillary services such as insurance. The third, much smaller division, Plan and Support Services, provides plan management and support coordination services to participants in the National Disability Insurance Scheme. The company operates through 15 subsidiary companies in Australia, four in the UK and two in New Zealand.

Latest business results (June 2022, full year)

Revenues and the after-tax profit were up. The biggest division, Asset Management Services, enjoyed double-digit increases in revenues and profits, thanks in particular to the continuing strength of used car prices, which generated substantial increases in remarketing profits. The Group Remuneration Services division achieved a small increase in revenues, with total salary packages under management rising 4 per cent to 370 902. Novated lease orders were up 3 per cent, but actual sales fell 4 per cent as the company struggled to source new car stock. At June 2022 the company had $26 million in vehicle orders waiting to be fulfilled, forcing up costs, and this division saw profits slightly down. Nevertheless, though only 35 per cent of company income, Group Remuneration Services contributed around 55 per cent of total profit. The new Plan and Support Services division achieved large increases in revenues and profits, thanks to a 64 per cent rise in customer numbers.

Outlook

McMillan Shakespeare occupies a strong position in its main businesses in Australia, with high profit margins and continuing growth from a strong pipeline of prospective customers. In April 2022 it received a credit licence for its new Onboard Finance operation, which will provide funding for novated leases, and it sees this as a new business with great profit potential. Its Asset Management Services division has achieved a significant turnaround in its limping British operations, thanks to restructuring efforts, helped by elevated used car prices, and profits soared. It sees opportunities for its novated lease business in planned new laws exempting many zero-emission and low-emission cars from the fringe benefits tax. It is seeking further acquisition opportunities for its fast-growing Plan and Support Services division.

Year to 30 June	2021	2022
Revenues ($mn)	544.2	593.8
Asset management services (%)	58	58
Group remuneration services (%)	37	35
Plan & support services (%)	5	7
EBIT ($mn)	99.5	99.6
EBIT margin (%)	18.3	16.8
Profit before tax ($mn)	97.1	97.8
Profit after tax ($mn)	61.1	70.3
Earnings per share (c)	78.91	90.91
Cash flow per share (c)	165.65	180.13
Dividend (c)	61.3	108
Percentage franked	100	100
Net tangible assets per share ($)	1.21	1.55
Interest cover (times)	12.2	21.4
Return on equity (%)	24.5	25.1
Debt-to-equity ratio (%)	6.8	2.4
Current ratio	1.7	2.1

Medibank Private Limited

ASX code: MPL   www.medibank.com.au

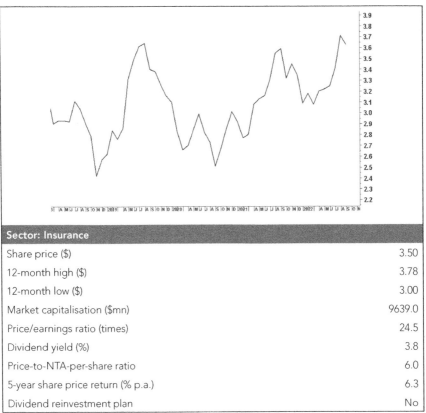

Sector: Insurance	
Share price ($)	3.50
12-month high ($)	3.78
12-month low ($)	3.00
Market capitalisation ($mn)	9639.0
Price/earnings ratio (times)	24.5
Dividend yield (%)	3.8
Price-to-NTA-per-share ratio	6.0
5-year share price return (% p.a.)	6.3
Dividend reinvestment plan	No

Melbourne-based Medibank Private was established by the Australian government in 1976 as a not-for-profit private health insurer under the Health Insurance Commission. It was privatised and listed on the ASX in 2014. Today it is Australia's largest private health insurer, with a market share of around 27 per cent, operating under the Medibank and ahm brands. It has also branched into other areas, including travel insurance, pet insurance, life insurance, income protection and funeral insurance. Its Medibank Health division specialises in the provision of healthcare services over the phone, online or face-to-face.

Latest business results (June 2022, full year)

Rising policyholder numbers meant higher revenues for Medibank, but profits were down. However, this was largely a result of volatility in financial markets, which led to a $24.8 million loss in net investment income, compared with a $120 million gain in the previous year. On an operational basis, profits rose 12.5 per cent, with underlying after-tax profit, which adjusts for the normalisation of investment returns, up 9.1 per cent. Policyholder numbers grew by a net 3.5 per cent during the year, with much of this increase again concentrated in the budget ahm health insurance brand, which is aimed at younger customers. Health insurance revenue rose 2.7 per cent, and net claims were up 1.9 per cent. Productivity benefits led to improved margins. The very small Medibank Health business saw double-digit rises in revenues and profits, thanks to strong growth in COVID-related services and a second-half recovery in travel insurance.

Outlook

Medibank occupies a central role in the national health sector. Nevertheless, its business is heavily regulated, and it is difficult to achieve significant growth. In addition, as the population ages, customer claim volumes have sometimes been growing faster than premium rises. Maintaining a tight control on expenses is important for the company, and it has a target of $40 million in annual productivity savings in the three years to June 2024. It is benefiting from an apparent new focus among Australians on their health and wellbeing, triggered by the COVID pandemic, with record numbers continuing to take out medical insurance and retention rates at their highest in a decade. Young people particularly — a lower-claiming customer demographic — are now more inclined than ever to seek out private health insurance. Medibank is investing in hospitals that provide members with short-stay surgical procedures and it is expanding its no-gap network of health providers who offer members a range of selected medical procedures with no out-of-pocket costs.

Year to 30 June	2021	2022
Revenues ($mn)	6910.4	7128.5
EBIT ($mn)	619.1	548.2
EBIT margin (%)	9.0	7.7
Profit before tax ($mn)	632.3	560.0
Profit after tax ($mn)	441.2	393.9
Earnings per share (c)	16.02	14.30
Cash flow per share (c)	20.45	18.48
Dividend (c)	12.7	13.4
Percentage franked	100	100
Net tangible assets per share ($)	0.57	0.59
Interest cover (times)	~	~
Return on equity (%)	23.8	20.5
Debt-to-equity ratio (%)	~	~
Current ratio	1.8	1.5

Metcash Limited

ASX code: MTS   www.metcash.com

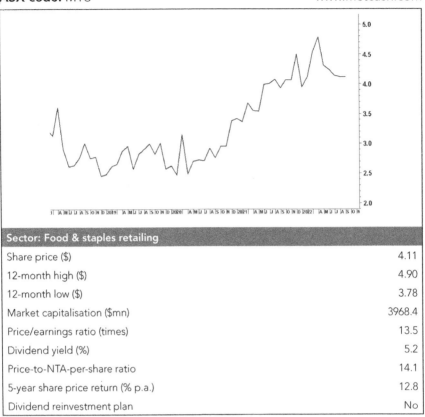

Sector: Food & staples retailing	
Share price ($)	4.11
12-month high ($)	4.90
12-month low ($)	3.78
Market capitalisation ($mn)	3968.4
Price/earnings ratio (times)	13.5
Dividend yield (%)	5.2
Price-to-NTA-per-share ratio	14.1
5-year share price return (% p.a.)	12.8
Dividend reinvestment plan	No

Sydney-based Metcash, with a history dating back to the 1920s, is a leading food and liquor wholesaler. Its Food division supports a network of more than 1600 independently owned grocery stores and supermarkets, mainly under the IGA and Foodland brands. The Liquor division is Australia's largest supplier of liquor to independently owned liquor retailers, with more than 12 000 customers. These include the Independent Brands Australia network of Cellarbrations, The Bottle-O, Duncans, Thirsty Camel, IGA Liquor, Big Bargain and Porters. The Hardware division operates the Independent Hardware Group which supplies more than 1500 stores, including the Mitre 10, Home Timber & Hardware and Total Tools chains.

Latest business results (April 2022, full year)

Metcash reported another strong result, with all divisions achieving growth. The core Food division saw EBIT up 4.1 per cent on a 0.8 per cent rise in sales, a solid performance in the face of significant supply chain disruptions and accelerating wholesale price inflation. The company reported that price increases were received from some 60 per cent of its suppliers in the second half. Liquor division EBIT rose

9.8 per cent, with sales revenues up 8.7 per cent, as customers maintained their preference for local shopping, along with the decline in overseas travel and duty-free shopping. Once again the best result came from the Hardware division, which recorded a 40.7 per cent jump in EBIT on a 25.4 per cent rise in sales. This partially reflected the addition of new stores, though on a like-for-like basis sales were up 9 per cent. Sales might have been higher but for the adverse impact of a tight labour market on construction and renovation activity. Though just 13 per cent of total revenues, the Hardware division now contributes some 39 per cent of company EBIT.

Outlook

Metcash is reaping the rewards of its five-year MFuture restructuring process that has cut costs and enhanced the attractiveness of its offerings. It expects by 2026 to have upgraded around 90 per cent of its store network. It also believes that it is a beneficiary of a move by consumers to local neighbourhood shopping. It is building a new, semi-automated 115 000-square-metre distribution centre in outer Melbourne aimed at expanding the range of goods that it can carry and boosting competitiveness, with completion expected by mid-2024. It continues to expand its investment in its high-margin hardware business. Nevertheless, it faces a series of challenges, including inflation, supply chain problems and a possible slowdown in consumer spending.

Year to 30 April	2021	2022
Revenues ($mn)	14 315.3	15 164.8
Food (%)	58	55
Liquor (%)	31	31
Hardware (%)	11	13
EBIT ($mn)	401.4	472.3
EBIT margin (%)	2.8	3.1
Gross margin (%)	10.3	11.1
Profit before tax ($mn)	358.8	423.8
Profit after tax ($mn)	252.7	299.6
Earnings per share (c)	24.75	30.48
Cash flow per share (c)	40.78	48.38
Dividend (c)	17.5	21.5
Percentage franked	100	100
Net tangible assets per share ($)	0.54	0.29
Interest cover (times)	68.0	65.6
Return on equity (%)	19.2	25.4
Debt-to-equity ratio (%)	~	17.3
Current ratio	1.2	1.1

Michael Hill International Limited

ASX code: MHJ   investor.michaelhill.com

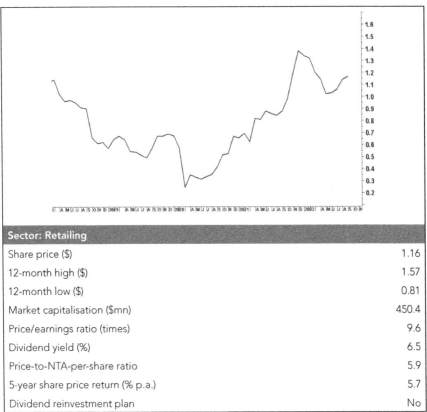

Sector: Retailing	
Share price ($)	1.16
12-month high ($)	1.57
12-month low ($)	0.81
Market capitalisation ($mn)	450.4
Price/earnings ratio (times)	9.6
Dividend yield (%)	6.5
Price-to-NTA-per-share ratio	5.9
5-year share price return (% p.a.)	5.7
Dividend reinvestment plan	No

Jewellery retailer Michael Hill dates back to the opening of its first store in Whangarei, New Zealand, in 1979. It grew steadily, expanding to Australia and Canada, and it moved its headquarters to Brisbane. Today it incorporates 280 stores, with 147 in Australia, 85 in Canada and 48 in New Zealand.

Latest business results (June 2022, full year)

Michael Hill overcame first-half lockdowns in Australia and New Zealand to post its second consecutive year of rising sales and profits. Revenues grew by 7 per cent, or 8 per cent on a same-store basis as the company closed six underperforming stores. Canada, which was barely affected by lockdowns, was the star, with sales soaring 40 per cent, or 35 per cent in local currency, and profits more than doubling, thanks especially to new leadership and productivity initiatives. Nevertheless, Canadian profitability remained below Australian and New Zealand levels. By contrast, both Australia and New Zealand posted declines in sales and profits. Digital sales rose 23 per cent to $42 million, delivering high margins. During the year the company opened one new store in Australia.

Outlook

Michael Hill has a combination of strategies that it believes can deliver sustainable long-term growth. A key tactic is the elevation of the Michael Hill brand, driving its transition from a name associated with discount-led promotions into a brand for unique high-margin, high-quality jewellery. It has launched emotive story-telling publicity campaigns that place a focus on craftsmanship, quality and sustainability, with the result that the average transaction value at its stores has risen 15 per cent over three years. The new Brilliance by Michael Hill loyalty program has grown from 200 000 members in June 2020 to more than 1.4 million in June 2022, and the company is already finding that members shop more frequently and spend considerably more than other customers. The company is also investing heavily to strengthen its online presence. It has launched an online brand, Medley, which has achieved $1 million in sales in its first full year of operation. It plans to initiate international shipping to all countries for online orders. Nevertheless, it views its physical stores as fundamental to its success, and continues to invest heavily in store upgrades. It is working to appeal to environmentally conscious customers with laboratory-grown diamonds, which are certified as sustainable and climate neutral, and which also deliver high margins. At June 2022 Michael Hill had no debt and more than $95 million in cash holdings.

Year to 26 June*	2021	2022
Revenues ($mn)	556.5	595.2
Australia (%)	56	51
Canada (%)	22	29
New Zealand (%)	21	20
EBIT ($mn)	66.7	73.2
EBIT margin (%)	12.0	12.3
Gross margin (%)	62.7	64.7
Profit before tax ($mn)	59.1	65.7
Profit after tax ($mn)	41.0	46.7
Earnings per share (c)	10.57	12.03
Cash flow per share (c)	22.96	25.41
Dividend (c)	4.5	7.5
Percentage franked	0	0
Net tangible assets per share ($)	0.21	0.20
Interest cover (times)	67.0	98.7
Return on equity (%)	23.6	25.3
Debt-to-equity ratio (%)	~	~
Current ratio	1.8	1.8

*27 June 2021

Mineral Resources Limited

ASX code: MIN   www.mineralresources.com.au

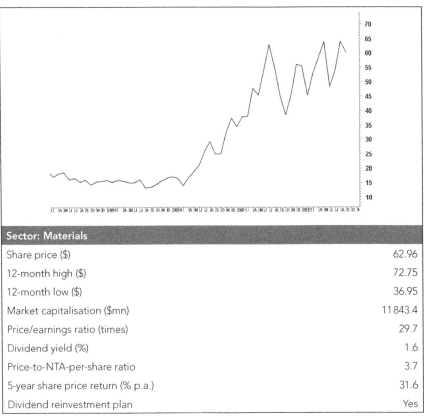

Sector: Materials	
Share price ($)	62.96
12-month high ($)	72.75
12-month low ($)	36.95
Market capitalisation ($mn)	11 843.4
Price/earnings ratio (times)	29.7
Dividend yield (%)	1.6
Price-to-NTA-per-share ratio	3.7
5-year share price return (% p.a.)	31.6
Dividend reinvestment plan	Yes

Mineral Resources, based in Perth, was founded in 1993, and is a mining and mining services company. Its mining side comprises iron ore production assets as well as holdings in the Wodgina lithium mine and the Mount Marion lithium project. The mining services side incorporates several subsidiaries: CSI Mining Services provides contract crushing, screening and processing services to the resources sector; Process Minerals International is a minerals processor and exporter, with a specialty in bringing new mines into production; and Mining Wear Parts is a newly acquired business that provides specialist parts to the mining, quarrying and recycling industries.

Latest business results (June 2022, full year)

A weaker iron ore price sent revenues and profits down, only partially offset by the company's lithium business. Total iron ore sales of 19.2 million tonnes were up 11 per cent from the previous year, but the average price received by the company of US$82 per tonne was 42 per cent lower, and the company actually reported a loss on this business at the EBIT level. In contrast, Mineral Resources was a significant beneficiary of a surging lithium price. Sales of spodumene concentrate — a lithium ore — fell 4 per cent to 464 tonnes, but average prices received more than quadrupled. The company reported underlying lithium EBIT of $565.7 million, compared with a $29.2 million loss in the previous year. Mining services operations again performed very well, with increases in revenues and profits, thanks to a high level of demand from the company's own mining activities as well as from external mine operators.

Outlook

Mineral Resources is set to expand substantially following the August 2022 announcement that it will proceed with its massive Onslow Iron Project. Situated in the West Pilbara region of Western Australia, it will become one of the state's largest-ever iron ore developments. Mineral Resources will hold a 40 per cent stake in the project, and its Mining Services division will be responsible for developing and operating the mine and its associated infrastructure. Initial iron ore shipments could begin as early as December 2023, with a target of 35 million tonnes annually from the first stage. The company has become a significant beneficiary of fast-growing global demand for lithium. It plans an expansion of its Mt Marion joint venture and is also considering an expansion of the Wodgina mine. At Wodgina it plans to develop plants to convert spodumene concentrate to higher-value lithium hydroxide. The company says its long-term vision is to manufacture the actual lithium batteries.

Year to 30 June	2021	2022
Revenues ($mn)	3733.6	3418.0
Iron ore (%)	82	58
Lithium (%)	3	23
Mining services (%)	15	19
EBIT ($mn)	1643.0	672.0
EBIT margin (%)	44.0	19.7
Profit before tax ($mn)	1557.0	559.0
Profit after tax ($mn)	1103.0	400.0
Earnings per share (c)	584.80	211.76
Cash flow per share (c)	721.58	398.22
Dividend (c)	275	100
Percentage franked	100	100
Net tangible assets per share ($)	16.83	17.02
Interest cover (times)	22.3	6.7
Return on equity (%)	40.3	12.4
Debt-to-equity ratio (%)	~	21.3
Current ratio	2.1	3.7

Monadelphous Group Limited

ASX code: MND   www.monadelphous.com.au

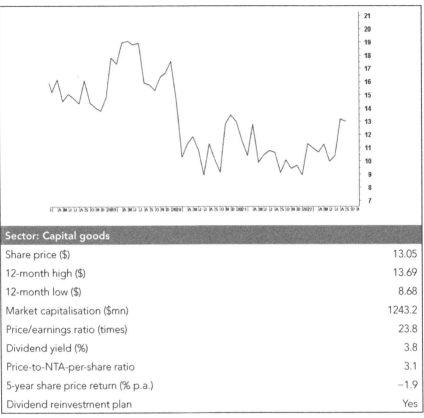

Sector: Capital goods	
Share price ($)	13.05
12-month high ($)	13.69
12-month low ($)	8.68
Market capitalisation ($mn)	1243.2
Price/earnings ratio (times)	23.8
Dividend yield (%)	3.8
Price-to-NTA-per-share ratio	3.1
5-year share price return (% p.a.)	−1.9
Dividend reinvestment plan	Yes

Perth-based Monadelphous, established in 1972, is an engineering company that provides a wide range of construction, maintenance, project management and support services to the minerals, energy and infrastructure industries. It operates from branches throughout Australia, with a client base that includes most of the country's resource majors. It has also established a presence in overseas markets that include New Zealand, China, Mongolia, Papua New Guinea, Chile and the Philippines. Its Zenviron joint venture is involved in large-scale renewable energy projects.

Latest business results (June 2022, full year)

Monadelphous reported a second year of rising revenues and profits, with $1.45 billion in new contracts and contract extensions secured during the year — up from $950 million in the previous year — with a particular focus on iron ore projects. The company classifies its activities into two broad segments. The Maintenance and Industrial Services division rebounded from the previous year's weakness with revenues up 19 per cent, and a significant volume of maintenance, shutdown and project contract work for the iron ore sector in Western Australia's Pilbara region. Both BHP and Rio Tinto were among the major clients. By contrast, the Engineering

Construction division, which in the previous year had seen its revenues jump 59 per cent, this time recorded a 21 per cent decline, with the completion of some large projects and the commencement of fewer new projects. Income from overseas operations — mainly in Chile and Papua New Guinea — jumped 51 per cent to represent 10 per cent of total revenues.

Outlook

Monadelphous plays an important role in the Australian minerals, energy and infrastructure industries, and it stands to benefit from growing demand for its services over coming years. More than 40 per cent of its income derives from the iron ore sector, where the outlook is increasingly buoyant. A further 20 per cent of its revenues comes from the oil and gas sector, and it is experiencing a steady flow of work for new LNG projects and strong demand for maintenance services. In addition, it sees strongly growing investment in projects relating to lithium and other battery metals as providing more opportunities. It is also optimistic about the outlook for clean energy, with its Zenviron joint venture actively involved in the wind energy sector, and with hydrogen developments showing potential. But the company is concerned about skills shortages, which are driving labour costs higher and leading to delays in completing projects. At June 2022 Monadelphous had net cash holdings of more than $170 million.

Year to 30 June	2021	2022
Revenues ($mn)	1754.2	1810.4
Maintenance & industrial services (%)	56	60
Engineering construction (%)	44	40
EBIT ($mn)	71.4	74.6
EBIT margin (%)	4.1	4.1
Gross margin (%)	6.4	6.8
Profit before tax ($mn)	70.4	73.5
Profit after tax ($mn)	47.1	52.2
Earnings per share (c)	49.70	54.90
Cash flow per share (c)	84.46	89.70
Dividend (c)	45	49
Percentage franked	100	100
Net tangible assets per share ($)	4.13	4.28
Interest cover (times)	67.3	67.8
Return on equity (%)	12.1	12.9
Debt-to-equity ratio (%)	~	~
Current ratio	1.9	2.0

National Australia Bank Limited

ASX code: NAB   www.nab.com.au

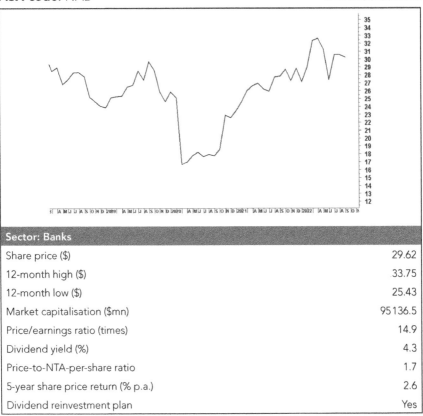

Sector: Banks	
Share price ($)	29.62
12-month high ($)	33.75
12-month low ($)	25.43
Market capitalisation ($mn)	95 136.5
Price/earnings ratio (times)	14.9
Dividend yield (%)	4.3
Price-to-NTA-per-share ratio	1.7
5-year share price return (% p.a.)	2.6
Dividend reinvestment plan	Yes

National Australia Bank, based in Melbourne, has a history dating back to the establishment of the National Bank of Australasia in 1858. It is one of Australia's largest banks, with a wide spread of financial activities and particular strength in business banking. It owns the Bank of New Zealand, and also operates offices in several countries in Asia. It is involved in financial planning and wealth management, including with its long-established JBWere advisory service. Other activities include the nabtrade online broking service and the UBank online bank.

Latest business results (March 2022, half year)

National Australia's strength in business banking helped it post an increase in profits. The Business and Private Banking division represents some 40 per cent of bank earnings, and profits rose 17.5 per cent, reflecting strong growth in lending and deposit volumes, a rise in fee income and reduced credit impairment charges. Partially offsetting these were higher operating expenses, particularly related to the bank's technology infrastructure. New Zealand business was also strong, thanks to lending growth and improved margins. The Corporate and Institutional Banking division recorded a 3.1 per cent rise in profits, with solid growth in lending and deposit volumes. However, the fourth division, Personal Banking, posted an 8.3 per cent drop in profits, as competitive pressures cut margins, despite growth in household deposits and an expanding home loans book.

Outlook

In an environment of growing inflation and rising interest rates, NAB is adjusting its priorities. In 2020 it announced that its goal was to lower absolute costs in the 2023–2025 period. It has now noted that it is becoming increasingly expensive to attract and retain sufficient numbers of qualified staff, with other costs also rising, so despite success in its drive to boost productivity it expects its expenses to continue to rise modestly. It is adding more bankers to its Business and Private Banking division, aimed particularly at expanding its exposure to the small and medium-sized enterprise sector. It is also working to speed up the process of approving business loans. The Personal Banking division has achieved success with its digital Simple Home Loans application platform, which has considerably simplified the mortgage process. The acquisition, completed in June 2022, of Citibank's Australian consumer business is expected to help the bank scale up its personal banking operations. It is also increasingly involved in environmental projects. It has launched the Agri Green Loan program to help agribusinesses reduce emissions and has helped found Carbonplace, a carbon credit settlement platform.

Year to 30 September	2020	2021
Operating income ($mn)	17319.0	16806.0
Net interest income ($mn)	13920.0	13797.0
Operating expenses ($mn)	7679.0	7817.0
Profit before tax ($mn)	6878.0	9206.0
Profit after tax ($mn)	4733.0	6558.0
Earnings per share (c)	154.27	199.33
Dividend (c)	60	127
Percentage franked	100	100
Non-interest income to total income (%)	19.6	17.9
Cost-to-income ratio (%)	53.6	46.5
Return on equity (%)	8.7	10.6
Return on assets (%)	0.6	0.7
Half year to 31 March	2021	2022
Operating income ($mn)	8439.0	8828.0
Profit before tax ($mn)	4704.0	4863.0
Profit after tax ($mn)	3343.0	3480.0
Earnings per share (c)	101.19	106.92
Dividend (c)	60	73
Percentage franked	100	100
Net tangible assets per share ($)	17.56	17.70

Netwealth Group Limited

ASX code: NWL   www.netwealth.com.au

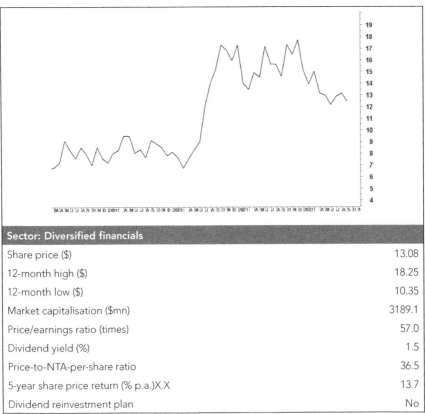

Sector: Diversified financials	
Share price ($)	13.08
12-month high ($)	18.25
12-month low ($)	10.35
Market capitalisation ($mn)	3189.1
Price/earnings ratio (times)	57.0
Dividend yield (%)	1.5
Price-to-NTA-per-share ratio	36.5
5-year share price return (% p.a.)X.X	13.7
Dividend reinvestment plan	No

Based in Melbourne, wealth management business Netwealth was founded in 1999. Through its wealth management platform it specialises in superannuation products, investor-directed portfolio services for self-managed superannuation, managed accounts and managed funds. The founding Heine family own more than half the company equity.

Latest business results (June 2022, full year)

In a volatile year for financial markets, Netwealth again saw strong demand for its business, delivering growth in revenues and profits. During the year it recorded net inflows to its funds of $13 billion. This offset negative market movements of $4.5 billion, and total funds under administration at June 2022 of $55.7 billion were up 18 per cent from a year earlier and the number of client accounts was up 19 per cent to 115 642. The acceleration of investment in IT infrastructure led to a 43 per cent jump in the IT and communication expense, with staffing costs up 32 per cent as the company continued its growth.

Outlook

Netwealth runs a wealth management platform, which is a comprehensive software system that is designed to help financial advisors, clients and others to track their investment portfolios, perform research on new investments and execute trades. It is estimated that as much as $1 trillion in investor assets are currently being managed on such platforms in Australia and it is a highly competitive business. The leaders are major financial institutions such as Insignia Financial, BT Financial Group, AMP Group, Colonial First State and Macquarie Group. But catching up on them are several smaller and fast-growing firms like Netwealth that have a particular strength in the development of user-friendly technology. These smaller companies were helped by the Financial Services Royal Commission of 2017, which led to many advisors separating themselves from the major legacy institutions and choosing to work independently, a trend that continues. Netwealth says that, based on industry analysis, it was Australia's fastest-growing platform provider by net fund flows in the 12 months to March 2022, and it is gaining market share. It continues to invest heavily in its IT infrastructure, in order to promote continuing growth, with a particular target of increased business from high net worth individuals. It also maintains a focus on securing and retaining key talent, despite a tight labour market. It will benefit from higher interest rates. It forecasts further net fund inflows of $11 billion to $13 billion in the June 2023 year. At June 2022 Netwealth had no debt and more than $88 million in cash holdings.

Year to 30 June	2021	2022
Revenues ($mn)	142.0	169.5
EBIT ($mn)	76.8	81.3
EBIT margin (%)	54.1	48.0
Profit before tax ($mn)	77.2	81.1
Profit after tax ($mn)	54.1	55.9
Earnings per share (c)	22.55	22.93
Cash flow per share (c)	23.40	24.15
Dividend (c)	18.56	20
Percentage franked	100	100
Net tangible assets per share ($)	0.31	0.36
Interest cover (times)	~	441.8
Return on equity (%)	63.9	56.6
Debt-to-equity ratio (%)	~	~
Current ratio	4.9	6.5

NIB Holdings Limited

ASX code: NHF

www.nib.com.au

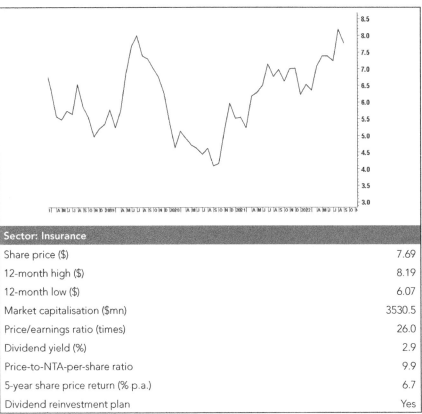

Sector: Insurance	
Share price ($)	7.69
12-month high ($)	8.19
12-month low ($)	6.07
Market capitalisation ($mn)	3530.5
Price/earnings ratio (times)	26.0
Dividend yield (%)	2.9
Price-to-NTA-per-share ratio	9.9
5-year share price return (% p.a.)	6.7
Dividend reinvestment plan	Yes

Newcastle private health insurer NIB Holdings was established as the Newcastle Industrial Benefits Hospital Fund in 1952 by workers at the BHP steelworks. It subsequently demutualised and became the first private health insurer to list on the ASX. It is also active in New Zealand. Other businesses are travel insurance and the provision of specialist insurance services to international students and workers in Australia. In April 2022 it acquired Kiwi Insurance for $42 million.

Latest business results (June 2022, full year)

Revenues rose but profits fell. However, this largely reflected losses in investment returns. The company said its underlying profit was up nearly 15 per cent. The company's flagship Australian Residents Health Insurance, representing 85 per cent of company income, saw premium revenues increase by 5.2 per cent. Policyholder numbers grew by 3.2 per cent. The total claims expense actually fell 3.1 per cent as COVID-related lockdowns affected both the willingness and the ability of Australians to access surgery and healthcare. New Zealand health insurance represents a further 11 per cent of company turnover. It enjoyed a solid year, with premium revenues up 12.8 per cent and policyholder numbers up 30 per cent. This included a two-month contribution from Kiwi Insurance. The company's formerly high-margin health insurance program for international students and workers in Australia continued to be hit by border restrictions. Premium revenue rose 7.1 per cent to $123.7 million, helped by price rises and a strong second half, but this business remained in the red. The travel insurance operation enjoyed an exceptionally strong fourth-quarter recovery, but it too made an operating loss for the year.

Outlook

NIB continues to see its policyholder base grow, with the COVID pandemic apparently raising community awareness of health issues and generating increased demand for health insurance. It benefits from its exposure in New Zealand, where it is the country's second-largest health insurer. However, it has noted that the pandemic has led some people to defer treatment, which could mean a higher level of claims in future. It is working to branch into new areas of business. It launched a new joint venture company, Honeysuckle Health, aimed at using data analytics to deliver healthcare programs. It holds a majority stake in out-of-hours prescription delivery service Midnight Health. It sees plan management work for participants in the National Disability Insurance Scheme as a new business opportunity. However, the COVID pandemic has made its Chinese health insurance joint venture unsustainable, and it will close this business.

Year to 30 June	2021	2022
Revenues ($mn)	2548.8	2703.4
EBIT ($mn)	237.8	197.5
EBIT margin (%)	9.3	7.3
Profit before tax ($mn)	231.0	190.8
Profit after tax ($mn)	161.1	135.7
Earnings per share (c)	35.24	29.60
Cash flow per share (c)	42.24	36.52
Dividend (c)	24	22
Percentage franked	100	100
Net tangible assets per share ($)	0.74	0.78
Interest cover (times)	35.0	29.5
Return on equity (%)	25.2	19.2
Debt-to-equity ratio (%)	2.6	7.4
Current ratio	1.9	1.7

Nick Scali Limited

ASX code: NCK www.nickscali.com.au

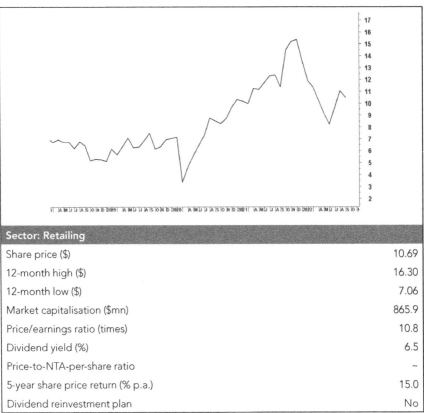

Sector: Retailing

Share price ($)	10.69
12-month high ($)	16.30
12-month low ($)	7.06
Market capitalisation ($mn)	865.9
Price/earnings ratio (times)	10.8
Dividend yield (%)	6.5
Price-to-NTA-per-share ratio	~
5-year share price return (% p.a.)	15.0
Dividend reinvestment plan	No

Sydney-based Nick Scali is one of Australia's largest furniture importers and retailers, with a history dating back more than 50 years. It specialises in leather and fabric lounge suites along with dining room and bedroom furniture. In November 2021 it acquired Plush-Think Sofas. At June 2022 it operated 57 Nick Scali Furniture stores in Australia, and five in New Zealand, and 46 Plush stores.

Latest business results (June 2022, full year)

An eight-month contribution of $88.8 million in sales from the Plush acquisition led to a jump in revenues, but underlying profits were down in a difficult year for the company. During the first half of the year over 55 per cent of the store network was closed for a period of three months. In addition, the company's ability to source its furniture was significantly affected by extended COVID-related closures of manufacturing facilities in Vietnam and of port facilities in China. The Plush acquisition led to a big rise in debt levels, and due to its lower levels of profitability the Plush business also helped push down the company's own profit margins. Total written sales orders for the year of $473.8 million represented growth of 18 per cent, with Plush contributing $98.7 million of this amount. The Nick Scali online business received orders of $37.6 million, more than double the figure for the previous year. At June 2022 Nick Scali had an order backlog of $185.3 million, which was 67 per cent higher than a year earlier. However, part of this was attributed to lockdowns in China in April and May 2022, which delayed deliveries to customers.

Outlook

Nick Scali is directly affected by trends in consumer spending, interest rates, currency movements, housing sales, renovation activity and the general economy. Thanks to its substantial order book, it is optimistic about the short-term outlook. However, for the longer term it is concerned about continuing inflationary pressures, as well as the possibility of a housing slowdown and a dampening of consumer spending. It sees great potential for its $102.5 million Plush acquisition. This has been successfully integrated into its own operations, and it expects to achieve significant cost synergies, including $13 million in the June 2023 year, as well as boosting margins as it changes the furniture mix at Plush. The company's long-term target is for at least 86 Nick Scali stores and 90 to 100 Plush stores across Australia and New Zealand, including four to six new stores that will open during the June 2023 year.

Year to 30 June	2021	2022
Revenues ($mn)	373.0	441.0
EBIT ($mn)	127.8	124.5
EBIT margin (%)	34.26	28.23
Gross margin (%)	63.47	61.00
Profit before tax ($mn)	121.21	115.30
Profit after tax ($mn)	84.24	80.20
Earnings per share (c)	104.00	99.01
Cash flow per share (c)	142.11	150.31
Dividend (c)	65	70
Percentage franked	100	100
Net tangible assets per share ($)	~	~
Interest cover (times)	19.4	13.6
Return on equity (%)	88.9	62.9
Debt-to-equity ratio (%)	~	12.1
Current ratio	1.2	0.8

Nine Entertainment Company Holdings Limited

ASX code: NEC   www.nineforbrands.com.au

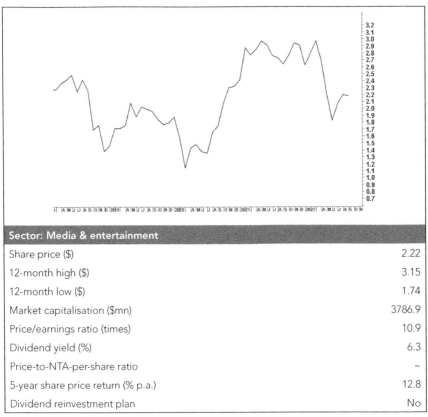

Sector: Media & entertainment	
Share price ($)	2.22
12-month high ($)	3.15
12-month low ($)	1.74
Market capitalisation ($mn)	3786.9
Price/earnings ratio (times)	10.9
Dividend yield (%)	6.3
Price-to-NTA-per-share ratio	~
5-year share price return (% p.a.)	12.8
Dividend reinvestment plan	No

With roots that stretch back to the first edition of the *Sydney Herald* in 1831 and the launch of channel TCN-9 in 1956, Sydney-based Nine Entertainment is today one of Australia's media giants. It divides its activities into four broad segments. The Broadcasting division incorporates its free-to-air television activities, its 9Now streaming video service and eight radio stations. Digital and Publishing comprises a portfolio of newspapers, including the *Sydney Morning Herald*, *The Age* and the *Australian Financial Review*, as well as magazines and online publications. The Stan division represents the Stan subscription video on demand service. The fourth segment, Domain Group, is a real estate media and services business.

Latest business results (June 2022, full year)

Nine Entertainment enjoyed an excellent year, with a big surge in revenues and profits. The best result came from the Digital and Publishing division, with revenues up 18 per cent and profits jumping 53 per cent. The continuing downward drift in print-edition subscription numbers was more than offset by a double-digit rise in digital subscriptions and strong growth in advertising revenues. With just a modest rise in costs, profit margins expanded. The Broadcasting division reported a 21 per cent increase in profits, with revenues up 10 per cent. Advertising revenues rose and there was a particularly strong performance from the 9Now streaming video service. The Domain Group benefited from a strong housing market as well as from acquisitions made during the year. Stan revenues grew 22 per cent as the number of subscribers exceeded 2.5 million, but profits fell 28 per cent as the company invested heavily in original programming and sport.

Outlook

Nine Entertainment has been a beneficiary of the COVID pandemic and of events such as the war in Ukraine, with Australians spending more to access entertainment and news. It has also benefited from a robust economy and from its own restructuring efforts, which have quite significantly reduced costs. The challenge now is to maintain this momentum as the economy slows and cost pressures grow. A key strategy is an acceleration of the shift to digital platforms for its content. Its 9Now business continues to grow strongly. An increasing share of the company's radio audience is listening online or via apps, and Nine targets a doubling of the number of digital subscribers to its newspapers within five years. With subscriber numbers at Stan continuing to expand, especially as it moves into sports broadcasting, Nine expects profits to start growing again for this business.

Year to 30 June	2021	2022
Revenues ($mn)	2342.2	2691.4
Broadcasting (%)	53	51
Digital & publishing (%)	21	22
Stan (%)	13	14
Domain Group (%)	12	13
EBIT ($mn)	415.6	551.6
EBIT margin (%)	17.7	20.5
Profit before tax ($mn)	388.1	526.4
Profit after tax ($mn)	261.0	348.5
Earnings per share (c)	15.31	20.46
Cash flow per share (c)	24.55	29.21
Dividend (c)	10.5	14
Percentage franked	100	100
Net tangible assets per share ($)	~	~
Interest cover (times)	36.3	54.4
Return on equity (%)	14.7	18.9
Debt-to-equity ratio (%)	12.8	15.7
Current ratio	1.0	1.0

NRW Holdings Limited

ASX code: NWH   www.nrw.com.au

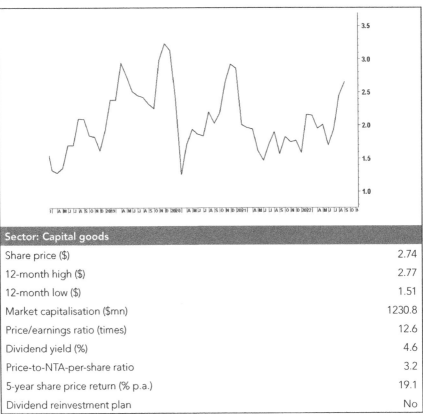

Sector: Capital goods	
Share price ($)	2.74
12-month high ($)	2.77
12-month low ($)	1.51
Market capitalisation ($mn)	1230.8
Price/earnings ratio (times)	12.6
Dividend yield (%)	4.6
Price-to-NTA-per-share ratio	3.2
5-year share price return (% p.a.)	19.1
Dividend reinvestment plan	No

Perth company NRW Holdings, a specialist provider of services to the mining and resources industries, was founded in 1994. It segments its operations into three divisions. The Mining division specialises in mine management, contract mining, drill and blast operations, and maintenance services. The Civil division is involved in the delivery of a wide range of private and public civil infrastructure projects, including roads, bridges and renewable energy facilities. The Minerals, Energy and Technologies division includes mining equipment manufacturer RCR Mining Technologies, specialist metals and mining engineer DIAB Engineering, and resources and energy construction specialist Primero.

Latest business results (June 2022, full year)

Strategic initiatives in recent years by NRW to diversify its revenue streams helped deliver higher revenues and a sharp increase in profits, despite the challenges of the COVID pandemic, labour shortages, rising inflation and some significant weather disruptions. The best result came from the Minerals, Energy and Technologies division, with sales surging 64 per cent and profits up 44 per cent, in large part due to a full year's benefit from the Primero business, acquired in February 2021. The division benefited from increasing work on Covalent Lithium's Mount Holland project and the Coburn Mineral Sands project for Strandline Resources. The Mining division was also strong, with sales up 8 per cent and profits jumping 27 per cent as the company closed out some lower-margin projects. By contrast, the Civil division experienced a 33 per cent fall in revenues, with profits down 11 per cent, following the completion in the previous year of some major Pilbara-based contracts.

Outlook

NRW had an order book of $5.2 billion at June 2022, compared with $3.4 billion a year earlier, and it is optimistic about future business. It expected some $19.8 billion worth of potential projects to be put up for tender during the June 2023 year, compared with $14.5 billion in the June 2022 year. Its early forecast for June 2023 is for revenues of $2.6 billion to $2.7 billion, with most of this already in the order book. It forecasts EBITA between $162 million and $172 million, compared to $157 million in June 2022. It sees particular potential over the coming three to five years for battery-related minerals and materials projects, and also forecasts an increase in iron ore projects. In August 2022 NRW made a takeover offer for Perth-based contractor MACA, which has a specialty in services for gold and iron ore mines. However, following a competing bid from Thiess Group Investments, NRW withdrew its offer.

Year to 30 June	2021	2022
Revenues ($mn)	2221.5	2377.7
Mining (%)	52	52
Minerals, energy & technologies (%)	19	28
Civil (%)	29	20
EBIT ($mn)	89.2	149.1
EBIT margin (%)	4.0	6.3
Profit before tax ($mn)	75.9	136.2
Profit after tax ($mn)	54.3	97.4
Earnings per share (c)	12.47	21.69
Cash flow per share (c)	50.65	49.14
Dividend (c)	9	12.5
Percentage franked	100	100
Net tangible assets per share ($)	0.75	0.87
Interest cover (times)	9.2	15.7
Return on equity (%)	10.7	17.0
Debt-to-equity ratio (%)	21.2	2.3
Current ratio	1.4	1.3

Objective Corporation Limited

ASX code: OCL

www.objective.com.au

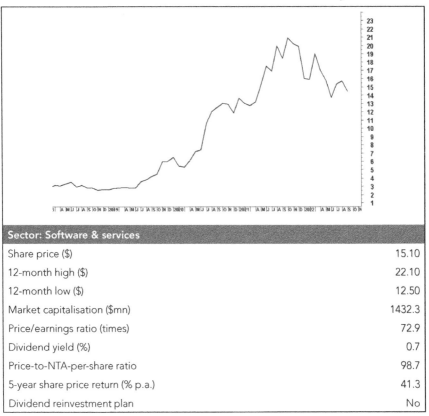

Sector: Software & services	
Share price ($)	15.10
12-month high ($)	22.10
12-month low ($)	12.50
Market capitalisation ($mn)	1432.3
Price/earnings ratio (times)	72.9
Dividend yield (%)	0.7
Price-to-NTA-per-share ratio	98.7
5-year share price return (% p.a.)	41.3
Dividend reinvestment plan	No

Sydney-based Objective, founded in 1987, provides information technology software and services. Its particular specialty is working with federal, state and local governments, as well as government agencies and regulated industries, and it has operations in Australia, New Zealand and the United Kingdom. It has grown substantially, organically and through acquisition, and now operates under numerous product categories.

Latest business results (June 2022, full year)

In another excellent result, Objective reported double-digit increases in revenues and profits. For reporting purposes, the company divides its businesses into three broad segments. The largest of these, Content and Process, representing around 70 per cent of total turnover, comprises the company's core products, which allow customers to manage, process and publish information and collaborate with external organisations. It recorded an 8 per cent rise in sales for the year. The best growth came from the company's RegTech segment, which comprises products that manage governmental safety and compliance regulatory processes and represents 19 per cent of income. This achieved a 34 per cent jump in revenues, thanks especially to a new five-year $13 million contract with New Zealand Police for software to help regulate the country's firearms. The third segment, Planning and Building, digitally manages the development and construction planning consent process, and it saw revenues up 10 per cent, despite labour shortages that delayed some projects. Overseas sales, primarily in New Zealand and the UK, represented about a quarter of total company income.

Outlook

Objective is a small company working in niche businesses, but with a solid reputation and a high level of profitability. The company's particular goal is to help customers digitalise and streamline the processes of compliance, accountability and governance. It is working to move its businesses as much as possible to a subscription model, which will make revenues and earnings more predictable each year. Already some 80 per cent of company income is of a recurring nature. Its products share a common interface, and as the product range grows it is increasingly able to cross-sell to its existing customer base. It spends heavily on research and development, and this reached $25 million in the June 2022 year, up from $23 million. In March 2022 it acquired American content management software developer Simflofy for US$5 million. It believes Simflofy will help Objective to broaden its offerings in its existing markets as well as extend its reach to North America. At June 2022 Objective had no debt and more than $63 million in cash holdings.

Year to 30 June	2021	2022
Revenues ($mn)	95.1	106.5
EBIT ($mn)	20.2	23.3
EBIT margin (%)	21.2	21.9
Profit before tax ($mn)	20.2	23.4
Profit after tax ($mn)	16.1	19.6
Earnings per share (c)	17.16	20.72
Cash flow per share (c)	22.36	26.57
Dividend (c)	9	11
Percentage franked	100	45
Net tangible assets per share ($)	0.03	0.15
Interest cover (times)	~	~
Return on equity (%)	39.1	35.9
Debt-to-equity ratio (%)	~	~
Current ratio	1.1	1.2

OZ Minerals Limited

ASX code: OZL   www.ozminerals.com

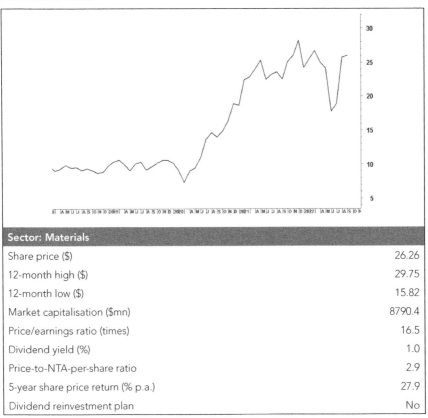

Sector: Materials	
Share price ($)	26.26
12-month high ($)	29.75
12-month low ($)	15.82
Market capitalisation ($mn)	8790.4
Price/earnings ratio (times)	16.5
Dividend yield (%)	1.0
Price-to-NTA-per-share ratio	2.9
5-year share price return (% p.a.)	27.9
Dividend reinvestment plan	No

OZ Minerals, based in Adelaide, dates back to the founding of gold mining company Golden Plateau in 1932. Golden Plateau later changed its name to Oxiana, and in 2008 merged with lead and zinc miner Zinifex — founded in 2004, when it was spun off from Pasminco — to form OZ Minerals. Today the company operates the Prominent Hill and Carrapateena underground copper–gold mines in the Gawler Craton of South Australia. It also mines copper and gold at Carajás in Brazil. It is working towards the launch of operations at its West Musgrave copper–nickel project in Western Australia, and it maintains exploration projects in several countries. In August 2022 BHP Group made a takeover bid for the company.

Latest business results (June 2022, half year)

Revenues and profits fell in a disappointing result, as the company was hit by higher costs, reduced sales volumes and weaker copper prices, only partially offset by higher gold prices. Total copper production of 57 745 tonnes was down 3 per cent from the June 2021 half, with gold production of 99 957 ounces down 12 per cent. The realised copper price fell 4 per cent, while the realised gold price rose 11 per cent. The company incurred substantially higher costs as a result of one-off production outages, repairs to the Carrapateena materials handling system, some extreme weather events and additional workforce costs due to COVID-related absenteeism. Mining costs of $298 million were up 22 per cent, with processing costs of $147.4 million up 15 per cent and freight charges of $47.8 million up 56 per cent. In addition, exploration and corporate development expenditure jumped 185 per cent to $68.3 million.

Outlook

OZ Minerals management are strongly resisting BHP's takeover bid, pointing to a bright and highly profitable future for their company. In particular, they say that the world is on the cusp of significant demand growth for copper and nickel, which are needed for electric vehicles and for such applications as wind turbines. It notes that quality copper assets are increasingly scarce and that new copper discoveries can take 17 years to come online. The company believes it has the capacity to more than double its current copper output. In September 2022 it announced plans to proceed with a major new $1.7 billion copper-nickel mine at West Musgrave. It describes this as one of the world's largest, longest-life and lowest-cost nickel projects. Having substantially reduced its borrowings, OZ Minerals at June 2022 had net cash holdings of some $82 million.

Year to 31 December	2020	2021
Revenues ($mn)	1342.0	2095.8
EBIT ($mn)	322.9	795.7
EBIT margin (%)	24.1	38.0
Profit before tax ($mn)	295.8	756.6
Profit after tax ($mn)	212.6	530.7
Earnings per share (c)	65.22	159.60
Cash flow per share (c)	152.16	269.88
Dividend (c)	25	26
Percentage franked	100	100
Interest cover (times)	11.9	20.4
Return on equity (%)	6.9	15.3
Half year to 30 June	2021	2022
Revenues ($mn)	986.1	908.6
Profit before tax ($mn)	367.5	178.2
Profit after tax ($mn)	268.6	109.2
Earnings per share (c)	80.90	32.70
Dividend (c)	8	8
Percentage franked	100	100
Net tangible assets per share ($)	8.24	9.17
Debt-to-equity ratio (%)	17.7	~
Current ratio	1.8	1.8

Pendal Group Limited

ASX code: PDL   www.pendalgroup.com

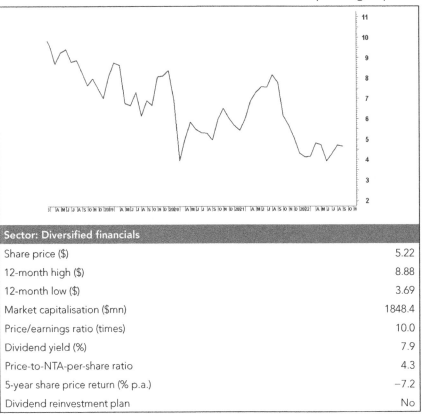

Sector: Diversified financials	
Share price ($)	5.22
12-month high ($)	8.88
12-month low ($)	3.69
Market capitalisation ($mn)	1848.4
Price/earnings ratio (times)	10.0
Dividend yield (%)	7.9
Price-to-NTA-per-share ratio	4.3
5-year share price return (% p.a.)	−7.2
Dividend reinvestment plan	No

Sydney-based funds management company Pendal Group started life as part of Ord-BT, an investment banking firm established in 1969. Ord-BT, later renamed as BT Financial Group, was subsequently acquired by Westpac Banking Corporation, which added to it some other funds management businesses, then created BT Investment Management as a new entity to be listed on the ASX. It was later renamed as Pendal Group. Today Pendal actively manages a wide range of investments in Australian equities, listed property and fixed interest, in international fixed interest, in multi-asset portfolios and in alternative investments. Its London-based subsidiary J O Hambro Capital Management, with offices in Singapore and the US, manages international funds. Pendal is set to be acquired by rival fund manager Perpetual.

Latest business results (March 2022, half year)

Revenues and profits rose, although this reflected in part a full six-month contribution from the Thompson, Siegel & Walmsley acquisition. Base management fees of $317.7 million were up 35 per cent from the March 2021 period. Performance fees increased 8 per cent to $44.5 million. Funds under management rose from $101.7 billion in March 2021 to $124.9 billion, though this largely reflected the addition of Thompson, Siegel & Walmsley funds. In the six months to March 2022 the company actually experienced a 10.3 per cent decline in funds under management, due to market weakness, adverse currency rate movements and net outflows of $7.5 billion. The company reported that over the 12 months to March 2022 only 36 per cent of its funds had outperformed their benchmarks, although, over three years, 86 per cent had outperformed.

Outlook

Pendal is heavily dependent on market activity and investor sentiment. Its business can also be buffeted by its own performance, which helps determine levels of performance fees. In addition, with a majority of its equities funds under management held in foreign currencies it is heavily influenced by currency fluctuations. However, it benefits from moves by Australian investors into overseas equities, while its Thompson, Siegel & Walmsley acquisition has given it significant exposure to the large US market as well as generating cross-selling opportunities. It sees great potential in its moves into environmental, social and governance (ESG) investing. Its subsidiary Regnan, an ESG specialist, plans a series of socially responsible funds. In August 2022 Pendal announced that it will be acquired by Perpetual in a Scheme of Arrangement agreed to by both companies, though also dependent on approval by Pendal shareholders.

Year to 30 September	2020	2021
Revenues ($mn)	474.8	581.9
EBIT ($mn)	152.8	219.6
EBIT margin (%)	32.2	37.7
Profit before tax ($mn)	151.4	217.9
Profit after tax ($mn)	116.4	164.7
Earnings per share (c)	39.76	51.96
Cash flow per share (c)	45.26	58.92
Dividend (c)	37	41
Percentage franked	10	10
Interest cover (times)	113.0	126.6
Return on equity (%)	12.9	14.4
Half year to 31 March	2021	2022
Revenues ($mn)	277.0	362.6
Profit before tax ($mn)	114.1	123.7
Profit after tax ($mn)	89.9	96.7
Earnings per share (c)	27.80	25.20
Dividend (c)	17	21
Percentage franked	10	10
Net tangible assets per share ($)	1.21	1.23
Debt-to-equity ratio (%)	~	~
Current ratio	1.8	2.2

PeopleIn Limited

ASX code: PPE www.peoplein.com.au

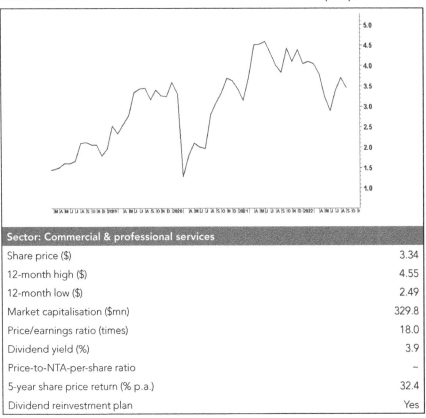

Sector: Commercial & professional services	
Share price ($)	3.34
12-month high ($)	4.55
12-month low ($)	2.49
Market capitalisation ($mn)	329.8
Price/earnings ratio (times)	18.0
Dividend yield (%)	3.9
Price-to-NTA-per-share ratio	~
5-year share price return (% p.a.)	32.4
Dividend reinvestment plan	Yes

Brisbane-based labour hire company PeopleIn, formerly called People Infrastructure Group, was founded in 1996. It has grown substantially — organically and through acquisition — and today comprises 26 brands across three broad segments: health and community, professional services, and industrial and specialist services. It has also expanded to New Zealand.

Latest business results (June 2022, full year)

A tight labour market and four acquisitions during the year generated strong growth in revenues. However, higher costs, including some COVID-related expenses, along with rising depreciation charges and interest payments, meant that profits were generally flat for the year. The company's largest segment, industrial and specialist services, enjoyed a good year, with strong double-digit growth in revenues and profits. A particular benefit came from the June 2021 acquisition of Techforce Personnel, thanks to growing mining and construction demand in Western Australia. By contrast, the health and community segment, providing staff to nursing, care, disability, mental health and child protection services, was hit by COVID-related lockdowns and the delay of elective surgeries, and profits fell sharply, despite a small increase in revenues.

The smaller professional services segment more than doubled its revenues and profits, with particularly strong demand for IT professionals.

Outlook

PeopleIn is a beneficiary of low unemployment levels in Australia and the inability of many companies to find sufficient numbers of qualified staff. It also benefits from wage inflation, which boosts its margins. It maintains a high organic growth rate, and also has a strong pipeline of potential acquisitions, with a focus on expanding its services within health, federal and state government, and professional services. In addition, it has other strategies for growth. As it expands it sees many cross-selling opportunities between its various brands. It is also working to boost its international recruitment services. It already has considerable experience in recruiting nurses from the UK and Ireland, and agricultural workers from the Pacific. As visa application times improve, it now hopes to leverage this experience into finding staff for a much broader range of industries. The company's Halcyon Knight specialist government division is experiencing a significant increase in government and education work. PeopleIn's June 2022 acquisition, Food Industry People Group, provides staff for the food services industry through the Pacific Australia Labour Mobility scheme, and the company believes it can expand the scheme to help solve critical staffing shortages in the aged care sector. The company's early forecast is for June 2023 EBITDA of $62 million to $66 million, up from $47.2 million in June 2022.

Year to 30 June	2021	2022
Revenues ($mn)	444.3	682.3
Industrial & specialist services (%)	57	61
Health & community (%)	30	20
Professional services (%)	13	19
EBIT ($mn)	28.3	29.1
EBIT margin (%)	6.4	4.3
Profit before tax ($mn)	26.8	27.0
Profit after tax ($mn)	17.7	17.7
Earnings per share (c)	19.27	18.60
Cash flow per share (c)	26.61	30.28
Dividend (c)	10.5	13
Percentage franked	100	100
Net tangible assets per share ($)	~	~
Interest cover (times)	34.0	22.1
Return on equity (%)	16.9	14.0
Debt-to-equity ratio (%)	12.9	32.2
Current ratio	1.4	1.2

Perpetual Limited

ASX code: PPT   www.perpetual.com.au

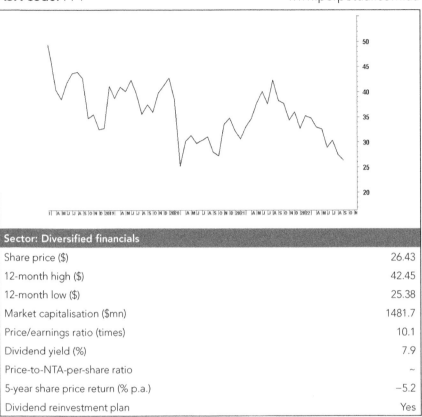

Sector: Diversified financials	
Share price ($)	26.43
12-month high ($)	42.45
12-month low ($)	25.38
Market capitalisation ($mn)	1481.7
Price/earnings ratio (times)	10.1
Dividend yield (%)	7.9
Price-to-NTA-per-share ratio	~
5-year share price return (% p.a.)	−5.2
Dividend reinvestment plan	Yes

Sydney-based financial services company Perpetual was established in 1886 as Perpetual Trustees. Following two major acquisitions in 2020, Perpetual divides its operations into four broad areas. Perpetual Private is a specialist boutique financial services business aimed at high-net-worth individuals, and providing its clients with access to tailored financial, tax, legal and estate planning advice. Two asset management divisions offer a range of managed domestic and international investment products to the retail, wholesale and institutional markets. The fourth division, Perpetual Corporate Trust, is a leading provider of corporate trustee and transaction support services to the financial services industry. In August 2022 Perpetual announced the planned acquisition of rival fund manager Pendal Group.

Latest business results (June 2022, full year)

Revenues and underlying profits rose for a second straight year, reversing two years of mediocre results, and with strength across all areas of business. Asset Management International has become the company's largest division, thanks to two recent American acquisitions, the specialist investment firm Trillium Asset Management and a 75 per cent stake in the investment management company Barrow Hanley. Revenues and profits rose strongly, in large part due to a full year's contribution from Barrow Hanley. Asset Management Australia also achieved a small increase in revenues, with profits rising, thanks to new products and disciplined cost management. Perpetual Private delivered an excellent result, with double-digit gains in revenues and profits, thanks to organic growth, an excellent funds performance and a 10-month contribution from the boutique wealth advisory firm Jacaranda Financial Planning. Perpetual Corporate Trust also generated double-digit increases in revenues and profits, with growth across all key business lines.

Outlook

Perpetual is set to be transformed by its planned $2.3 billion acquisition of Pendal Group in a Scheme of Arrangement that has been agreed to by the two companies. However, the deal must first be approved by Pendal shareholders, and the actual implementation is not expected until around the end of 2022 or early 2023. Pendal — which is included in this book — is a leading Australian funds management group with specialties that include international equities and also, through its subsidiary Regnan, environmental, social and governance (ESG) investing. The acquisition is intended to create a global asset manager with a strong presence across all major markets — including a leadership position in ESG investing — more than $200 billion in assets and significant capacity for growth. Perpetual also envisages substantial cost synergies from bringing together the two companies, and it expects strong growth for the June 2023 year.

Year to 30 June	2021	2022
Revenues ($mn)	652.1	749.6
Asset management international (%)	22	29
Perpetual Private (%)	29	28
Asset management Australia (%)	27	22
Perpetual Corporate Trust (%)	22	21
EBIT ($mn)	170.3	204.3
EBIT margin (%)	26.1	27.3
Profit before tax ($mn)	169.3	201.2
Profit after tax ($mn)	122.8	148.2
Earnings per share (c)	221.43	262.97
Cash flow per share (c)	300.23	356.48
Dividend (c)	180	209
Percentage franked	100	100
Net tangible assets per share ($)	0.79	~
Interest cover (times)	170.3	65.9
Return on equity (%)	15.7	16.2
Debt-to-equity ratio (%)	20.1	29.2
Current ratio	1.3	1.3

Pinnacle Investment Management Group Limited

ASX code: PNI   www.pinnacleinvestment.com

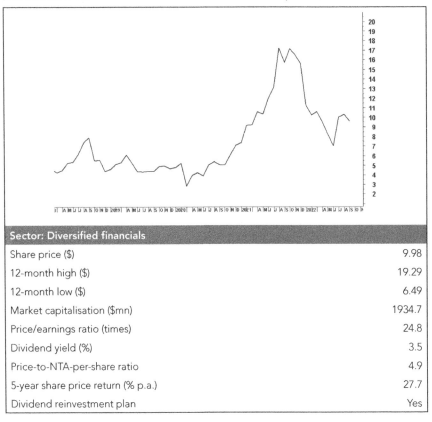

Sector: Diversified financials	
Share price ($)	9.98
12-month high ($)	19.29
12-month low ($)	6.49
Market capitalisation ($mn)	1934.7
Price/earnings ratio (times)	24.8
Dividend yield (%)	3.5
Price-to-NTA-per-share ratio	4.9
5-year share price return (% p.a.)	27.7
Dividend reinvestment plan	Yes

Sydney-based Pinnacle Investment Management started life in 2006 as a boutique funds management company that was majority-owned by Wilson HTM Investment Group. In 2016 it was fully acquired by Wilson Group, with Wilson Group changing its own name to Pinnacle. Today it is a prominent adviser to small funds management groups, providing them with distribution services, business support and responsible entity services, while also holding an equity stake in these companies.

Latest business results (June 2022, full year)

Pinnacle overcame stock market volatility to post another solid result, though with a notable slowdown in the second half. At June 2022 the company comprised 15 fund management affiliates, and it held shareholdings in these that ranged from 23.5 per cent to 49.9 per cent. Total revenues during the year for the 15 fund managers of $505.5 million were up from $415.5 million in the previous year. Of this amount,

$57.8 million came from performance fees, down from $86.2 million. There were net inflows during the year to the 15 fund manager affiliates of $0.6 billion, but falling markets meant that total funds under management declined to $83.7 billion at June 2022, down from $89.4 billion a year before. During the year Pinnacle acquired a 25 per cent equity interest in the Australian private equity firm Five V Capital and a 32.5 per cent stake in Toronto-based Langdon Equity Partners.

Outlook

Pinnacle's initial role is to provide its fund manager affiliates with equity, seed capital and working capital. It then allows its managers to focus on investment performance by providing them with marketing and other support services. Pinnacle's own revenues and profits derive from the revenues it receives from its affiliates for its services, together with its share of their profits, and performance is important. It has achieved success with the fund management companies it has chosen to join its group, reporting that 83 per cent of funds with a five-year track record had by June 2022 outperformed their benchmarks during this period. Pinnacle has been steadily boosting its exposure to retail funds, which provide higher margins than institutional funds, and these now represent around one quarter of total funds under management. The company believes its business model could work well overseas, and it has expressed a desire to expand abroad, though the COVID pandemic has forced it to delay any such moves. With its businesses directly tied to trends in global financial markets, Pinnacle could suffer in any prolonged market downturn.

Year to 30 June	2021	2022
Revenues ($mn)	98.9	121.7
EBIT ($mn)	67.6	78.6
EBIT margin (%)	68.3	64.6
Profit before tax ($mn)	67.0	76.4
Profit after tax ($mn)	67.0	76.4
Earnings per share (c)	38.23	40.21
Cash flow per share (c)	38.76	40.73
Dividend (c)	28.7	35
Percentage franked	100	100
Net tangible assets per share ($)	1.35	2.06
Interest cover (times)	125.6	34.8
Return on equity (%)	31.0	23.6
Debt-to-equity ratio (%)	1.6	20.3
Current ratio	8.4	14.5

Platinum Asset Management Limited

ASX code: PTM

www.platinum.com.au

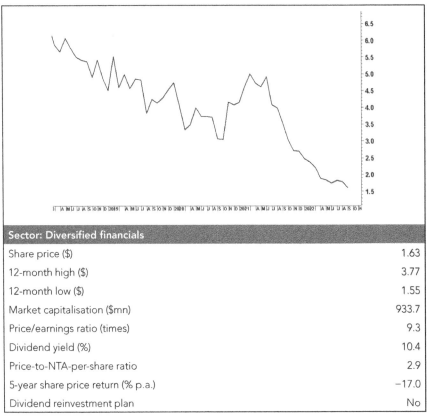

Sector: Diversified financials	
Share price ($)	1.63
12-month high ($)	3.77
12-month low ($)	1.55
Market capitalisation ($mn)	933.7
Price/earnings ratio (times)	9.3
Dividend yield (%)	10.4
Price-to-NTA-per-share ratio	2.9
5-year share price return (% p.a.)	−17.0
Dividend reinvestment plan	No

Sydney funds management company Platinum Asset Management was established in 1994. It has developed a specialty in managing portfolios of international equities. Its primary product is the $6.5 billion Platinum International Fund. Other funds specialise in Europe, Asia, Japan, health care, technology and international brands. Much of the company equity is held by Platinum directors and staff members.

Latest business results (June 2022, full year)

Revenues slipped again, reflecting a reduction in management fees, and profits fell sharply. Management fees of $246 million were down 7 per cent from June 2021 as average funds under management during the year fell from $23.4 billion to $21.4 billion. Performance fees rose 69 per cent to $6.7 million. The main contributor to the decline in profits was a large unrealised loss on the company's investments, compared with a gain in the previous year. Platinum said that on an underlying basis its after-tax profit fell 10.9 per cent to $118.2 million. Staff costs edged down. At June 2022 Platinum held funds under management of $18.2 billion, down from $23.5

billion in June 2021, driven by negative investment returns of $2.2 billion, net fund outflows also of $2.2 billion and $0.9 billion in net distributions.

Outlook

Platinum has gained a degree of renown among Australian investors for an impressive long-term period of outperformance for its international equity funds, thanks to its stock-picking skills, and this has sparked some solid growth in funds under management. However, the more recent performance has been mixed. The company has attributed this to its preference for value stocks, at a time when growth stocks were leading global markets higher. The company is now forecasting a deep bear market, with the possibility of markets falling 50 per cent from their peaks. It suggests that this could lead to a reversal of recent trends favouring growth-stock funds and passive funds, and a move back to value-stock funds of the kind managed by Platinum. It says that as global economies weaken and markets remain volatile, it sees attractive opportunities in many places, with significant differences in stock market performance by sector and geography in the years ahead. Platinum is planning to launch a new ASX-listed carbon transition fund, investing in companies that are enabling or contributing to the transition away from fossil fuel–derived energy and goods production and consumption. Responding to investor concerns, it has also recruited a dedicated ESG (environmental, social and governance) analyst to help integrate ethical concerns into the company's investment analysis.

Year to 30 June	2021	2022
Revenues ($mn)	269.2	252.7
EBIT ($mn)	233.7	146.2
EBIT margin (%)	86.8	57.9
Profit before tax ($mn)	234.2	146.7
Profit after tax ($mn)	163.3	101.5
Earnings per share (c)	28.17	17.54
Cash flow per share (c)	28.72	18.03
Dividend (c)	24	17
Percentage franked	100	100
Net tangible assets per share ($)	0.58	0.56
Interest cover (times)	~	~
Return on equity (%)	49.4	30.5
Debt-to-equity ratio (%)	~	~
Current ratio	10.1	12.8

Premier Investments Limited

ASX code: PMV   www.premierinvestments.com.au

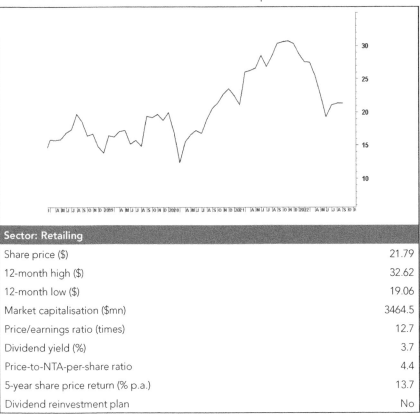

Sector: Retailing	
Share price ($)	21.79
12-month high ($)	32.62
12-month low ($)	19.06
Market capitalisation ($mn)	3464.5
Price/earnings ratio (times)	12.7
Dividend yield (%)	3.7
Price-to-NTA-per-share ratio	4.4
5-year share price return (% p.a.)	13.7
Dividend reinvestment plan	No

Melbourne-based Premier was founded in 1987 and operates as an investment company. Its main holding is a 100-per-cent stake in the retailer Just Group, which was founded in 1970. The Just Group incorporates the brands Just Jeans, Smiggle, Peter Alexander, Jay Jays, Portmans, Jacqui E and Dotti. Premier also holds 28 per cent of the equity in home appliance specialist Breville Group and a significant equity stake in department store chain Myer.

Latest business results (January 2022, half year)

Sales and profits fell, although the company said that on a like-for-like basis— excluding some significant items and adjusting for the fact that the January 2021 half comprised 27 weeks and the January 2022 half 26 weeks—sales and profits were up. This came despite COVID-related lockdown measures, which led to the closure of many stores for extended periods, followed by disruption from the fast-spreading Omicron variant. The Peter Alexander sleepwear chain was again an excellent performer, with sales of $227.4 million, up 11.4 per cent from a year before. Smiggle, which specialises in colourful school stationery and other products for children, with stores around the world, rebounded from the previous year's decline with sales of

$146.3 million, up 5.6 per cent. The five other apparel brands delivered sales of $396.2 million, just slightly higher than a year earlier, though up 5.3 per cent on a like-for-like basis, with particular strength for Portmans. Total group online sales of $195.4 million were 27.3 per cent higher than the January 2021 half and more than double the figure for January 2020.

Outlook

Premier operates seven strong brands and continues to expand. Nevertheless, as much retail activity moves online it is rationalising its activities, including the closure of many stores, particularly when it is unable to negotiate rent adjustments. It is working to expand online sales, which generate significantly higher profit margins than the retail store network, and is currently selling online in three countries. After a restructuring of its Smiggle business, which was particularly hard hit by pandemic-mandated school closures, the company believes this division is set for continuing solid growth. At January 2022 Premier held net cash holdings of around $400 million. Its shareholding in Breville Group, worth around $1 billion, was on the books for just $289 million. However, with most of its product lines sourced from overseas manufacturers, the company can be affected by currency rate fluctuations and shipping fee increases. It is also vulnerable to inflationary pressures and trends in consumer spending.

Year to 31 July*	2020	2021
Revenues ($mn)	1216.3	1443.2
EBIT ($mn)	209.6	390.0
EBIT margin (%)	17.2	27.0
Profit before tax ($mn)	195.2	379.6
Profit after tax ($mn)	137.8	271.8
Earnings per share (c)	86.89	171.15
Cash flow per share (c)	223.38	283.39
Dividend (c)	70	80
Percentage franked	100	100
Interest cover (times)	14.5	37.4
Return on equity (%)	10.2	18.9
Half year to 29 January**	2021	2022
Revenues ($mn)	784.6	769.9
Profit before tax ($mn)	262.1	229.3
Profit after tax ($mn)	188.2	163.6
Earnings per share (c)	118.50	102.97
Dividend (c)	34	46
Percentage franked	100	100
Net tangible assets per share ($)	4.06	4.99
Debt-to-equity ratio (%)	~	~
Current ratio	1.3	1.7

*25 July 2020
**30 January 2021

Pro Medicus Limited

ASX code: PME www.promed.com.au

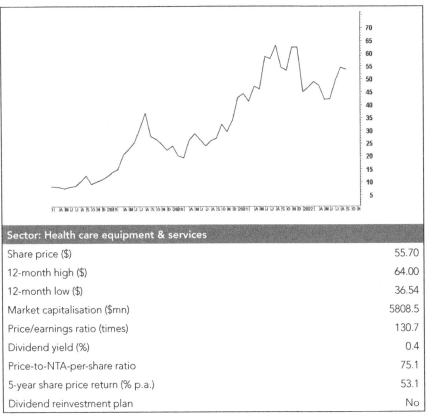

Sector: Health care equipment & services	
Share price ($)	55.70
12-month high ($)	64.00
12-month low ($)	36.54
Market capitalisation ($mn)	5808.5
Price/earnings ratio (times)	130.7
Dividend yield (%)	0.4
Price-to-NTA-per-share ratio	75.1
5-year share price return (% p.a.)	53.1
Dividend reinvestment plan	No

Melbourne-based Pro Medicus, established in 1983, provides software and internet products and services to the medical profession. Its Visage 7.0 medical imaging software provides radiologists and clinicians with advanced visualisation capability for the rapid viewing of medical images. Its Radiology Information Systems (RIS) product provides proprietary medical software for practice management. In Australia it operates the Promedicus.net online network for doctors. It has extensive business operations throughout Australia, the US and Germany, and overseas sales represent nearly 85 per cent of total turnover.

Latest business results (June 2022, full year)

Pro Medicus enjoyed another successful year of strong double-digit revenue and profit growth. America is by far the company's largest market, accounting for 79 per cent of sales, and revenues there soared 47 per cent, with the signing of three major new contracts and the renewal of a further three. The relatively small German operation achieved 24 per cent growth in sales, thanks to an extension of the German government hospital contract to a fourth site. Australian sales rose 8 per cent, again due especially to RIS contracts with Healius and I-MED Radiology Network. The result benefited from a weaker dollar.

Outlook

Pro Medicus continues to enjoy some outstanding success in America for its Visage 7 software, which has the speed and functionality to meet the requirements of many different kinds of users. The company is now one of the market leaders in this business, with nine of the 20 leading American hospitals using its products. It is making a substantial investment in research and development activities aimed at new products and enhancements to existing products, including artificial intelligence–based products and cloud-based systems. It has established an R&D centre in New York in order to collaborate with customer research projects. It is working on the addition of a cardiology application to its existing imaging platform, and together with Yale New Haven Health has developed a promising breast density algorithm based on artificial intelligence. With cash holdings of more than $63 million in June 2022 it is also seeking out acquisition opportunities offering access to new technologies. It has a retention rate of 100 per cent for its US business. The three US contracts renewed in the June 2022 year were done so with contract periods of five years or more and with an increased fee per transaction. Most of the company's revenue is recurring in nature, and, with three new contract signings in the June 2022 year, the outlook for June 2023 is very positive.

Year to 30 June	2021	2022
Revenues ($mn)	67.9	93.5
EBIT ($mn)	42.7	62.4
EBIT margin (%)	62.9	66.8
Profit before tax ($mn)	42.9	63.1
Profit after tax ($mn)	30.9	44.4
Earnings per share (c)	29.62	42.60
Cash flow per share (c)	36.53	49.62
Dividend (c)	15	22
Percentage franked	100	100
Net tangible assets per share ($)	0.57	0.74
Interest cover (times)	~	~
Return on equity (%)	43.5	48.5
Debt-to-equity ratio (%)	~	~
Current ratio	5.0	4.5

PWR Holdings Limited

ASX code: PWH   www.pwr.com.au

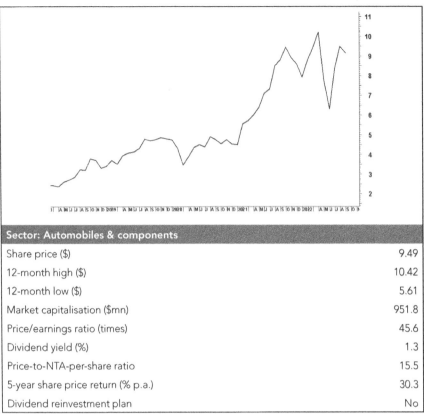

Sector: Automobiles & components	
Share price ($)	9.49
12-month high ($)	10.42
12-month low ($)	5.61
Market capitalisation ($mn)	951.8
Price/earnings ratio (times)	45.6
Dividend yield (%)	1.3
Price-to-NTA-per-share ratio	15.5
5-year share price return (% p.a.)	30.3
Dividend reinvestment plan	No

Based on the Gold Coast, automotive products company PWR got its start in 1987. It specialises in cooling systems, including aluminium radiators, intercoolers and oil coolers. It has a particular specialty in the supply of cooling systems to racing car teams. Other customers include the automotive original equipment manufacturing (OEM) sector and the automotive aftermarket sector, along with the aerospace, defence and renewable energy industries. It operates from manufacturing and distribution facilities in Australia and the United States, with a European distribution centre in the United Kingdom. It owns the American cooling products manufacturer C&R Racing. More than 85 per cent of company sales are to customers overseas, mainly in Europe and North America.

Latest business results (June 2022, full year)

Revenues and profits enjoyed a second year of double-digit rises, with growth across all key markets and regions. The car racing business remains responsible for more than half the company's sales, and revenues grew 23 per cent to $55 million. However, the best growth came from other sectors. Automotive OEM sales now represent 21 per cent of company income, and revenues surged 65 per cent. The aerospace and defence sector achieved 56 per cent growth, although this business represents just 7 per cent of total sales. Automotive aftermarket revenues rose 6 per cent. The company also classifies its sales into its core advanced cooling activities and emerging technologies. The latter remained relatively small, at 19 per cent of total revenue, but with sales more than doubling during the year.

Outlook

PWR supplies its cooling systems to most Formula One racing teams, as well as to teams in other motor sports around the world, including Nascar and Indycar. It also supplies bespoke cooling systems to a range of high-performance automobile companies such as Aston Martin. It spends heavily on research and development in order to maintain its market-leading position, and it is working to move into other market areas with high growth potential. It believes revenues from these emerging technologies could overtake motor sport revenues by 2024. Its new North American aerospace and defence machining centre was due to open in September 2022 and it may also build production facilities in the UK. It sees particular potential in the advance of electric vehicles, and it is working with several electric car manufacturers for the supply of sophisticated cooling technology. Other applications include helicopters, drones and storage batteries for alternative energy systems. PWR is also working with companies involved in the development of hydrogen fuel-cell technology.

Year to 30 June	2021	2022
Revenues ($mn)	79.2	101.1
PWR performance products (%)	69	72
PWR North America (%)	31	28
EBIT ($mn)	23.2	28.5
EBIT margin (%)	29.3	28.2
Profit before tax ($mn)	22.5	28.5
Profit after tax ($mn)	16.8	20.8
Earnings per share (c)	16.78	20.79
Cash flow per share (c)	22.52	28.00
Dividend (c)	8.8	12
Percentage franked	100	100
Net tangible assets per share ($)	0.49	0.61
Interest cover (times)	34.3	950.7
Return on equity (%)	28.4	29.7
Debt-to-equity ratio (%)	~	~
Current ratio	2.8	3.5

REA Group Limited

ASX code: REA   www.rea-group.com

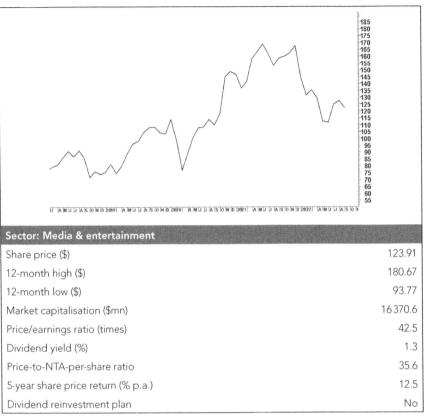

Sector: Media & entertainment	
Share price ($)	123.91
12-month high ($)	180.67
12-month low ($)	93.77
Market capitalisation ($mn)	16 370.6
Price/earnings ratio (times)	42.5
Dividend yield (%)	1.3
Price-to-NTA-per-share ratio	35.6
5-year share price return (% p.a.)	12.5
Dividend reinvestment plan	No

Melbourne-based REA was founded in 1995. Through its websites realestate.com.au and realcommercial.com.au it is a leader in the provision of online real estate advertising services in Australia. It also owns Flatmates.com.au, as well as the residential property data company PropTrack Australia and the mortgage broking franchise group Smartline. It has interests in property websites throughout Asia, and holds a 20 per cent shareholding in the Move online property marketing company in the US. In 2021 it acquired the mortgage broker Mortgage Choice. News Corp owns more than 60 per cent of REA's equity.

Latest business results (June 2022, full year)

A buoyant housing market and the Mortgage Choice acquisition helped generate a solid rise in revenues and profits. Australian residential revenue was up 24 per cent to $776 million, thanks to increases in new listings, price rises and the growing strength of the company's premium and add-on products. Commercial and developer revenues rose 3 per cent to $134 million, with strength in commercial business offsetting a decline in developer income. The company's media, data and other segment grew 9 per cent to $97 million, thanks especially to the strength of the PropTrack market intelligence operation. The addition of Mortgage Choice helped REA's financial services business enjoy a good rise in revenues and profits. A new REA India business saw expanding revenues, but was in the red. American business, represented by the company's 20-per-cent shareholding in Move, was hit by rising costs, and profits were down.

Outlook

REA is heavily geared to trends in the domestic housing market, and it expects continuing growth, despite a market slowdown as interest rates rise. It will benefit from price increases and planned new product launches. Its acquisition of Mortgage Choice gives it more than 5 per cent of the Australian mortgage market, and it plans to build on this business, hoping in the longer term to double its market share. The full integration of Mortgage Choice is expected during 2023. It has also expressed a desire for more acquisitions, and has flagged property insurance as a sector it could enter. REA is also actively working to develop its Asian businesses. It has sold its Malaysian and Thai interests to Singaporean company PropertyGuru, in return for a 17.5 per cent equity stake in PropertyGuru. It is also investing heavily in strengthening its Indian operations. REA's shareholding in Move, one of the largest real estate websites in the US, has given the company a foothold in the vast American property market.

Year to 30 June	2021	2022
Revenues ($mn)	927.8	1160.2
EBIT ($mn)	472.8	554.7
EBIT margin (%)	51.0	47.8
Profit before tax ($mn)	468.4	547.9
Profit after tax ($mn)	322.7	384.8
Earnings per share (c)	244.60	291.26
Cash flow per share (c)	307.22	361.72
Dividend (c)	131	164
Percentage franked	100	100
Net tangible assets per share ($)	1.76	3.48
Interest cover (times)	107.6	81.6
Return on equity (%)	33.4	32.5
Debt-to-equity ratio (%)	28.7	17.5
Current ratio	2.0	1.6

Reece Limited

ASX code: REH

group.reece.com

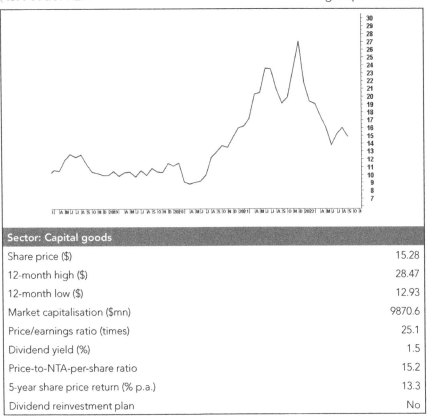

Sector: Capital goods	
Share price ($)	15.28
12-month high ($)	28.47
12-month low ($)	12.93
Market capitalisation ($mn)	9870.6
Price/earnings ratio (times)	25.1
Dividend yield (%)	1.5
Price-to-NTA-per-share ratio	15.2
5-year share price return (% p.a.)	13.3
Dividend reinvestment plan	No

Melbourne-based plumbing supplies company Reece traces its origins back to 1919, when Harold Reece started selling his products from the back of a truck. It is today one of the country's leading suppliers of plumbing products, with operations also in the US and New Zealand, and it has expanded into related fields. These include a network of businesses in the heating, ventilation, air conditioning and refrigeration sectors and specialist stores for the landscape and agricultural industries. At June 2022 it operated 645 branches in Australia and New Zealand, up from 642 a year earlier, and 204 in the US, up from 189.

Latest business results (June 2022, full year)

Sales and profits rose strongly in another good year for the company, driven by solid demand and rising prices across all markets. COVID lockdowns had a significant impact on Australia and New Zealand operations in the first half, but sales for the year rose 12 per cent, with EBIT up 4 per cent. American operations, now representing 54 per cent of total company turnover, increased sales by 33 per cent, or 28 per cent on a US dollar basis, with EBIT soaring 63 per cent, as Reece restructured this business and expanded margins. There was also a benefit from some bolt-on acquisitions during the year. Nevertheless, though now more than half of company turnover, US operations contributed less than a third of after-tax profit. The company made a strategic investment in boosting inventory during the year, due to fears of supply chain disruptions, and inventory levels at June 2022 were substantially higher than a year earlier.

Outlook

Reece continues to benefit from the strength of housing and renovation markets in Australia, New Zealand and the US. However, amid signs of a possible slowdown, there are also growing concerns about rising interest rates, inflationary pressures, labour shortages, a weakening of consumer sentiment and some continuing supply chain issues. In the US in particular many projects are now delayed because of problems in finding tradespeople. In Australia the company is investing heavily in digital innovation, to make business as smooth as possible for customers, and it also expects to open new branches. However, it is in the US that Reece sees its best growth prospects, and its restructuring efforts there are steadily raising margins. It operates in 16 states and is carrying out trials of new branch formats and service concepts, in order to expand business and lower costs. It is also seeking further US acquisitions.

Year to 30 June	2021	2022
Revenues ($mn)	6270.7	7654.0
EBIT ($mn)	493.0	578.0
EBIT margin (%)	7.9	7.6
Gross margin (%)	28.1	27.9
Profit before tax ($mn)	380.3	509.4
Profit after tax ($mn)	285.6	392.5
Earnings per share (c)	44.21	60.76
Cash flow per share (c)	79.44	100.73
Dividend (c)	18	22.5
Percentage franked	100	100
Net tangible assets per share ($)	0.73	1.01
Interest cover (times)	7.2	12.5
Return on equity (%)	10.1	12.6
Debt-to-equity ratio (%)	17.5	26.2
Current ratio	2.4	2.1

Reliance Worldwide Corporation Limited

ASX code: RWC

www.rwc.com

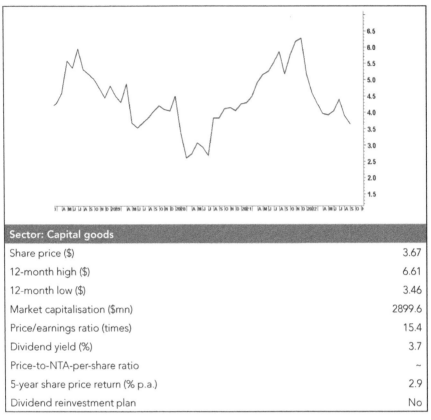

Sector: Capital goods	
Share price ($)	3.67
12-month high ($)	6.61
12-month low ($)	3.46
Market capitalisation ($mn)	2899.6
Price/earnings ratio (times)	15.4
Dividend yield (%)	3.7
Price-to-NTA-per-share ratio	~
5-year share price return (% p.a.)	2.9
Dividend reinvestment plan	No

Melbourne-based engineering firm Reliance dates back to 1949 and the establishment of a small tool shop in Brisbane. It is today a major global manufacturer and distributor of a range of products, particularly for the plumbing and heating industries. Its businesses and brands include SharkBite, Speedfit, HoldRite, CashAcme, StreamLabs and John Guest. In August 2021 it acquired the business interests of LCL, one of Australia's largest producers of copper-based alloys, and in November 2021 it acquired the US plumbing products manufacturer EZ-Flo.

Latest business results (June 2022, full year)

Revenues rose but profits fell in a mixed year for the company, with rapidly rising costs and supply chain disruptions partially offset by price rises implemented by the company. However, Reliance reported that the result was held back by costs associated with its two acquisitions during the year, and that without these its profits edged up. American revenues were up 26 per cent, although this largely reflected the EZ-Flo acquisition, and on a like-for-like basis sales rose 6 per cent. Asia Pacific sales rose 6 per cent, thanks especially to continuing strength in the Australian home-building and renovations markets. The Europe/Middle East/Africa segment saw sales up 1 per cent, with weakness in the UK offset by continuing strength in continental Europe, driven especially by growing demand for water filtration and drinks dispensing products. Note that Reliance now reports its results in US dollars. The June 2022 figures have been converted at prevailing exchange rates and are for guidance only.

Outlook

Reliance sees plumbing industry backlogs across many of its markets, in part driven by labour shortages, as supporting its operations in the short term. In addition, much of its output is used in plumbing repair work, which is generally non-discretionary in nature. However, it is concerned that rising inflation and higher interest rates will put a dent in consumer spending, particularly in the UK, and this could lead to a slowdown in home renovation business. In addition, it has noted that US retailers have been keeping higher inventory levels of the company's fixtures and fittings to guard against supply chain interruptions, which could foreshadow a period of weaker demand. It also faces the challenge that as its costs continue to escalate it must implement price rises in order to maintain margins. It sees great potential in its US$332 million EZ-Flo acquisition. This business has particular strength in the US$1.2 billion large appliance connector market, and Reliance expects significant cross-selling opportunities as well as cost-saving synergies.

Year to 30 June	2021	2022
Revenues ($mn)	1340.8	1605.7
Americas (%)	63	67
Europe/Middle East/Africa (%)	25	22
Asia Pacific (%)	12	11
EBIT ($mn)	289.3	285.4
EBIT margin (%)	21.6	17.8
Gross margin (%)	44.0	39.3
Profit before tax ($mn)	280.9	268.3
Profit after tax ($mn)	211.9	188.3
Earnings per share (c)	26.82	23.83
Cash flow per share (c)	33.95	32.07
Dividend (c)	13	13.42
Percentage franked	20	15
Net tangible assets per share ($)	0.34	~
Interest cover (times)	34.6	16.7
Return on equity (%)	14.1	11.7
Debt-to-equity ratio (%)	10.9	48.7
Current ratio	2.0	3.2

Ridley Corporation Limited

ASX code: RIC   www.ridley.com.au

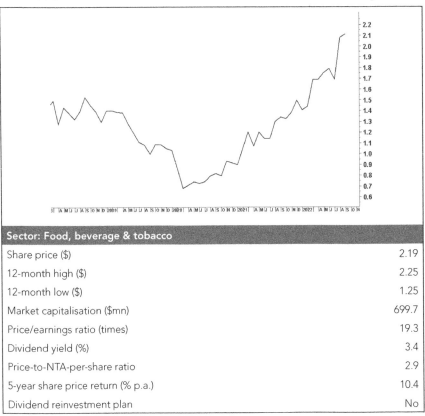

Sector: Food, beverage & tobacco	
Share price ($)	2.19
12-month high ($)	2.25
12-month low ($)	1.25
Market capitalisation ($mn)	699.7
Price/earnings ratio (times)	19.3
Dividend yield (%)	3.4
Price-to-NTA-per-share ratio	2.9
5-year share price return (% p.a.)	10.4
Dividend reinvestment plan	No

Melbourne-based Ridley, founded in 1987, is a leading producer of animal feed. It operates from some 20 sites in Victoria, New South Wales, Queensland and South Australia, producing around two million tonnes annually of finished feeds and feed ingredients based on locally grown cereal grains. It also owns an aquafeed manufacturing facility in Thailand. It classifies its production into two broad segments. Bulk stockfeeds comprises the company's animal nutrition feed that is delivered in bulk. Packaged feeds and ingredients represents animal nutrition feed and ingredients that are delivered in packaged form, ranging from three-kilogram bags to one-tonne containers.

Latest business results (June 2022, full year)

Ridley enjoyed a good year, with double-digit rises in revenues and profits. The packaged feeds and ingredients operation was notably strong, with an excellent contribution from the company's rendering business unit, which is benefiting from the continuing premiumisation of its products and higher market prices for rendered tallows and oils. There was also strong growth for Ridley's branded packaged products as the company was able to expand its product lines into urban pet specialty chains and boost market share. However, aquafeed volumes were down, following the sale of the company's Westbury production facility in Tasmania. The bulk stockfeeds segment benefited from increased production efficiencies and the company also reported gains in market share, led by increased sales volumes in the poultry and dairy sectors. The repayment of a substantial amount of company debt led to reduced interest payments.

Outlook

Ridley occupies a prominent place in the Australian agricultural sector as one of the leading producers of stockfeeds, nutritional blocks, mineral concentrates, supplements and other products for a wide range of animal species that include dairy cows, poultry, pigs, beef cattle, horses, sheep, working dogs, pets and fish. It has an extensive research and development program and strong partnerships with industry bodies, universities and key research organisations. It benefits as the Australian agricultural sector expands and has adopted an ambitious three-year growth plan. Expanding output is providing scale benefits and enhanced profit margins. It is seeking to introduce new products to the bulk stockfeeds segment and to move into new markets, and wishes to boost exports for the packaged feeds and ingredients segment. It says that it is gaining market share in many areas, which will help it increase revenues in the June 2023 year. It benefits from a flourishing prawn and barramundi industry in Northern Australia. With lower debt levels, Ridley is now seeking appropriate merger and acquisition opportunities.

Year to 30 June	2021	2022
Revenues ($mn)	927.7	1049.1
Bulk stockfeeds (%)	66	66
Packaged feeds & ingredients (%)	34	34
EBIT ($mn)	39.5	54.4
EBIT margin (%)	4.3	5.2
Gross margin (%)	8.5	9.5
Profit before tax ($mn)	35.0	51.6
Profit after tax ($mn)	24.9	36.2
Earnings per share (c)	7.81	11.33
Cash flow per share (c)	17.10	19.40
Dividend (c)	2	7.4
Percentage franked	100	100
Net tangible assets per share ($)	0.66	0.75
Interest cover (times)	8.8	19.1
Return on equity (%)	9.1	12.0
Debt-to-equity ratio (%)	28.9	7.3
Current ratio	1.5	1.2

Rio Tinto Limited

ASX code: RIO

www.riotinto.com

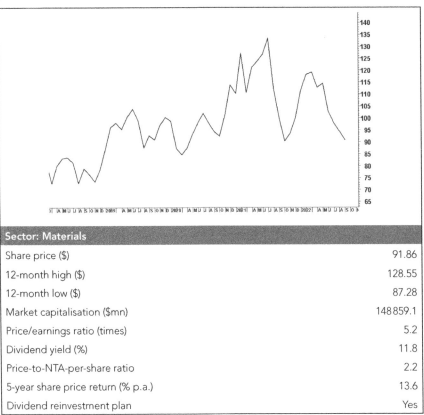

Sector: Materials	
Share price ($)	91.86
12-month high ($)	128.55
12-month low ($)	87.28
Market capitalisation ($mn)	148859.1
Price/earnings ratio (times)	5.2
Dividend yield (%)	11.8
Price-to-NTA-per-share ratio	2.2
5-year share price return (% p.a.)	13.6
Dividend reinvestment plan	Yes

British-based Rio Tinto, one of the world's largest mining companies, was founded by European investors in 1873 in order to reopen some ancient copper mines at the Tinto River in Spain. It maintains an ASX presence in a dual-listing structure and continues to pay franked dividends to Australian shareholders. Its products include iron ore, copper, gold, industrial minerals, diamonds and aluminium. Subsidiaries include the 86-per-cent-owned uranium miner Energy Resources of Australia.

Latest business results (June 2022, half year)

Falling iron ore prices caused a fall in revenues and profits compared with the June 2021 half. The average price for the period was down 28 per cent, compounded by rising inflationary pressures at the company's operations, though partially offset by a weaker Australian dollar, and iron ore profits for the company fell 35 per cent. Iron ore represented 53 per cent of total company turnover and around 72 per cent of the profit. By contrast, the Aluminium division, representing 25 per cent of sales, achieved an excellent 68 per cent jump in profits, thanks to a 45 per cent rise in the average realised aluminium price. Copper division profits fell, despite a higher copper price, due to a significant rise in production costs. The company's Minerals division, incorporating iron ore pellets and concentrates, titanium dioxide, borates and diamonds, also posted an earnings decline, primarily due to rising operational costs, energy price increases and lower volumes. Altogether, 52 per cent of total company sales were to China—down from 60 per cent a year earlier—and a further 16 per cent to the rest of Asia. Note that Rio Tinto reports its results in US dollars. The tables in this book are based on Australian dollar figures and exchange rates supplied by the company.

Outlook

Rio Tinto maintains a substantial portfolio of well-run assets across many countries, and with generally low operating costs. It forecasts capital expenditure of US$9 billion to US$10 billion in each of 2023 and 2024. A major growth project is the Oyu Tolgoi copper-gold mine development in Mongolia. Despite delays, the company believes sustainable production will begin in 2023. In March 2022 it acquired for US$825 million the Rincon lithium project in Argentina, and it will spend a further US$190 million to build a small battery lithium carbonate plant. However, its planned US$2.4 billion lithium project in Serbia, intended as Europe's largest source of lithium for electric vehicle batteries, has stalled in the face of community protests.

Year to 31 December	2020	2021
Revenues ($mn)	64 577.0	84 488.0
EBIT ($mn)	25 753.6	41 272.2
EBIT margin (%)	39.9	48.8
Profit before tax ($mn)	25 569.6	41 027.0
Profit after tax ($mn)	18 019.0	28 449.0
Earnings per share (c)	1114.07	1757.85
Cash flow per share (c)	1497.49	2144.81
Dividend (c)	613.95	1086.46
Percentage franked	100	100
Interest cover (times)	139.9	168.3
Return on equity (%)	30.3	43.2
Half year to 30 June	2021	2022
Revenues ($mn)	42 876.0	41 374.0
Profit before tax ($mn)	23 392.0	17 112.0
Profit after tax ($mn)	15 767.0	11 988.0
Earnings per share (c)	974.40	740.30
Dividend (c)	509.42	383.7
Percentage franked	100	100
Net tangible assets per share ($)	40.54	41.23
Debt-to-equity ratio (%)	~	4.1
Current ratio	2.1	1.8

Schaffer Corporation Limited

ASX code: SFC   schaffer.com.au

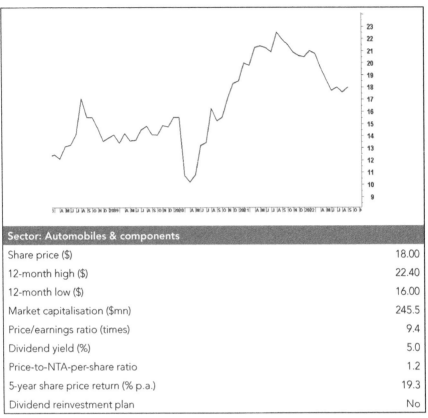

Sector: Automobiles & components	
Share price ($)	18.00
12-month high ($)	22.40
12-month low ($)	16.00
Market capitalisation ($mn)	245.5
Price/earnings ratio (times)	9.4
Dividend yield (%)	5.0
Price-to-NTA-per-share ratio	1.2
5-year share price return (% p.a.)	19.3
Dividend reinvestment plan	No

Perth company Schaffer was founded in 1955 to manufacture sand-lime bricks for the construction industry. Today its Delta Corporation subsidiary produces precast and prestressed concrete floors, beams and wall products, aimed mainly at the Western Australian construction market. However, its primary business now is the manufacture of leather goods, with a particular emphasis on products for the automotive industry, through its 83-per-cent-owned subsidiary Automotive Leather. This business operates from facilities in Australia, China and Slovakia and supplies leading auto makers around the world. A third business for Schaffer is investments and property development, and it owns a growing portfolio of rental and development sites, mainly in Western Australia.

Latest business results (June 2022, full year)

Revenues and profits fell sharply, with weakness across all businesses. The core Automotive Leather division saw sales down 18 per cent to $136 million and the after-tax profit down 26 per cent to $18.1 million as the semiconductor shortage reduced demand for the company's products from automakers. Second-half profits were higher than the first half, despite adverse currency movements. Property sales boosted the company's investments business, with revenues rising 20 per cent to $17.2 million, but unrealised revaluations forced the after-tax profit down 37 per cent to $11.4 million. The company's Delta Corporation concrete products operation continued to struggle in a challenging Western Australian construction market, with revenues up 5 per cent to $17.3 million, but with the business falling into the red as it was hit by project delays, severe labour shortages and rising costs.

Outlook

Schaffer's core automotive leather goods business is highly dependent on trends in the global car-making sector. The company has reported that it has been experiencing a recovery in demand, including a renewal of key programs with Jaguar Land Rover and new contracts with Mercedes and Audi. In advance of this new business the company has been increasing hide inventory levels and installing additional machinery, including new computer numerical controlled cutting machines, and it forecasts rising automotive leather revenues in the June 2023 year. It also expects continuing growth in its investment portfolio, valued at $187.7 million — or $13.78 per share — at June 2022. It has started development work on its 34-hectare Jandakot Road land holding, 15 minutes from the Perth CBD, and also expects further profits from land sales at its North Coogee site. Schaffer forecasts that, thanks to its strong order book, the concrete products business will return to profit during the first half of the June 2023 year.

Year to 30 June	2021	2022
Revenues ($mn)	196.3	170.4
EBIT ($mn)	63.7	43.8
EBIT margin (%)	32.5	25.7
Gross margin (%)	33.8	28.5
Profit before tax ($mn)	62.9	42.8
Profit after tax ($mn)	41.0	26.2
Earnings per share (c)	300.57	191.05
Cash flow per share (c)	356.10	244.29
Dividend (c)	90	90
Percentage franked	100	100
Net tangible assets per share ($)	14.10	15.16
Interest cover (times)	76.0	46.7
Return on equity (%)	22.8	13.0
Debt-to-equity ratio (%)	1.7	~
Current ratio	2.0	2.2

Seek Limited

ASX code: SEK

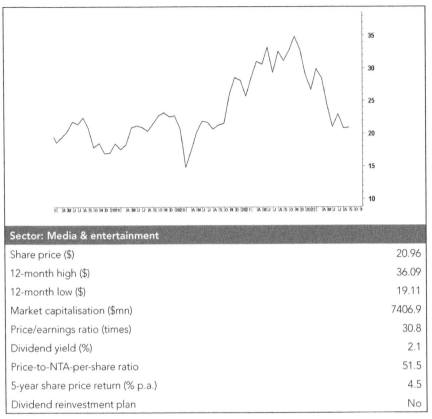

Sector: Media & entertainment	
Share price ($)	20.96
12-month high ($)	36.09
12-month low ($)	19.11
Market capitalisation ($mn)	7406.9
Price/earnings ratio (times)	30.8
Dividend yield (%)	2.1
Price-to-NTA-per-share ratio	51.5
5-year share price return (% p.a.)	4.5
Dividend reinvestment plan	No

Melbourne-based Seek, founded in 1997, operates Australia's largest website for job-seekers. It has expanded to New Zealand, and also has equity stakes in leading online employment businesses in Asia and Latin America, with nearly a third of company revenues deriving from outside Australia. In Asia it operates employment platforms in Hong Kong, the Philippines, Thailand, Malaysia, Singapore and Indonesia under the brands JobStreet and JobsDB. In Brazil it runs the Brasil Online business and in Mexico it operates Online Career Centre (OCC). It also holds a 23.5 per cent equity stake in Zhaopin, a Chinese recruitment business.

Latest business results (June 2022, full year)

A tight employment market led to a surge in online jobs advertising, and a resounding result for Seek. The core Australia/New Zealand segment achieved a 53 per cent jump in revenues, with profits up 60 per cent, as the company benefited from higher prices and decisions by employers to pay more for premium products in order to attract job candidates. Seek Asia also benefited from an increase in job advertising volumes, with revenues up 37 per cent, though the profit rise was a more modest 9 per cent, due to a significant investment during the year in marketing and technology. The small

Mexican operation enjoyed double-digit growth in revenues and profits, but Brazilian business slumped, with revenues and profits down due to a weak economy and higher costs.

Outlook

Seek has changed its corporate structure with the establishment in 2021 of the Seek Growth Fund, which will be run as an independent operation. The new fund includes a portfolio of start-up companies in which Seek had invested, along with Seek's holdings in Online Education Services. This new structure is intended to allow Seek to focus on its core online recruitment business. The company maintains its dominance of this market in Australia, providing very high profit margins. It attributes its continuing strength to an ongoing reinvestment strategy, with continuing new products and enhanced services. It sees great potential for its Asian activities, and is working to build a unified online marketplace platform across Australia, New Zealand and Asia. It believes that when this work is completed, by the end of the June 2024 year, it will allow new products to be deployed at scale across all markets, as well as enabling rapid innovation and enhanced reliability and security. Seek's early forecast is for June 2023 revenues of $1.25 billion to $1.3 billion and an after-tax profit of $250 million to $270 million.

Year to 30 June	2021	2022
Revenues ($mn)	760.3	1116.5
Australia/New Zealand (%)	61	74
Seek Asia (%)	26	18
Brasil Online (%)	8	3
OCC (%)	4	3
EBIT ($mn)	188.6	393.5
EBIT margin (%)	24.8	35.2
Profit before tax ($mn)	138.3	341.9
Profit after tax ($mn)	104.9	240.8
Earnings per share (c)	29.71	68.05
Cash flow per share (c)	53.47	93.40
Dividend (c)	40	44
Percentage franked	100	100
Net tangible assets per share ($)	0.74	0.41
Interest cover (times)	3.7	7.6
Return on equity (%)	7.2	13.2
Debt-to-equity ratio (%)	32.1	55.2
Current ratio	1.8	2.0

Servcorp Limited

ASX code: SRV   www.servcorp.com

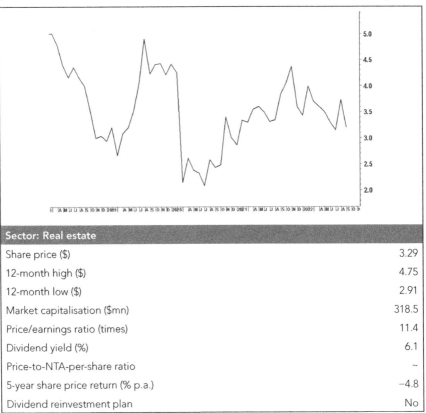

Sector: Real estate	
Share price ($)	3.29
12-month high ($)	4.75
12-month low ($)	2.91
Market capitalisation ($mn)	318.5
Price/earnings ratio (times)	11.4
Dividend yield (%)	6.1
Price-to-NTA-per-share ratio	~
5-year share price return (% p.a.)	−4.8
Dividend reinvestment plan	No

Sydney-based Servcorp was founded in 1978 to provide serviced office space to small businesses. It has expanded to provide advanced corporate infrastructure, including IT and telecommunications services, and office support services. It also offers what it terms virtual offices, providing a prestigious address and a range of services — such as message forwarding and access to meeting rooms — for people or businesses not needing a physical office. More than 40 per cent of the company's business is in North Asia, with nearly 30 per cent from Europe and the Middle East. In June 2022 it was operating 129 floors of offices in 41 cities across 20 countries.

Latest business results (June 2022, full year)

Revenues edged up and profits bounced back as most parts of the world gradually returned to a state of normalcy, following a year in which the COVID pandemic badly hit the company. The best performance came from the Europe/Middle East region, with an 80 per cent jump in profits. The largest segment, North Asia, was hurt by COVID-related lockdowns in China, with revenues down 5 per cent and profits falling 30 per cent. The Australia/New Zealand/South East Asia segment recorded a 12 per cent decline in revenues, but rationalisation efforts led to an increase in profits.

The small American operation achieved higher revenues and moved from loss to profit. During the year the company opened 12 new floors and closed five. The total occupancy rate at June 2022 of 72 per cent was in line with the previous year.

Outlook

Servcorp is a world leader in its business, with good market shares and a reputation for quality. However, it was badly hurt by the COVID pandemic, which led many workers to abandon their offices and work from home. Now, as conditions recover, and with high levels of client retention, the company is investing heavily in further expansion, with moves into five new locations set for the June 2023 year. It expects its total portfolio to rise to 5318 offices by June 2023, up from 5162 at June 2022. Servcorp has completed work on a new IT platform, which it is steadily introducing to all its global businesses. It is expected to be completely installed by early 2024, streamlining operations and providing a future avenue for growth. At June 2022 Servcorp had no debt and more than $100 million in cash holdings. Its early forecast is for underlying profits to rise by at least 16 per cent in the June 2023 year.

Year to 30 June	2021	2022
Revenues ($mn)	269.7	271.6
EBIT ($mn)	29.9	33.3
EBIT margin (%)	11.1	12.2
Profit before tax ($mn)	30.6	34.4
Profit after tax ($mn)	23.5	28.0
Earnings per share (c)	24.26	28.94
Cash flow per share (c)	151.05	153.05
Dividend (c)	18	20
Percentage franked	0	0
Net tangible assets per share ($)	~	~
Interest cover (times)	~	~
Return on equity (%)	11.3	14.3
Debt-to-equity ratio (%)	~	~
Current ratio	0.9	0.9

Smartgroup Corporation Limited

ASX code: SIQ · www.smartgroup.com.au

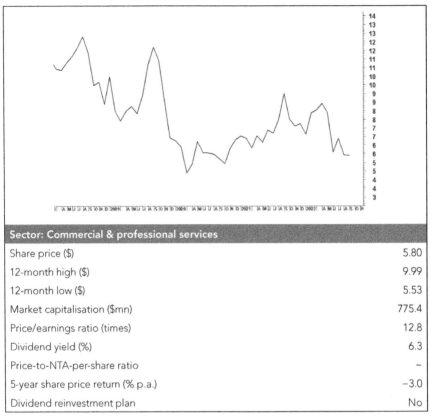

Sector: Commercial & professional services	
Share price ($)	5.80
12-month high ($)	9.99
12-month low ($)	5.53
Market capitalisation ($mn)	775.4
Price/earnings ratio (times)	12.8
Dividend yield (%)	6.3
Price-to-NTA-per-share ratio	~
5-year share price return (% p.a.)	−3.0
Dividend reinvestment plan	No

Sydney-based specialist employee management services provider Smartgroup got its start in 1999 as Smartsalary, a salary packaging specialist. It later branched into other businesses, and has grown significantly, both organically and through acquisition. It is now engaged in salary packaging services, as well as vehicle novated leasing, fleet management, payroll administration, share plan administration and workforce optimisation consulting services.

Latest business results (June 2022, half year)

Revenues and profits rose, in a pleasing result for the company. Salary packages of 383 000 were up from 373 500 in the June 2021 half, thanks to a number of new clients and organic growth from existing clients. However, the company's vehicle-related businesses were hit by continuing supply disruptions, resulting in lengthening sales lead times, despite firm demand. It meant that novated leases under management fell 4 per cent to 62 800, and managed fleet vehicle numbers edged down to 24 850. At June 2022 the company had a pipeline of unfulfilled vehicle orders worth approximately $14 million.

Outlook

Smartgroup is one of Australia's largest companies involved in the salary packaging and novated leasing businesses. Essentially this latter business involves taking advantage of complex legislation to provide tax deductions for employees, mainly those working in charities or in the public sector. Smartgroup has grown considerably through a series of acquisitions, with around 4000 clients. As it grows it achieves economies of scale, and profit margins increase. It has been achieving success in renewing or extending the contracts of its leading clients. However, it has noted that as households face rising cost pressures, potential customers have been delaying vehicle buying decisions, with the problem compounded by extended vehicle delivery delays. It has announced a strategic plan, named Smart Future, aimed at boosting annual EBITDA by $15 million to $20 million from 2024. This involves spending $5 million to $6 million per year over three years to redesign client and customer portals, migrating to cloud infrastructure and software, and investing in business automation and enhanced data analytics capability. Under this scheme, a new Smartsalary website has been launched. Under development is a new vehicle sales portal that, when fully functional, will take customers through the entire sales process. The company is also working to boost cross-selling of its various products among existing clients. In addition, it sees a great opportunity among the employees of its current clients. Though most of these employees own cars, only around 66 000 are using novated leases, and Smartgroup has initiated a scheme to target them as potential customers.

Year to 31 December	2020	2021
Revenues ($mn)	216.3	221.8
EBIT ($mn)	64.2	86.8
EBIT margin (%)	29.7	39.2
Profit before tax ($mn)	61.5	85.2
Profit after tax ($mn)	41.3	58.8
Earnings per share (c)	31.88	45.41
Cash flow per share (c)	51.39	55.19
Dividend (c)	34.5	36.5
Percentage franked	100	100
Interest cover (times)	23.9	52.0
Return on equity (%)	15.1	21.9
Half year to 30 June	2021	2022
Revenues ($mn)	109.4	113.6
Profit before tax ($mn)	38.8	44.7
Profit after tax ($mn)	26.6	30.9
Earnings per share (c)	20.50	23.80
Dividend (c)	17.5	17
Percentage franked	100	100
Net tangible assets per share ($)	~	~
Debt-to-equity ratio (%)	1.7	11.0
Current ratio	0.9	0.9

Sonic Healthcare Limited

ASX code: SHL   www.sonichealthcare.com

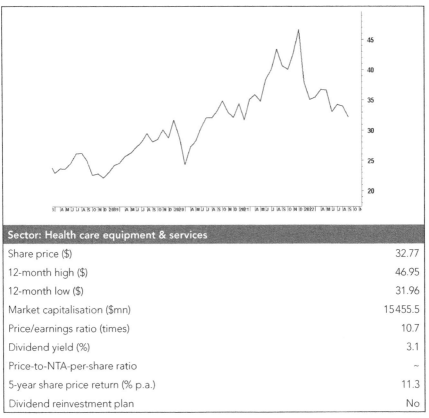

Sector: Health care equipment & services	
Share price ($)	32.77
12-month high ($)	46.95
12-month low ($)	31.96
Market capitalisation ($mn)	15455.5
Price/earnings ratio (times)	10.7
Dividend yield (%)	3.1
Price-to-NTA-per-share ratio	~
5-year share price return (% p.a.)	11.3
Dividend reinvestment plan	No

Sydney-based Sonic Healthcare has its roots in the pathology practice of Douglass Laboratories, which it acquired in 1987. It has since expanded significantly through acquisition and organic growth, and now operates through numerous separate companies. It has become Australia's largest private provider of pathology services and second-largest provider of radiology services. It is also now the world's third-largest pathology services provider, with activities in the United States, Germany, Switzerland, Belgium, the United Kingdom and New Zealand. Its Sonic Clinical Services division operates around 240 medical centres in Australia.

Latest business results (June 2022, full year)

Sonic's exposure to the COVID testing business once again helped boost revenues and profits. The company reported that COVID revenues rose 13 per cent on a constant currency basis to $2.4 billion, with other revenues up 2 per cent. In contrast to some previous years, most growth this year came from domestic businesses, with revenues for Australian and New Zealand laboratory operations up 24.2 per cent. By contrast, reduced demand for COVID testing at its overseas laboratories meant that European revenues rose just 3.3 per cent and American revenues fell 5.9 per cent.

Australian radiology also performed strongly, with revenues up 13.9 per cent, mainly reflecting the acquisitions of Canberra Imaging Group and Epworth Medical Imaging. The relatively small Sonic Clinical Services business saw revenues up 5 per cent, with occupational health and vaccination income partially offset by general medical centre weakness. During the year the company invested $628 million in acquisitions and joint ventures.

Outlook

Sonic expects demand for its COVID testing services to continue. It also forecasts accelerated growth from its other businesses, thanks to ageing and growing populations, market share gains and the clearing of backlogged testing that was postponed during the pandemic. It continues to work at building its pathology businesses. It achieved sustained success through its drive to consolidate the once-fragmented Australian pathology industry, and is now doing the same abroad. It has become the market leader in Germany, Switzerland and Britain, and one of the leaders in Belgium and the United States. Thanks to strong profit growth it continues to reduce its debt levels, and it has declared that it is now seeking further major acquisition opportunities. In the UK it is seeing a significant increase in private-sector GP referrals. It has launched a joint venture company, Franklin.ai, aimed at using artificial intelligence to speed up the diagnosis and detection of cancer and other diseases, with the first product release expected within two years.

Year to 30 June	2021	2022
Revenues ($mn)	8754.1	9340.2
Laboratory — Europe (%)	40	38
Laboratory — Australia/NZ (%)	23	27
Laboratory — USA (%)	26	23
Radiology — Australia (%)	7	8
EBIT ($mn)	1918.5	2155.0
EBIT margin (%)	21.9	23.1
Profit before tax ($mn)	1828.6	2077.2
Profit after tax ($mn)	1315.0	1460.6
Earnings per share (c)	275.47	305.47
Cash flow per share (c)	409.87	446.72
Dividend (c)	91	100
Percentage franked	51	100
Net tangible assets per share ($)	~	~
Interest cover (times)	21.3	27.7
Return on equity (%)	22.0	21.4
Debt-to-equity ratio (%)	14.2	10.7
Current ratio	1.0	1.1

Steadfast Group Limited

ASX code: SDF   www.steadfast.com.au

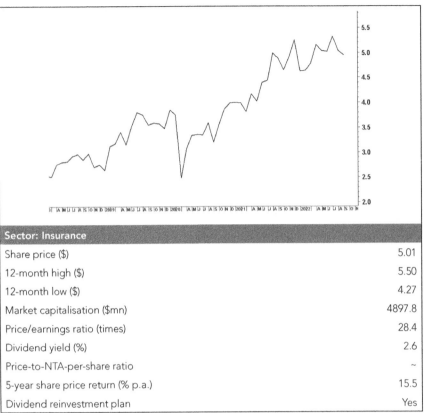

Sector: Insurance	
Share price ($)	5.01
12-month high ($)	5.50
12-month low ($)	4.27
Market capitalisation ($mn)	4897.8
Price/earnings ratio (times)	28.4
Dividend yield (%)	2.6
Price-to-NTA-per-share ratio	~
5-year share price return (% p.a.)	15.5
Dividend reinvestment plan	Yes

Melbourne-based insurance broking firm Steadfast launched in 1996 with the aim of boosting the buying power of small independent general insurance brokers in their dealings with insurers. It has since grown to become the largest insurance broker network and underwriting group in Australasia, with further operations in Asia and Europe. It also manages a range of complementary businesses that include back-office services, risk services guidance, work health consultancy, reinsurance and legal advice. It has taken a 60 per cent stake in Hamburg-based UnisonSteadfast, one of the world's largest networks of general insurance brokers. In August 2022 it acquired insurance distribution business Insurance Brands Australia.

Latest business results (June 2022, full year)

Steadfast enjoyed another excellent year, with solid rises in revenues and profits. Its core Steadfast Broking business recorded gross written premium of $11.1 billion, up 13.1 per cent from the previous year. A particular benefit came from $552 million of acquisitions made during the year, as well as from organic growth and further premium rate increases, and together these easily offset rising costs, resulting in underlying profit growth of 23.6 per cent. At June 2022 Steadfast incorporated a network of 355 brokerages in Australia, 50 in New Zealand and 22 in Singapore. It had equity holdings in 67 of the brokerages. The Steadfast Underwriting Agencies business, comprising 28 specialist agencies offering over 100 niche products, generated gross written premium of $1.8 billion, up 19.9 per cent, with price rises contributing to expanding profit margins.

Outlook

Steadfast is involved in an assortment of initiatives aimed at delivering long-term growth. Insurance Brands Australia, which it has acquired at a price of up to $301 million, is a large insurance broking and underwriting firm with a network of 400 professionals at more than 70 locations. It is expected to deliver a substantial boost to business, including significant cost synergies. The company also expects to make a series of further accretive acquisitions during the June 2023 year. UnisonSteadfast is a network of 272 insurance brokerages in 140 countries, and in June 2022 Steadfast introduced a series of risk services products to UnisonSteadfast members. In addition, it is involved in a series of technology initiatives, including its fast-growing Steadfast Client Trading Platform, which provides brokers with automated access to its network, with significant efficiency gains. The company's early forecast is for a June 2023 after-tax profit of $190 million to $202 million and earnings per share growth of five per cent to 11 per cent.

Year to 30 June	2021	2022
Revenues ($mn)	899.9	1135.9
EBIT ($mn)	205.1	262.0
EBIT margin (%)	22.8	23.1
Profit before tax ($mn)	194.9	247.4
Profit after tax ($mn)	130.7	169.0
Earnings per share (c)	15.12	17.62
Cash flow per share (c)	22.17	25.26
Dividend (c)	11.4	13
Percentage franked	100	100
Net tangible assets per share ($)	~	~
Interest cover (times)	20.1	17.9
Return on equity (%)	11.5	11.9
Debt-to-equity ratio (%)	41.0	33.4
Current ratio	1.6	1.6

Super Retail Group Limited

ASX code: SUL www.superretailgroup.com.au

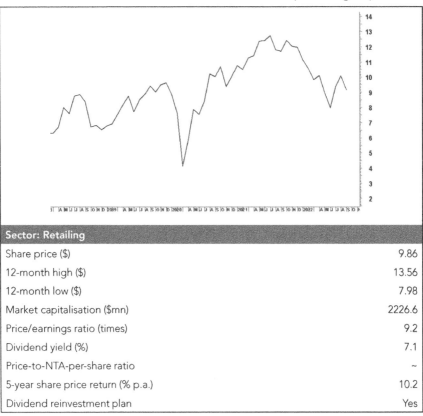

Sector: Retailing	
Share price ($)	9.86
12-month high ($)	13.56
12-month low ($)	7.98
Market capitalisation ($mn)	2226.6
Price/earnings ratio (times)	9.2
Dividend yield (%)	7.1
Price-to-NTA-per-share ratio	~
5-year share price return (% p.a.)	10.2
Dividend reinvestment plan	Yes

Specialist retail chain Super Retail Group was established as a mail-order business in 1972 and has its headquarters in Strathpine, Queensland. It now comprises a number of key retail brands, with more than 700 stores throughout Australia and New Zealand. Supercheap Auto is a retailer of automotive spare parts and related products. Rebel is a prominent sporting goods chain. BCF is a retailer of boating, camping and fishing products. Macpac is an outdoor adventure and activity specialist retailer.

Latest business results (July 2022, full year)

The opening of 21 new stores helped deliver a modest rise in sales for the year, but on a like-for-like basis sales were down 0.6 per cent — though with a solid second half, after first-half weakness — and with profits falling by double-digit amounts as the company's businesses were hit by pandemic-related store closures, rising costs and supply chain disruptions. The best result came from the small Macpac division, with 4.4 per cent like-for-like sales growth. This included strong growth in Australia, partly offset by a decline in New Zealand. BCF too enjoyed a modest rise, with strong sales over the summer and Easter holiday periods. The largest business, Supercheap Auto, saw like-for-like sales largely flat for the year, while Rebel like-for-like sales fell 2.8 per cent. Total group online sales of $601 million were up 44 per cent for the year. Note that the July 2022 result represented 53 weeks, compared with 52 weeks for the June 2021 result.

Outlook

Super Retail controls four prominent brands with strong positions in their respective markets and it has been experiencing a good recovery in business during 2022. Nevertheless, it operates in a challenging and competitive retail environment. With much of its product range imported, it is vulnerable to currency fluctuations and supply chain disruptions, along with rising costs. In addition, as interest rates edge up and inflation increasingly affects household budgets, it could see an easing of consumer spending. It plans a steady rollout of new stores, with as many as 30 expected to open during the June 2023 year. It will also upgrade five Rebel stores to the attractive new rCX (Rebel Customer Experience) format, aimed at giving shoppers a more interactive and immersive experience. It is increasing its range of higher-margin own-brand and exclusive products at its stores, and is harnessing customer loyalty through the promotion of members' clubs. It is also boosting its digital capacity, and expects online sales to continue their strong growth.

Year to 2 July*	2021	2022
Revenues ($mn)	3453.1	3550.9
Supercheap Auto (%)	38	38
Rebel (%)	35	34
BCF (%)	23	23
Macpac (%)	4	5
EBIT ($mn)	468.6	392.7
EBIT margin (%)	13.6	11.1
Gross margin (%)	48.0	46.8
Profit before tax ($mn)	427.6	345.7
Profit after tax ($mn)	301.0	241.2
Earnings per share (c)	133.44	106.81
Cash flow per share (c)	266.16	241.96
Dividend (c)	88	70
Percentage franked	100	100
Net tangible assets per share ($)	~	~
Interest cover (times)	11.4	8.4
Return on equity (%)	27.1	19.2
Debt-to-equity ratio (%)	~	~
Current ratio	1.1	1.2

*26 June 2021

Supply Network Limited

ASX code: SNL   www.supplynetwork.com.au

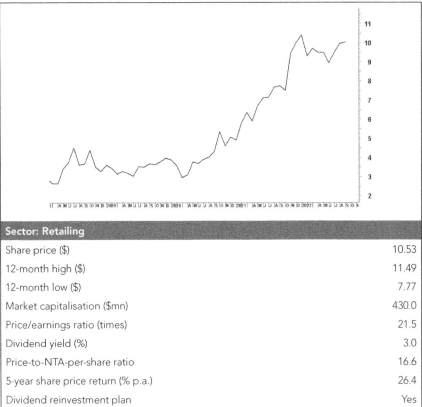

Sector: Retailing	
Share price ($)	10.53
12-month high ($)	11.49
12-month low ($)	7.77
Market capitalisation ($mn)	430.0
Price/earnings ratio (times)	21.5
Dividend yield (%)	3.0
Price-to-NTA-per-share ratio	16.6
5-year share price return (% p.a.)	26.4
Dividend reinvestment plan	Yes

Sydney-based Supply Network is a supplier of bus and truck parts in the commercial vehicle aftermarket, operating under the brand name Multispares, which was established in 1976. It manages offices, distribution centres and workshops at 18 locations throughout Australia and five in New Zealand.

Latest business results (June 2022, full year)

A rebounding economy generated strong rises in sales and profits for Supply Network, with efficiency gains helping to boost margins. There was strength across most product areas, although bus customers continued to experience COVID-related constraints. Sales in Australia were up 24 per cent, with pre-tax profit up 44 per cent. New Zealand, representing 17.5 per cent of total income, saw revenues up 12 per cent and the pre-tax profit jumping 50 per cent. Supply chain interruptions were a problem, forcing the company to accelerate purchases of its supplies in order to have sufficient product in stock, and it was generally able to meet its customers' requirements in a timely fashion. The company continued its practice of passing on product cost increases in higher prices, maintaining profit margins. During the year Supply Network relocated its Newcastle and Mackay branches to larger and more accessible sites, with a positive impact on sales. It also completed the extension of its New Zealand distribution facilities in Hamilton.

Outlook

Supply Network is one of the leaders in the Australian market for the supply of truck and bus parts. With a great diversity of vehicle makes and models, and with a considerable difference in requirements between various regions of the country, the company has established a decentralised management structure with a strong regional focus. Its core activity in recent years has become the supply of truck components, and this now represents more than 80 per cent of total income. Company fleets are the largest customer group, and these are sophisticated buyers of parts with a focus on costs, making this business highly competitive. Independent repair workshops are the next-largest customer group. The company is a beneficiary of the increasing complexity of trucks, which require an ever-growing range of expensive components. It plans two new branches during the June 2023 year, at Truganina, near Port Melbourne, and at Yatala in south-east Queensland. The company says that its recent strong growth has opened new product and market opportunities, and that projects under way will give it the capacity to exceed $250 million in annual revenues. It has started investigating further investment requirements to support annual revenues of $300 million.

Year to 30 June	2021	2022
Revenues ($mn)	162.6	198.4
EBIT ($mn)	21.1	29.9
EBIT margin (%)	13.0	15.1
Profit before tax ($mn)	19.7	28.5
Profit after tax ($mn)	13.8	20.0
Earnings per share (c)	33.91	49.02
Cash flow per share (c)	48.39	65.31
Dividend (c)	20	32
Percentage franked	100	100
Net tangible assets per share ($)	0.52	0.63
Interest cover (times)	14.9	20.5
Return on equity (%)	30.2	36.9
Debt-to-equity ratio (%)	7.1	4.1
Current ratio	2.4	2.4

Technology One Limited

ASX code: TNE   www.technologyonecorp.com

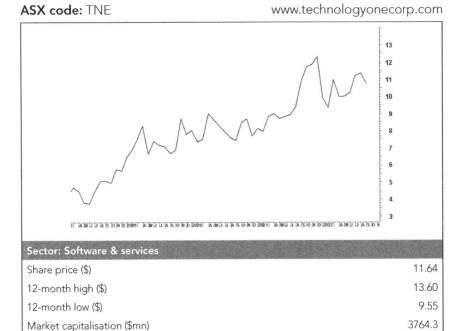

Sector: Software & services	
Share price ($)	11.64
12-month high ($)	13.60
12-month low ($)	9.55
Market capitalisation ($mn)	3764.3
Price/earnings ratio (times)	51.4
Dividend yield (%)	1.2
Price-to-NTA-per-share ratio	483.0
5-year share price return (% p.a.)	19.4
Dividend reinvestment plan	No

Brisbane-based Technology One, founded in 1987, designs, develops, implements and supports a wide range of financial management, accounting and business software. It enjoys particular strength in local government. Its software is also used by educational institutions, including many Australian universities. Other key markets are financial services, central government, and health and community services. It derives revenues not only from the supply of its products but also from annual licence fees. It operates from offices in Australia, New Zealand, Malaysia and the UK. In 2021 it acquired British educational software company Scientia Resource Management.

Latest business results (March 2022, half year)

Technology One posted another strong result, with profits up for the thirteenth straight March half year. Once again the company enjoyed success in moving its customers onto its Software as a Service (SaaS) cloud platforms. The number of large-scale enterprise SaaS customers rose to 714, up from 576 a year earlier. SaaS annual recurring revenue saw a 44 per cent jump from a year before. Consulting services — essentially the business of implementing the company's software, and representing about 18 per cent of company turnover — achieved low double-digit growth in sales and profits. The pre-tax profit for UK operations doubled to $2.3 million. The company maintained its high level of research and development spending, up 20 per cent to $41.5 million.

Outlook

Technology One has become a star among Australian high-tech companies, with growing profits and regular dividend increases. In large part this reflects a strong product line, a solid flow of recurring income and a heavy investment in new products and services. It is achieving great success with its SaaS offerings, which put software in the cloud, rather than on the customers' own computers, meaning that the customers always have the latest software versions, and giving them greater flexibility than previously. It says it has now largely completed moving its customer base to SaaS platforms. It currently receives annual recurring revenues of $288 million from its SaaS business, and believes it is on track to boost this to more than $500 million in 2026, with growing profit margins. It is developing a new product, known as 'Local Government—Digital Experience Platform', designed to transform the way local councils interact with residents, and believes this could become another long-term platform for future growth. It believes it can enhance its competitive position in the UK through its new Scientia business, which provides academic timetabling and resource scheduling software to educational institutions.

Year to 30 September	2020	2021
Revenues ($mn)	298.3	311.3
EBIT ($mn)	83.6	99.1
EBIT margin (%)	28.0	31.8
Profit before tax ($mn)	82.5	97.8
Profit after tax ($mn)	62.9	72.7
Earnings per share (c)	19.75	22.64
Cash flow per share (c)	25.60	30.69
Dividend (c)	12.88	13.91
Percentage franked	60	60
Interest cover (times)	73.2	78.2
Return on equity (%)	50.6	43.7
Half year to 31 March	2021	2022
Revenues ($mn)	144.3	172.0
Profit before tax ($mn)	37.3	42.6
Profit after tax ($mn)	28.2	33.2
Earnings per share (c)	8.80	10.29
Dividend (c)	3.82	4.2
Percentage franked	60	60
Net tangible assets per share ($)	0.09	0.02
Debt-to-equity ratio (%)	~	~
Current ratio	1.0	1.0

Telstra Corporation Limited

ASX code: TLS   www.telstra.com.au

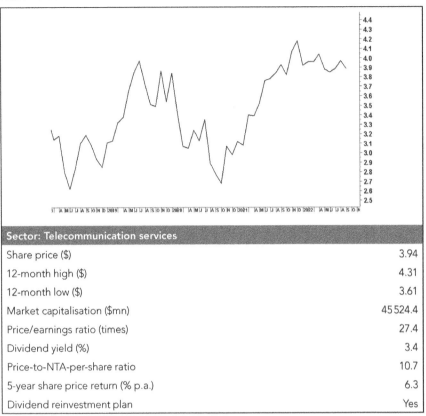

Sector: Telecommunication services	
Share price ($)	3.94
12-month high ($)	4.31
12-month low ($)	3.61
Market capitalisation ($mn)	45 524.4
Price/earnings ratio (times)	27.4
Dividend yield (%)	3.4
Price-to-NTA-per-share ratio	10.7
5-year share price return (% p.a.)	6.3
Dividend reinvestment plan	Yes

Melbourne-based Telstra traces its origins back to the construction of Australia's first telegraph line in 1854. It later became part of the Postmaster-General's department. Subsequently, a privatisation process began in 1997. It is today Australia's premier provider of telecommunication services, with 20.8 million retail mobile services, two million wholesale mobile services and 3.5 million consumer and small business bundle and data services. It also has substantial business interests throughout the Asia-Pacific, including operation of the region's largest sub-sea cable network. In July 2022, working with the Australian government, it completed the $2.4 billion acquisition of Digicel Pacific, a major Pacific-region telecommunication services provider with some 2.8 million customers.

Latest business results (June 2022, full year)

Revenues and profits fell, although this partly reflected some one-off gains in the previous year. The company said that underlying EBITDA rose 8.4 per cent, with a particular surge in the second half. The company's mobile activities continued to grow, with revenues up 1.7 per cent to $9.47 billion and profits strongly higher, despite a decline in hardware income. By contrast, the fixed-line consumer and small business segment saw sales down 5.3 per cent to $4.49 billion and a sharp decline in profits. Revenues were largely flat at $3.73 billion for the fixed-line enterprise business, with profits higher. Underlying fixed costs of $5.1 billion were down 8.1 per cent.

Outlook

Telstra has completed its T22 restructuring plan, and has now embarked on its three-year T25 strategy. This involves a significant reorganisation of its corporate structure and an ambitious range of performance targets. It plans to expand its mobile network, which already covers more than 2.6 million square kilometres of land and is providing the company with some of its best growth. It is also working to expand its international business, with its Digicel Pacific acquisition providing an important foothold in some Pacific-region countries. It sees good potential for its Telstra Health business, with revenues expected to double to $500 million by June 2025. It is also moving into the field of renewable energy, and will introduce initiatives to provide customers with carbon-neutral energy plans. Nevertheless, the company is vulnerable to any economic downturn, with rising inflation another negative. It is also affected by high levels of competition. The company's early forecast is for June 2023 revenues of $23 billion to $25 billion, underlying EBITDA of $7.8 billion to $8 billion — compared with $7.3 billion in June 2022 — with expected capital spending of $3.5 billion to $3.7 billion.

Year to 30 June	2021	2022
Revenues ($mn)	21 558.0	21 277.0
Mobility (%)	40	43
Fixed — consumer & small business (%)	20	20
Fixed — enterprise (%)	16	17
International (%)	6	7
InfraCo Fixed (%)	7	7
EBIT ($mn)	2992.0	2898.0
EBIT margin (%)	13.9	13.6
Profit before tax ($mn)	2441.0	2481.0
Profit after tax ($mn)	1857.0	1688.0
Earnings per share (c)	15.64	14.36
Cash flow per share (c)	54.76	51.43
Dividend (c)	10	13.5
Percentage franked	100	100
Net tangible assets per share ($)	0.39	0.37
Interest cover (times)	5.4	6.9
Return on equity (%)	12.8	11.3
Debt-to-equity ratio (%)	85.2	59.0
Current ratio	0.7	0.6

Wesfarmers Limited

ASX code: WES   www.wesfarmers.com.au

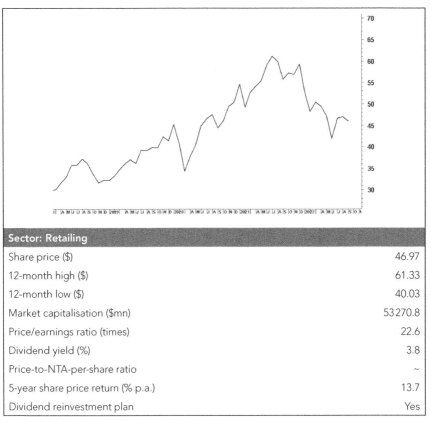

Sector: Retailing	
Share price ($)	46.97
12-month high ($)	61.33
12-month low ($)	40.03
Market capitalisation ($mn)	53 270.8
Price/earnings ratio (times)	22.6
Dividend yield (%)	3.8
Price-to-NTA-per-share ratio	~
5-year share price return (% p.a.)	13.7
Dividend reinvestment plan	Yes

Perth-based Wesfarmers, founded in 1914 as a farmers' cooperative, is now a conglomerate with many areas of operation. Its primary business is the Bunnings network of hardware stores. Other retail businesses include the Officeworks, Kmart and Target chains and the Catch online marketplace. In addition, it produces fertilisers, chemicals and industrial safety products. It has a 5 per cent equity stake in Coles, holds 50 per cent of the Flybuys loyalty card business, owns a 25 per cent interest in the ASX-listed BWP property trust — which owns many Bunnings warehouses — and holds half the equity in the financial services business Gresham Partners, the timber business Wespine Industries and the lithium producer Covalent Lithium. In November 2021 it acquired Beaumont Tiles and in March 2022 it acquired the pharmaceuticals wholesaler and retailer Australian Pharmaceutical Industries (API). At June 2022 Wesfarmers operated 1779 stores in Australia and New Zealand.

Latest business results (June 2022, full year)

Sales rose but profits edged down, as COVID-related lockdowns forced the closure of many stores in the first half. The core Bunnings business actually managed a small rise in profits, helped by new store openings. But the Kmart Group recorded a small decline in revenues and with profits crashing 40 per cent, despite a second-half recovery. Officeworks achieved increased sales, but with profits down. The WesCEF Chemicals, Energy and Fertilisers division enjoyed double-digit rises in sales and profits, thanks especially to higher global prices for LPG, fertiliser and other ammonia-related products. Strong demand for safety gear and workwear helped the Industrial and Safety division to a 31 per cent earnings increase. There was an initial contribution from the API acquisition.

Outlook

Wesfarmers has a variety of strategies for growth, although it is concerned about the impact that cost inflation, supply and labour shortages and shipping disruptions could have on its operations. It expects sales growth across its retail businesses, as customers become increasingly value-conscious, switching from high-priced to more affordable products. It has formed a new Health division, based on the API acquisition, and sees great potential in the Australian health, beauty and wellbeing sector. In April 2022 it created the OneDigital division to bring together its digital activities and to promote operational efficiencies and digital growth across its diverse range of businesses. The company's Covalent Lithium joint venture is constructing a $1.9 billion mine and refinery in Western Australia with the goal of producing up to 50 000 tonnes annually of lithium hydroxide, for use in lithium batteries, from late 2024.

Year to 30 June	2021	2022
Revenues ($mn)	33 941.0	36 838.0
Bunnings (%)	50	48
Kmart Group (%)	29	26
Officeworks (%)	9	9
WesCEF (%)	6	8
Industrial & safety (%)	5	5
EBIT ($mn)	3550.0	3416.0
EBIT margin (%)	10.5	9.3
Profit before tax ($mn)	3373.0	3320.0
Profit after tax ($mn)	2421.0	2352.0
Earnings per share (c)	214.06	207.77
Cash flow per share (c)	347.48	346.91
Dividend (c)	178	180
Percentage franked	100	100
Net tangible assets per share ($)	~	~
Interest cover (times)	33.2	37.5
Return on equity (%)	25.4	26.6
Debt-to-equity ratio (%)	~	53.3
Current ratio	1.1	1.1

Wisetech Global Limited

ASX code: WTC

www.wisetechglobal.com

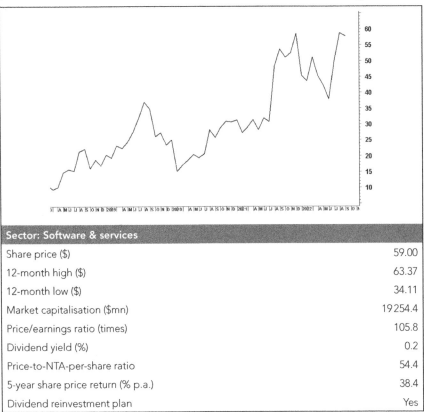

Sector: Software & services	
Share price ($)	59.00
12-month high ($)	63.37
12-month low ($)	34.11
Market capitalisation ($mn)	19 254.4
Price/earnings ratio (times)	105.8
Dividend yield (%)	0.2
Price-to-NTA-per-share ratio	54.4
5-year share price return (% p.a.)	38.4
Dividend reinvestment plan	Yes

Sydney-based logistics software specialist Wisetech was founded in 1994 to supply code for local freight forwarders. Today it is a global leader in international logistics software, with customers that include most of the world's largest freight forwarders and logistics providers. It has more that 50 offices worldwide and 35 product development centres. Its key product CargoWise is available in 30 languages and is sold in 170 countries, with more than 18 000 customers.

Latest business results (June 2022, full year)

Revenues and profits rose strongly in a sparkling result for Wisetech. With profits rising at a faster pace than revenues, the company achieved enhanced margins. It realised solid organic growth, with increasing usage of its CargoWise products by its existing large customer base, and it also won new customers during the year, including UPS and FedEx. It benefited from price increases, implemented in part to offset the impact of rising costs. Recurring revenue slipped from 90 per cent of the total to 89 per cent. With its sales invoiced in a range of currencies, it incurred a $9.4 million foreign exchange loss. The research and development expense rose 8 per cent to $180.8 million. By geography, the company received 41 per cent of its revenues from the Europe/Middle East/Africa sector, 32 per cent from the Asia Pacific sector and the remainder from the Americas.

Outlook

Wisetech's key strategy is to target the 25 leading global freight forwarders and the 200 leading global logistics providers, and it benefits as these companies consolidate and increasingly dominate their industries. It says its focus is on growth through six key development priorities — landside container haulage logistics, warehousing, Neo (the company's global integrated platform for consumers of logistics services), digital documents, customs and compliance, and international eCommerce. It benefits from a customer attrition rate of less than 1 per cent. Having completed 41 acquisitions in six years, the company has a highly experienced mergers and acquisitions division. It is now seeking further acquisitions to help introduce new technology to its operations. However, with its high levels of R&D spending it also expects further strong organic growth. It continues to benefit from a major two-year efficiency and streamlining program that has significantly reduced costs. At June 2022 Wisetech had no debt and cash holdings of more than $480 million. Its early forecast is for June 2023 revenues of $755 million to $780 million, with EBITDA of $385 million to $415 million, compared with $319 million in June 2022.

Year to 30 June	2021	2022
Revenues ($mn)	507.5	632.2
EBIT ($mn)	149.8	255.0
EBIT margin (%)	29.5	40.3
Profit before tax ($mn)	145.7	252.3
Profit after tax ($mn)	105.8	181.8
Earnings per share (c)	32.56	55.77
Cash flow per share (c)	50.05	75.40
Dividend (c)	6.55	11.15
Percentage franked	100	100
Net tangible assets per share ($)	0.62	1.08
Interest cover (times)	36.5	94.4
Return on equity (%)	10.0	15.0
Debt-to-equity ratio (%)	~	~
Current ratio	2.2	2.9

Woolworths Group Limited

ASX code: WOW   www.woolworthsgroup.com.au

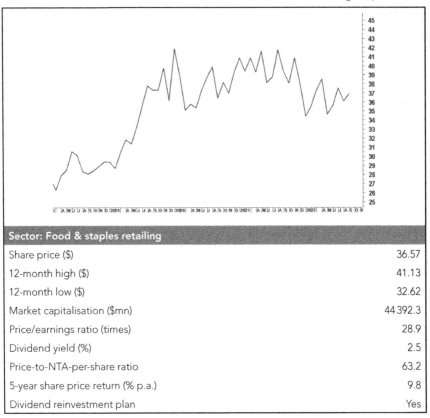

Sector: Food & staples retailing	
Share price ($)	36.57
12-month high ($)	41.13
12-month low ($)	32.62
Market capitalisation ($mn)	44 392.3
Price/earnings ratio (times)	28.9
Dividend yield (%)	2.5
Price-to-NTA-per-share ratio	63.2
5-year share price return (% p.a.)	9.8
Dividend reinvestment plan	Yes

Woolworths, founded in Sydney in 1924, is one of Australia's retail giants. Its 1450 outlets across Australia and New Zealand are centred on Woolworths and Countdown supermarkets and Big W mixed goods stores. It has created a new wholesale food and drinks business, called Australian B2B, based in part on the 2020 acquisition of food distribution business PFD Food Services. It has demerged its majority-owned drinks and hotels business Endeavour Group.

Latest business results (June 2022, full year)

Woolworths recorded higher sales. But increased costs related to the COVID pandemic forced profits down, despite a second-half recovery. The core Australian Food division was hit by supply chain disruption and product availability challenges, but recorded a 4.5 per cent rise in sales, with profits edging up. The company reported eCommerce sales of $4.7 billion, up 42.3 per cent from the previous year. The New Zealand Food division also recorded higher sales, but EBIT fell 12.5 per cent in NZ dollars, hurt by widespread COVID community transmission, shipping challenges and a three-day strike, which disrupted the supply chain. Big W was hit by lockdowns in the first half, forcing the closure of many stores, and sales fell 3.3

per cent, despite a strong fourth-quarter recovery, with EBIT crashing 68.2 per cent. The new Australian B2B segment achieved sales of $4 billion. The company also recorded a significant item that is not included in the figures in this book, a $6.4 billion profit from the demerger of its drinks and hotels business Endeavour Group.

Outlook

Despite its higher costs, Woolworths has actually benefited during the COVID pandemic as consumers have spent more time in their homes and have bought more from supermarkets. Now it faces an array of challenges, most notably rising business costs and price inflation from its suppliers, which force it either to raise its own prices or to accept lower margins. It has already reported that many customers are trading down from higher-priced to more affordable items. With COVID community spread continuing, the company is also being hit hard by staff absenteeism, while supply chain disruptions linger. The company expects conditions in New Zealand to remain challenging, but sees a turnaround in Big W. It continues to strengthen its fast-growing eCommerce activities and has acquired a majority stake in MyDeal, an online retail marketplace focused on home and lifestyle goods. It also expects continuing good growth from its new B2B operation, boosted by a major supply chain contract with Endeavour Group.

Year to 26 June*	2021	2022
Revenues ($mn)	55 733.0	60 849.0
Australian food (%)	78	75
New Zealand food (%)	12	11
Big W (%)	8	7
Australian B2B (%)	2	7
EBIT ($mn)	2764.0	2690.0
EBIT margin (%)	5.0	4.4
Gross margin (%)	29.4	29.7
Profit before tax ($mn)	2210.0	2091.0
Profit after tax ($mn)	1606.0	1547.0
Earnings per share (c)	127.77	126.65
Cash flow per share (c)	293.18	319.93
Dividend (c)	108	92
Percentage franked	100	100
Net tangible assets per share ($)	~	0.58
Interest cover (times)	29.1	37.9
Return on equity (%)	31.7	42.0
Debt-to-equity ratio (%)	107.1	53.4
Current ratio	0.7	0.6

*27 June 2021

PART II
THE TABLES

Table A

Market capitalisation

A company's market capitalisation is determined by multiplying the share price by the number of shares. To be included in this book, a company must be in the All Ordinaries Index, which comprises the 500 largest companies by market capitalisation.

	$mn
BHP Group	186 901.0
Commonwealth Bank	162 667.1
Rio Tinto	148 859.1
CSL	144 324.0
National Australia Bank	95 136.5
Macquarie Group	68 435.1
ANZ Banking	63 884.4
Wesfarmers	53 270.8
Fortescue Metals Group	51 624.3
Telstra Corporation	45 524.4
Woolworths Group	44 392.3
Aristocrat Leisure	23 456.9
Wisetech Global	19 254.4
REA Group	16 370.6
Sonic Healthcare	15 455.5
Computershare	14 942.3
ASX	14 506.1
Cochlear	14 281.1
Mineral Resources	11 843.4
IGO	10 253.4
Reece	9 870.6
Medibank Private	9 639.0
OZ Minerals	8 790.4
IDP Education	7 938.1
BlueScope Steel	7 486.6
Seek	7 406.9
Aurizon Holdings	6 865.8
Carsales.com	6 250.9
Pro Medicus	5 808.5
Harvey Norman Holdings	5 320.4
Altium	4 898.5
Steadfast Group	4 897.8
JB Hi-Fi	4 428.0
Iluka Resources	4 153.3
Alumina	4 004.3
Metcash	3 968.4
Nine Entertainment	3 786.9
Technology One	3 764.3
Beach Energy	3 764.2
NIB Holdings	3 530.5
Premier Investments	3 464.5
Ansell	3 422.3
Netwealth Group	3 189.1
Brickworks	3 143.3
Reliance Worldwide Corporation	2 899.6
Breville Group	2 876.4

ARB Corporation	2 523.6
Magellan Financial Group	2 322.9
Bapcor	2 318.2
Super Retail Group	2 226.6
CSR	2 193.9
IRESS	2 182.5
Healius	2 071.9
IPH	2 054.7
Pinnacle Investment	1 934.7
AUB Group	1 932.3
Elders	1 906.6
Pendal Group	1 848.4
Lifestyle Communities	1 808.6
Johns Lyng Group	1 736.6
Perpetual	1 481.7
Objective Corporation	1 432.3
Credit Corp Group	1 331.5
Monadelphous Group	1 243.2
NRW Holdings	1 230.8
GUD Holdings	1 180.7
Collins Foods	1 133.1
Codan	1 110.6
McMillan Shakespeare	1 105.8
Clinuvel Pharmaceuticals	1 042.6
Hansen Technologies	984.0
Data#3	977.1
PWR Holdings	951.8
Platinum Asset Management	933.7
Grange Resources	902.7
Nick Scali	865.9
Jumbo Interactive	840.6
Smartgroup Corporation	775.4
Ridley Corporation	699.7
Australian Ethical Investment	676.6
Baby Bunting Group	565.6
GWA Group	525.1
Beacon Lighting Group	498.0
Michael Hill International	450.4
Supply Network	430.0
Adairs	359.8
PeopleIn	329.8
Servcorp	318.5
Enero Group	294.5
Schaffer Corporation	245.5
Fiducian Group	239.2
Clover Corporation	168.4
Globe International	149.3

Table B

Revenues

This list ranks the companies in the book according to their most recent full-year revenues figures (operating income for the banks). The figures include revenues from sales and services, but other revenues — such as interest receipts and investment income — are not generally included.

	$mn
BHP Group	89 175.3
Rio Tinto	84 488.0
Woolworths Group	60 849.0
Wesfarmers	36 838.0
Commonwealth Bank	24 935.0
Fortescue Metals Group	23 821.9
Telstra Corporation	21 277.0
BlueScope Steel	19 029.9
ANZ Banking	17 447.0
Macquarie Group	17 324.0
National Australia Bank	16 806.0
Metcash	15 164.8
CSL	13 885.3
Sonic Healthcare	9 340.2
JB Hi-Fi	9 232.0
Reece	7 654.0
Medibank Private	7 128.5
Aristocrat Leisure	4 736.6
Harvey Norman Holdings	4 505.7
Super Retail Group	3 550.9
Computershare	3 509.7
Mineral Resources	3 418.0
Aurizon Holdings	3 075.3
NIB Holdings	2 703.4
Nine Entertainment	2 691.4
Ansell	2 674.1
Elders	2 548.9
NRW Holdings	2 377.7
Healius	2 337.7
CSR	2 311.6
Data#3	2 192.4
OZ Minerals	2 095.8
Bapcor	1 841.9
Monadelphous Group	1 810.4
Beach Energy	1 771.4
Cochlear	1 648.3
Reliance Worldwide Corporation	1 605.7
Iluka Resources	1 559.4
Premier Investments	1 443.2
Breville Group	1 418.4
Collins Foods	1 184.5
REA Group	1 160.2
Steadfast Group	1 135.9
Seek	1 116.5
Ridley Corporation	1 049.1
ASX	1 041.8

IGO	902.8
Johns Lyng Group	895.0
Brickworks	890.3
GUD Holdings	835.5
IDP Education	793.3
Grange Resources	781.7
Perpetual	749.6
ARB Corporation	694.5
PeopleIn	682.3
Wisetech Global	632.2
Magellan Financial Group	605.6
IRESS	595.9
Michael Hill International	595.2
McMillan Shakespeare	593.8
Pendal Group	581.9
Adairs	564.5
Enero Group	522.1
Carsales.com	509.1
Baby Bunting Group	507.3
Codan	506.1
Nick Scali	441.0
GWA Group	418.7
Credit Corp Group	411.2
IPH	385.1
AUB Group	332.5
Technology One	311.3
Beacon Lighting Group	304.8
Altium	302.5
Hansen Technologies	296.5
Globe International	274.5
Alumina	272.8
Servcorp	271.6
Platinum Asset Management	252.7
Lifestyle Communities	224.2
Smartgroup Corporation	221.8
Supply Network	198.4
Schaffer Corporation	170.4
Netwealth Group	169.5
Pinnacle Investment	121.7
Objective Corporation	106.5
Jumbo Interactive	104.3
PWR Holdings	101.1
Pro Medicus	93.5
Australian Ethical Investment	70.8
Fiducian Group	69.3
Clinuvel Pharmaceuticals	65.7
Clover Corporation	60.5

Table C

Year-on-year revenues growth

Companies generally strive for growth, though profit growth is usually of far more significance than a boost in revenues. In fact, it is possible for a company to increase its revenues by all kinds of means—including cutting profit margins or acquiring other companies—and year-on-year revenues growth is of little relevance if other ratios are not also improving. The figures used for this calculation are the latest full-year figures.

	%
Lifestyle Communities	62.7
Johns Lyng Group	57.5
Iluka Resources	57.4
OZ Minerals	56.2
PeopleIn	53.6
IDP Education	50.0
GUD Holdings	50.0
Grange Resources	48.5
BlueScope Steel	47.8
Seek	46.8
Pro Medicus	37.7
Clinuvel Pharmaceuticals	37.0
Macquarie Group	35.6
IGO	34.4
Rio Tinto	30.8
Enero Group	29.7
PWR Holdings	27.6
Altium	27.6
Steadfast Group	26.2
Jumbo Interactive	25.1
REA Group	25.0
Wisetech Global	24.6
Pinnacle Investment	23.0
Pendal Group	22.6
Healius	22.2
Reece	22.1
Supply Network	22.1
Elders	21.8
Australian Ethical Investment	20.6
Reliance Worldwide Corporation	19.8
Breville Group	19.4
Netwealth Group	19.4
Carsales.com	19.2
BHP Group	19.1
Premier Investments	18.7
Nick Scali	18.2
Fiducian Group	18.2
Computershare	16.9
Codan	15.8
Perpetual	15.0
Nine Entertainment	14.9
Aristocrat Leisure	14.4
Alumina	14.3
Beach Energy	13.4
Ridley Corporation	13.1
Adairs	12.9

Data#3	12.1
Objective Corporation	12.0
ARB Corporation	11.5
Collins Foods	11.1
Cochlear	10.1
IRESS	9.8
Credit Corp Group	9.7
Woolworths Group	9.2
McMillan Shakespeare	9.1
CSR	8.9
Wesfarmers	8.5
Baby Bunting Group	8.3
ASX	8.3
IPH	7.1
NRW Holdings	7.0
Michael Hill International	7.0
Sonic Healthcare	6.7
AUB Group	6.1
NIB Holdings	6.1
Metcash	5.9
CSL	5.7
Beacon Lighting Group	5.4
Bapcor	4.6
Technology One	4.4
JB Hi-Fi	3.5
Commonwealth Bank	3.4
Monadelphous Group	3.2
GWA Group	3.2
Medibank Private	3.2
Globe International	3.0
Super Retail Group	2.8
Smartgroup Corporation	2.5
Aurizon Holdings	1.9
Harvey Norman Holdings	1.5
Servcorp	0.7
Ansell	0.3
Telstra Corporation	−1.3
ANZ Banking	−1.7
National Australia Bank	−3.0
Hansen Technologies	−3.6
Platinum Asset Management	−6.2
Brickworks	−6.3
Mineral Resources	−8.5
Magellan Financial Group	−9.2
Schaffer Corporation	−13.2
Fortescue Metals Group	−18.8
Clover Corporation	−31.5

Table D
EBIT margin

A company's earnings before interest and taxation (EBIT) is sometimes regarded as a better measure of its profitability than the straight pre-tax or post-tax profit figure. EBIT is derived by adding net interest payments (that is, interest payments minus interest receipts) to the pre-tax profit. Different companies choose different methods of financing their operations; by adding back interest payments to their profits we can help minimise these differences and make comparisons between companies more valid.

The EBIT margin is the EBIT figure as a percentage of annual sales. Clearly a high figure is to be desired, though of course this can be achieved artificially by inflating borrowings (and hence interest payments). And it is noteworthy that efficient companies with strong cashflow like some of the retailers can operate most satisfactorily on low margins.

The EBIT margin figure has little relevance for banks, and they have been excluded.

	%
Alumina	93.5
Magellan Financial Group	85.4
Pro Medicus	66.8
ASX	66.2
Pinnacle Investment	64.6
Platinum Asset Management	57.9
Grange Resources	56.2
Carsales.com	53.6
BHP Group	52.4
Clinuvel Pharmaceuticals	51.9
IGO	51.8
Fortescue Metals Group	51.7
Rio Tinto	48.8
Netwealth Group	48.0
REA Group	47.8
Lifestyle Communities	45.0
Jumbo Interactive	43.5
Brickworks	43.4
Beach Energy	41.2
Wisetech Global	40.3
Smartgroup Corporation	39.2
OZ Minerals	38.0
Pendal Group	37.7
Credit Corp Group	36.0
Seek	35.2
AUB Group	34.8
Technology One	31.8
IPH	31.3
Iluka Resources	30.9
Altium	30.4
CSL	28.9
Aurizon Holdings	28.5
Nick Scali	28.2
PWR Holdings	28.2
Perpetual	27.3
Fiducian Group	27.2
Premier Investments	27.0
Codan	26.8
Harvey Norman Holdings	26.5
Schaffer Corporation	25.7
Aristocrat Leisure	24.3
ARB Corporation	24.1
Cochlear	23.2
Sonic Healthcare	23.1
Steadfast Group	23.1
Objective Corporation	21.9
Healius	21.1
Beacon Lighting Group	20.9
Nine Entertainment	20.5
IDP Education	20.0
BlueScope Steel	19.9
Mineral Resources	19.7
Australian Ethical Investment	19.4
Hansen Technologies	18.4
GWA Group	17.9
Reliance Worldwide Corporation	17.8
GUD Holdings	17.7
IRESS	17.1
McMillan Shakespeare	16.8
Supply Network	15.1
Computershare	14.3
Clover Corporation	14.2
Telstra Corporation	13.6
Adairs	13.5
CSR	12.6
Michael Hill International	12.3
Servcorp	12.2
Ansell	11.7
Enero Group	11.4
Bapcor	11.2
Super Retail Group	11.1
Breville Group	10.8
Globe International	10.0
Baby Bunting Group	9.7
Collins Foods	9.4
Wesfarmers	9.3
JB Hi-Fi	8.6
Medibank Private	7.7
Reece	7.6
NIB Holdings	7.3
Johns Lyng Group	6.6
Elders	6.5
NRW Holdings	6.3
Ridley Corporation	5.2
Woolworths Group	4.4
PeopleIn	4.3
Monadelphous Group	4.1
Metcash	3.1
Data#3	2.1

Table E
Year-on-year EBIT margin growth

The EBIT (earnings before interest and taxation) margin is one of the measures of a company's efficiency. So a rising margin is much to be desired, as it suggests that a company is achieving success in cutting its costs. This table does not include banks.

	%
Brickworks	100.2
IGO	92.9
IDP Education	65.2
Aristocrat Leisure	62.3
OZ Minerals	57.8
Premier Investments	56.8
NRW Holdings	56.2
Healius	51.2
BlueScope Steel	48.6
Seek	42.1
Wisetech Global	36.7
Smartgroup Corporation	31.9
Grange Resources	31.6
Iluka Resources	28.2
Beach Energy	23.0
Rio Tinto	22.5
Ridley Corporation	21.6
Pendal Group	17.3
BHP Group	16.9
Supply Network	16.2
Altium	15.7
Nine Entertainment	15.5
Technology One	13.6
Elders	13.3
CSR	12.5
Metcash	11.1
Collins Foods	10.5
Servcorp	10.4
IRESS	7.7
Baby Bunting Group	7.7
Data#3	7.0
Enero Group	6.9
Cochlear	6.6
Pro Medicus	6.2
GWA Group	5.9
Sonic Healthcare	5.3
Perpetual	4.4
IPH	3.9
JB Hi-Fi	3.3
Objective Corporation	3.1
AUB Group	3.1
Michael Hill International	2.6
Credit Corp Group	2.5
Beacon Lighting Group	1.8
Monadelphous Group	1.2

Steadfast Group	1.2
Carsales.com	1.1
Alumina	1.1
Computershare	0.8
ASX	–0.7
ARB Corporation	–1.0
Clinuvel Pharmaceuticals	–1.8
Telstra Corporation	–1.9
Bapcor	–2.1
GUD Holdings	–2.6
Magellan Financial Group	–3.2
PWR Holdings	–3.8
Reece	–3.9
Breville Group	–4.0
Harvey Norman Holdings	–4.7
Fiducian Group	–4.8
Aurizon Holdings	–4.8
Pinnacle Investment	–5.4
REA Group	–6.2
Jumbo Interactive	–6.8
CSL	–7.9
Johns Lyng Group	–8.2
McMillan Shakespeare	–8.3
Woolworths Group	–10.9
Wesfarmers	–11.3
Netwealth Group	–11.3
Medibank Private	–14.2
Codan	–15.5
Nick Scali	–17.6
Reliance Worldwide Corporation	–17.6
Super Retail Group	–18.5
Lifestyle Communities	–19.6
Schaffer Corporation	–20.8
NIB Holdings	–21.7
Fortescue Metals Group	–22.5
Hansen Technologies	–24.2
Australian Ethical Investment	–26.4
Ansell	–29.9
Clover Corporation	–31.4
PeopleIn	–33.0
Platinum Asset Management	–33.3
Adairs	–38.0
Globe International	–42.8
Mineral Resources	–55.3

Table F
After-tax profit

This table ranks all the companies according to their most recent full-year after-tax profit.

	$mn
BHP Group	30 684.9
Rio Tinto	28 449.0
Commonwealth Bank	9 595.0
Fortescue Metals Group	8 489.0
National Australia Bank	6 558.0
ANZ Banking	6 198.0
Macquarie Group	4 706.0
CSL	3 088.6
BlueScope Steel	2 701.1
Wesfarmers	2 352.0
Telstra Corporation	1 688.0
Woolworths Group	1 547.0
Sonic Healthcare	1 460.6
Harvey Norman Holdings	811.5
Aristocrat Leisure	765.6
JB Hi-Fi	544.9
OZ Minerals	530.7
Aurizon Holdings	524.9
ASX	508.5
Beach Energy	504.0
Mineral Resources	400.0
Magellan Financial Group	399.7
Medibank Private	393.9
Reece	392.5
REA Group	384.8
Nine Entertainment	348.5
IGO	330.9
Grange Resources	322.3
Iluka Resources	314.8
Computershare	311.9
Healius	309.3
Metcash	299.6
Brickworks	285.2
Cochlear	277.0
Premier Investments	271.8
Alumina	250.1
Super Retail Group	241.2
Seek	240.8
Ansell	217.4
Carsales.com	194.8
CSR	192.6
Reliance Worldwide Corporation	188.3
Wisetech Global	181.8
Steadfast Group	169.0
Pendal Group	164.7
Elders	151.1

Perpetual	148.2
NIB Holdings	135.7
Bapcor	131.6
ARB Corporation	122.0
Breville Group	105.7
IDP Education	102.6
Platinum Asset Management	101.5
Codan	100.7
Credit Corp Group	100.7
NRW Holdings	97.4
GUD Holdings	88.9
IPH	86.7
Nick Scali	80.2
Pinnacle Investment	76.4
Altium	76.0
AUB Group	74.0
IRESS	73.8
Technology One	72.7
McMillan Shakespeare	70.3
Lifestyle Communities	61.4
Smartgroup Corporation	58.8
Netwealth Group	55.9
Collins Foods	54.8
Monadelphous Group	52.2
Adairs	51.6
GWA Group	47.3
Michael Hill International	46.7
Pro Medicus	44.4
Hansen Technologies	41.9
Beacon Lighting Group	40.7
Ridley Corporation	36.2
Jumbo Interactive	31.2
Data#3	30.3
Baby Bunting Group	29.6
Servcorp	28.0
Enero Group	27.1
Schaffer Corporation	26.2
Johns Lyng Group	25.1
Clinuvel Pharmaceuticals	20.9
PWR Holdings	20.8
Supply Network	20.0
Objective Corporation	19.6
Globe International	18.6
PeopleIn	17.7
Fiducian Group	13.3
Australian Ethical Investment	9.5
Clover Corporation	6.0

Table G

Year-on-year earnings per share growth

The earnings per share (EPS) figure is a crucial one. It tells you — the shareholder — what your part is of the company's profits, for each of your shares. So investors invariably look for EPS growth in a stock. The year-on-year EPS growth figure is often one of the first ratios that investors look to when evaluating a stock. The figures used for this calculation are the latest full-year figures.

	%
IDP Education	158.6
IGO	153.9
OZ Minerals	144.7
BlueScope Steel	137.2
Seek	129.1
Healius	121.3
Aristocrat Leisure	114.6
Iluka Resources	108.3
Premier Investments	97.0
Brickworks	93.4
NRW Holdings	74.0
Wisetech Global	71.3
BHP Group	70.4
Lifestyle Communities	69.2
ANZ Banking	64.5
Altium	63.5
Grange Resources	57.8
Rio Tinto	57.8
Macquarie Group	50.6
Collins Foods	46.9
Ridley Corporation	45.1
Supply Network	44.6
Pro Medicus	43.9
Smartgroup Corporation	42.4
Beach Energy	38.9
Elders	38.3
Reece	37.4
Nine Entertainment	33.6
Pendal Group	30.7
National Australia Bank	29.2
Johns Lyng Group	24.5
PWR Holdings	23.9
Metcash	23.2
Objective Corporation	20.7
CSR	20.2
IRESS	20.1
Servcorp	19.3
REA Group	19.1
Data#3	18.8
Perpetual	18.8
Cochlear	18.2
Enero Group	17.2
Alumina	17.2
Steadfast Group	16.5
Computershare	16.2
Breville Group	15.4

McMillan Shakespeare	15.2
Technology One	14.6
Commonwealth Bank	14.0
Michael Hill International	13.8
Credit Corp Group	13.7
IPH	12.7
Carsales.com	12.1
Baby Bunting Group	11.5
GWA Group	11.2
Sonic Healthcare	10.9
Monadelphous Group	10.5
AUB Group	10.0
Jumbo Interactive	9.8
Fiducian Group	9.2
JB Hi-Fi	8.7
Beacon Lighting Group	7.7
ARB Corporation	6.7
GUD Holdings	5.8
ASX	5.7
Pinnacle Investment	5.2
Codan	3.3
Netwealth Group	1.7
Bapcor	1.2
Aurizon Holdings	–0.1
Woolworths Group	–0.9
Wesfarmers	–2.9
PeopleIn	–3.5
Harvey Norman Holdings	–3.6
Magellan Financial Group	–4.0
CSL	–4.1
Nick Scali	–4.8
Telstra Corporation	–8.2
Medibank Private	–10.7
Reliance Worldwide Corporation	–11.1
Australian Ethical Investment	–14.4
Clinuvel Pharmaceuticals	–15.6
NIB Holdings	–16.0
Super Retail Group	–20.0
Hansen Technologies	–27.4
Adairs	–32.0
Ansell	–32.2
Schaffer Corporation	–36.4
Fortescue Metals Group	–37.3
Platinum Asset Management	–37.7
Globe International	–44.0
Clover Corporation	–51.9
Mineral Resources	–63.8

Table H

Return on equity

Shareholders' equity is the company's assets minus its liabilities. It is, in theory, the amount owned by the shareholders of the company. Return on equity is the after-tax profit expressed as a percentage of that equity. Thus, it is the amount of profit that the company managers made for you — the shareholder — from your assets. For many investors it is one of the most important gauges of how well a company is doing. It is one of the requirements for inclusion in this book that all companies have a return on equity of at least 10 per cent in their latest financial year.

	%
Nick Scali	62.9
Netwealth Group	56.6
Data#3	51.3
Pro Medicus	48.5
BHP Group	46.0
Technology One	43.7
Rio Tinto	43.2
JB Hi-Fi	42.1
Woolworths Group	42.0
Grange Resources	40.7
Magellan Financial Group	39.6
Australian Ethical Investment	38.9
Supply Network	36.9
Objective Corporation	35.9
Jumbo Interactive	35.0
Fortescue Metals Group	34.8
Beacon Lighting Group	33.1
REA Group	32.5
BlueScope Steel	31.0
Platinum Asset Management	30.5
Codan	30.0
PWR Holdings	29.7
Fiducian Group	29.3
Adairs	28.5
Baby Bunting Group	26.8
Wesfarmers	26.6
Globe International	25.5
Metcash	25.4
Michael Hill International	25.3
McMillan Shakespeare	25.1
IDP Education	24.3
Pinnacle Investment	23.6
ARB Corporation	23.4
Smartgroup Corporation	21.9
Iluka Resources	21.8
Aristocrat Leisure	21.8
Sonic Healthcare	21.4
Elders	20.9
Altium	20.6
Medibank Private	20.5
IPH	20.2
Carsales.com	20.0
Harvey Norman Holdings	20.0
Enero Group	19.7
NIB Holdings	19.2
Super Retail Group	19.2

CSR	19.1
CSL	19.1
Nine Entertainment	18.9
Premier Investments	18.9
Breville Group	18.9
Clinuvel Pharmaceuticals	18.6
Macquarie Group	18.6
NRW Holdings	17.0
Cochlear	16.4
Healius	16.4
Perpetual	16.2
GWA Group	15.8
OZ Minerals	15.3
Beach Energy	15.2
Wisetech Global	15.0
Lifestyle Communities	14.8
Collins Foods	14.5
Pendal Group	14.4
GUD Holdings	14.4
Credit Corp Group	14.3
Servcorp	14.3
PeopleIn	14.0
Hansen Technologies	13.9
ASX	13.5
Seek	13.2
IRESS	13.1
Schaffer Corporation	13.0
Johns Lyng Group	13.0
Monadelphous Group	12.9
Commonwealth Bank	12.7
Reece	12.6
Mineral Resources	12.4
Bapcor	12.3
Aurizon Holdings	12.1
Ridley Corporation	12.0
Steadfast Group	11.9
Brickworks	11.7
Reliance Worldwide Corporation	11.7
Telstra Corporation	11.3
AUB Group	11.1
Alumina	11.0
National Australia Bank	10.6
Clover Corporation	10.4
Ansell	10.1
ANZ Banking	10.0
Computershare	10.0
IGO	10.0

Table I
Year-on-year return on equity growth

Company managers have a variety of strategies they can use to boost profits. It is much harder to lift the return on equity (ROE). Find a company with a high ROE figure, and one that is growing year by year, and it is possible that you have found a real growth stock. This figure is simply the percentage change in the ROE figure from the previous year to the latest year.

	%
IDP Education	136.5
OZ Minerals	122.7
IGO	118.9
Healius	109.0
BlueScope Steel	88.5
Premier Investments	84.8
Seek	83.4
Brickworks	82.5
BHP Group	75.9
ANZ Banking	62.4
Aristocrat Leisure	62.3
NRW Holdings	59.7
Wisetech Global	49.7
Smartgroup Corporation	45.1
Iluka Resources	44.4
Rio Tinto	42.8
Collins Foods	40.1
Lifestyle Communities	35.8
Altium	34.7
Macquarie Group	33.0
Woolworths Group	32.5
Metcash	32.5
Ridley Corporation	31.8
CSR	30.2
Nine Entertainment	28.8
Servcorp	26.2
Reece	24.8
Grange Resources	24.1
Alumina	23.9
Beach Energy	23.7
Supply Network	21.9
National Australia Bank	21.0
IRESS	13.7
IPH	12.8
Elders	12.8
Pendal Group	12.1
Pro Medicus	11.4
Commonwealth Bank	10.2
Data#3	9.5
Cochlear	8.8
Enero Group	8.3
Computershare	7.7
GWA Group	7.3
Monadelphous Group	7.2
Michael Hill International	7.0
Wesfarmers	4.6

ASX	4.5
PWR Holdings	4.5
Steadfast Group	3.6
Baby Bunting Group	2.8
Perpetual	2.8
Credit Corp Group	2.4
McMillan Shakespeare	2.4
Jumbo Interactive	1.3
JB Hi-Fi	0.4
Magellan Financial Group	-2.2
Aurizon Holdings	-2.2
Fiducian Group	-2.7
Sonic Healthcare	-2.8
REA Group	-2.8
Bapcor	-4.1
Breville Group	-4.5
Objective Corporation	-8.1
ARB Corporation	-10.9
Netwealth Group	-11.4
Telstra Corporation	-11.8
Beacon Lighting Group	-12.5
Harvey Norman Holdings	-13.2
Technology One	-13.5
Medibank Private	-14.1
Codan	-15.1
PeopleIn	-17.0
Reliance Worldwide Corporation	-17.2
Carsales.com	-19.6
Australian Ethical Investment	-20.7
AUB Group	-22.8
Pinnacle Investment	-23.7
NIB Holdings	-23.8
GUD Holdings	-25.4
Nick Scali	-29.3
Super Retail Group	-29.4
Hansen Technologies	-34.2
Clinuvel Pharmaceuticals	-35.7
Ansell	-36.6
CSL	-36.9
Platinum Asset Management	-38.3
Adairs	-42.4
Schaffer Corporation	-42.8
Fortescue Metals Group	-45.0
Globe International	-56.0
Clover Corporation	-57.4
Johns Lyng Group	-58.8
Mineral Resources	-69.2

Table J
Debt-to-equity ratio

A company's borrowings as a percentage of its shareholders' equity is one of the most common measures of corporate debt. Many investors will be wary of a company with a ratio that is too high. However, a company with a steady business and a regular income flow — such as an electric power company or a large supermarket chain — is generally considered relatively safe with a high level of debt, whereas a small company in a new business field might be thought at risk with even moderate debt levels. Much depends on surrounding circumstances, including the prevailing interest rates. Of course, it is often from borrowing that a company grows, and some investors are not happy buying shares in a company with little or no debt.

There are various ways to calculate the ratio, but for this book the net debt position is used. That is, a company's cash has been deducted from its borrowings. For inclusion in this book no company was allowed a debt-to-equity ratio of more than 70 per cent. Some of the companies had no net debt — their cash position was greater than the amount of their borrowings, or they had no borrowings at all — and so have been assigned a zero figure in this table. The ratio has no relevance for banks, and they have been excluded.

	%
Altium	0.0
Alumina	0.0
ARB Corporation	0.0
Aristocrat Leisure	0.0
ASX	0.0
AUB Group	0.0
Australian Ethical Investment	0.0
Beach Energy	0.0
Beacon Lighting Group	0.0
BHP Group	0.0
BlueScope Steel	0.0
Clinuvel Pharmaceuticals	0.0
Cochlear	0.0
CSL	0.0
CSR	0.0
Data#3	0.0
Enero Group	0.0
Fiducian Group	0.0
Grange Resources	0.0
IDP Education	0.0
Iluka Resources	0.0
JB Hi-Fi	0.0
Johns Lyng Group	0.0
Jumbo Interactive	0.0
Magellan Financial Group	0.0
Medibank Private	0.0
Michael Hill International	0.0
Monadelphous Group	0.0
Netwealth Group	0.0

Objective Corporation	0.0
OZ Minerals	0.0
Pendal Group	0.0
Platinum Asset Management	0.0
Premier Investments	0.0
Pro Medicus	0.0
PWR Holdings	0.0
Schaffer Corporation	0.0
Servcorp	0.0
Super Retail Group	0.0
Technology One	0.0
Wisetech Global	0.0
Baby Bunting Group	0.6
Breville Group	0.7
Globe International	1.2
NRW Holdings	2.3
McMillan Shakespeare	2.4
Rio Tinto	4.1
Supply Network	4.1
Fortescue Metals Group	5.1
Clover Corporation	7.0
IPH	7.0
Ridley Corporation	7.3
NIB Holdings	7.4
Codan	8.0
Hansen Technologies	9.0
Harvey Norman Holdings	10.5
IGO	10.7
Sonic Healthcare	10.7
Smartgroup Corporation	11.0

Nick Scali	12.1
Credit Corp Group	13.4
Ansell	14.1
Nine Entertainment	15.7
Metcash	17.3
REA Group	17.5
Pinnacle Investment	20.3
Brickworks	20.9
Mineral Resources	21.3
Bapcor	24.4
Reece	26.2
Healius	27.3
Perpetual	29.2
Elders	32.1
PeopleIn	32.2
Steadfast Group	33.4
Collins Foods	44.2
GWA Group	45.1
Adairs	47.1
Reliance Worldwide Corporation	48.7
Carsales.com	52.5
Wesfarmers	53.3
Woolworths Group	53.4
Lifestyle Communities	53.6
GUD Holdings	55.1
Seek	55.2
Telstra Corporation	59.0
IRESS	62.9
Computershare	63.9
Aurizon Holdings	69.1

Table K
Current ratio

The current ratio is simply the company's current assets divided by its current liabilities. Current assets are cash or assets that can, in theory, be converted quickly into cash. Current liabilities are normally those payable within a year. The current ratio helps measure the ability of a company to repay in a hurry its short-term debt, should the need arise. Banks are not included.

Pinnacle Investment	14.5	Fiducian Group	1.7
Platinum Asset Management	12.8	BHP Group	1.7
Alumina	12.8	IGO	1.7
Clinuvel Pharmaceuticals	10.2	NIB Holdings	1.7
Clover Corporation	6.9	Premier Investments	1.7
Netwealth Group	6.5	Codan	1.7
Credit Corp Group	6.2	BlueScope Steel	1.7
Grange Resources	5.1	IDP Education	1.6
Pro Medicus	4.5	REA Group	1.6
Aristocrat Leisure	3.8	Steadfast Group	1.6
Mineral Resources	3.7	Computershare	1.6
ARB Corporation	3.6	Medibank Private	1.5
PWR Holdings	3.5	Beacon Lighting Group	1.5
Reliance Worldwide Corporation	3.2	AUB Group	1.5
Altium	3.1	IRESS	1.5
Iluka Resources	3.0	Beach Energy	1.4
Wisetech Global	2.9	Perpetual	1.3
Fortescue Metals Group	2.9	NRW Holdings	1.3
IPH	2.8	Elders	1.3
Ansell	2.7	CSR	1.3
Jumbo Interactive	2.6	Baby Bunting Group	1.3
Cochlear	2.5	PeopleIn	1.2
Breville Group	2.5	Objective Corporation	1.2
Magellan Financial Group	2.4	Ridley Corporation	1.2
Supply Network	2.4	Adairs	1.2
Bapcor	2.4	Super Retail Group	1.2
Brickworks	2.3	Johns Lyng Group	1.2
CSL	2.3	Metcash	1.1
Schaffer Corporation	2.2	Sonic Healthcare	1.1
Pendal Group	2.2	JB Hi-Fi	1.1
GUD Holdings	2.2	ASX	1.1
Globe International	2.2	Wesfarmers	1.1
Reece	2.1	Data#3	1.1
McMillan Shakespeare	2.1	Technology One	1.0
GWA Group	2.0	Nine Entertainment	1.0
Seek	2.0	Servcorp	0.9
Monadelphous Group	2.0	Smartgroup Corporation	0.9
Harvey Norman Holdings	1.9	Aurizon Holdings	0.9
Australian Ethical Investment	1.9	Lifestyle Communities	0.8
Michael Hill International	1.8	Nick Scali	0.8
Hansen Technologies	1.8	Collins Foods	0.7
OZ Minerals	1.8	Telstra Corporation	0.6
Enero Group	1.8	Healius	0.6
Rio Tinto	1.8	Woolworths Group	0.6
Carsales.com	1.7		

Table L
Price/earnings ratio

The price/earnings ratio (PER) — the current share price divided by the earnings per share figure — is one of the best known of all sharemarket ratios. Essentially it expresses the amount of money investors are ready to pay for each cent or dollar of a company's profits, and it allows you to compare the share prices of different companies of varying sizes and with widely different profits. A high PER suggests the market has a high regard for the company and its growth prospects; a low one may mean that investors are disdainful of the stock. The figures in this table are based on share prices as of 8 September 2022.

Company	PER	Company	PER
Grange Resources	2.8	PeopleIn	18.0
BlueScope Steel	2.9	Fiducian Group	18.0
Rio Tinto	5.2	Baby Bunting Group	19.0
Magellan Financial Group	5.8	Ridley Corporation	19.3
Fortescue Metals Group	6.1	ARB Corporation	20.6
BHP Group	6.1	Collins Foods	20.7
Harvey Norman Holdings	6.6	Supply Network	21.5
Healius	6.9	AUB Group	21.6
Adairs	6.9	Wesfarmers	22.6
Beach Energy	7.5	Hansen Technologies	23.4
Globe International	8.0	IPH	23.6
JB Hi-Fi	8.5	Monadelphous Group	23.8
Super Retail Group	9.2	Medibank Private	24.5
Platinum Asset Management	9.3	Pinnacle Investment	24.8
Schaffer Corporation	9.4	Reece	25.1
Michael Hill International	9.6	NIB Holdings	26.0
Pendal Group	10.0	Jumbo Interactive	26.9
Perpetual	10.1	Breville Group	27.2
Enero Group	10.4	Telstra Corporation	27.4
ANZ Banking	10.5	Clover Corporation	28.0
Sonic Healthcare	10.7	Steadfast Group	28.4
Nick Scali	10.8	ASX	28.5
Nine Entertainment	10.9	Woolworths Group	28.9
Brickworks	11.0	Aristocrat Leisure	29.2
Codan	11.0	Lifestyle Communities	29.3
GWA Group	11.1	Mineral Resources	29.7
GUD Holdings	11.3	IRESS	30.0
Servcorp	11.4	Seek	30.8
CSR	11.4	IGO	31.0
Beacon Lighting Group	12.2	Carsales.com	32.0
Elders	12.6	Data#3	32.2
NRW Holdings	12.6	REA Group	42.5
Premier Investments	12.7	CSL	45.5
Smartgroup Corporation	12.8	PWR Holdings	45.6
Aurizon Holdings	13.1	Computershare	47.4
Iluka Resources	13.1	Clinuvel Pharmaceuticals	49.9
Credit Corp Group	13.2	Technology One	51.4
Metcash	13.5	Cochlear	51.6
Macquarie Group	13.6	Netwealth Group	57.0
National Australia Bank	14.9	Altium	64.4
Reliance Worldwide Corporation	15.4	Johns Lyng Group	64.8
Ansell	15.7	Australian Ethical Investment	70.3
McMillan Shakespeare	15.7	Objective Corporation	72.9
Alumina	16.0	IDP Education	77.4
OZ Minerals	16.5	Wisetech Global	105.8
Commonwealth Bank	17.2	Pro Medicus	130.7
Bapcor	17.6		

Table M

Price-to-NTA-per-share ratio

The NTA-per-share figure expresses the worth of a company's net tangible assets — that is, its assets minus its liabilities and intangible assets — for each share of the company. Intangible assets, such as goodwill or the value of newspaper mastheads, are excluded because it is deemed difficult to place a value on them (though this proposition is debatable), and also because they might not have much worth if separated from the company. The price-to-NTA-per-share ratio relates this figure to the share price.

A ratio of one means that the company is valued exactly according to the value of its assets. A ratio below one suggests that the shares are a bargain, though usually there is a good reason for this. Profits are more important than assets.

In some respects, this is an 'old economy' ratio. For many high-tech companies in the 'new economy' the most important assets are human ones, whose worth does not appear on the balance sheet.

Companies with a negative NTA-per-share figure, as a result of having intangible assets valued at more than their net assets, have been omitted from this table.

Grange Resources	1.0	Enero Group	7.0
BlueScope Steel	1.1	Bapcor	7.4
Beach Energy	1.1	AUB Group	8.3
ANZ Banking	1.1	Clinuvel Pharmaceuticals	8.4
Schaffer Corporation	1.2	Breville Group	8.8
Brickworks	1.2	Baby Bunting Group	8.8
Harvey Norman Holdings	1.5	McMillan Shakespeare	9.2
Aurizon Holdings	1.6	CSL	9.4
National Australia Bank	1.7	NIB Holdings	9.9
Alumina	1.8	Telstra Corporation	10.7
Credit Corp Group	1.9	Codan	12.0
Fortescue Metals Group	2.1	Aristocrat Leisure	12.1
Iluka Resources	2.2	Cochlear	12.8
Rio Tinto	2.2	ASX	13.1
Globe International	2.4	Metcash	14.1
Commonwealth Bank	2.5	Reece	15.2
Magellan Financial Group	2.6	Altium	15.2
CSR	2.7	PWR Holdings	15.5
Macquarie Group	2.8	Supply Network	16.6
OZ Minerals	2.9	Carsales.com	17.8
Ridley Corporation	2.9	JB Hi-Fi	17.8
Platinum Asset Management	2.9	Jumbo Interactive	21.4
Clover Corporation	2.9	Fiducian Group	24.5
BHP Group	3.0	Australian Ethical Investment	27.5
IGO	3.0	Beacon Lighting Group	32.7
Monadelphous Group	3.1	REA Group	35.6
NRW Holdings	3.2	Netwealth Group	36.5
Mineral Resources	3.7	Data#3	46.8
Lifestyle Communities	4.0	Seek	51.5
Pendal Group	4.3	Wisetech Global	54.4
Premier Investments	4.4	Woolworths Group	63.2
Elders	4.7	Pro Medicus	75.1
Pinnacle Investment	4.9	Johns Lyng Group	78.4
Ansell	5.4	Objective Corporation	98.7
ARB Corporation	5.5	Technology One	483.0
Michael Hill International	5.9	IRESS	2182.5
Medibank Private	6.0		

Table N
Dividend yield

Many investors buy shares for income, rather than for capital growth. They look for companies that offer a high dividend yield (the dividend expressed as a percentage of the share price). Table N ranks the companies in this book according to their historic dividend yields. Note that the franking credits available from most companies in this book can make the dividend yield substantially higher. The dividend yield changes with the share price. The figures in this table are based on share prices as of 8 September 2022.

	%
Grange Resources	15.4
Magellan Financial Group	14.3
BHP Group	12.5
Fortescue Metals Group	12.3
Rio Tinto	11.8
Platinum Asset Management	10.4
Globe International	8.9
Harvey Norman Holdings	8.8
Adairs	8.6
Perpetual	7.9
Pendal Group	7.9
JB Hi-Fi	7.8
GWA Group	7.6
McMillan Shakespeare	7.6
Super Retail Group	7.1
CSR	7.0
Nick Scali	6.5
Michael Hill International	6.5
Nine Entertainment	6.3
Smartgroup Corporation	6.3
ANZ Banking	6.2
Alumina	6.2
Servcorp	6.1
Aurizon Holdings	5.7
Metcash	5.2
Schaffer Corporation	5.0
GUD Holdings	4.7
NRW Holdings	4.6
Codan	4.6
Healius	4.4
National Australia Bank	4.3
Beacon Lighting Group	4.2
Commonwealth Bank	4.0
IRESS	4.0
Fiducian Group	3.9
Enero Group	3.9
PeopleIn	3.9
Wesfarmers	3.8
Medibank Private	3.8
Credit Corp Group	3.8
Monadelphous Group	3.8
Premier Investments	3.7
Reliance Worldwide Corporation	3.7
Baby Bunting Group	3.7
Pinnacle Investment	3.5
Macquarie Group	3.5

Elders	3.4
Telstra Corporation	3.4
Ridley Corporation	3.4
IPH	3.2
Jumbo Interactive	3.2
ASX	3.2
Bapcor	3.1
BlueScope Steel	3.1
Sonic Healthcare	3.1
Supply Network	3.0
Brickworks	2.9
Ansell	2.9
NIB Holdings	2.9
Data#3	2.8
Collins Foods	2.8
AUB Group	2.6
Steadfast Group	2.6
Woolworths Group	2.5
Iluka Resources	2.5
Hansen Technologies	2.4
ARB Corporation	2.3
Carsales.com	2.3
Computershare	2.2
Seek	2.1
Mineral Resources	1.6
Netwealth Group	1.5
Reece	1.5
Breville Group	1.5
Cochlear	1.4
REA Group	1.3
PWR Holdings	1.3
Altium	1.3
Beach Energy	1.2
Technology One	1.2
Aristocrat Leisure	1.2
CSL	1.1
Australian Ethical Investment	1.0
Clover Corporation	1.0
OZ Minerals	1.0
IDP Education	0.9
Johns Lyng Group	0.9
IGO	0.7
Objective Corporation	0.7
Lifestyle Communities	0.6
Pro Medicus	0.4
Clinuvel Pharmaceuticals	0.2
Wisetech Global	0.2

Table O
Year-on-year dividend growth

Most investors hope for a rising dividend, and this table tells how much each company raised or lowered its dividend in its latest financial year.

	%
Iluka Resources	1100.0
Aristocrat Leisure	310.0
Grange Resources	300.0
Ridley Corporation	270.0
IDP Education	237.5
ANZ Banking	136.7
National Australia Bank	111.7
Elders	90.9
Rio Tinto	77.0
McMillan Shakespeare	76.2
Wisetech Global	70.2
Michael Hill International	66.7
BlueScope Steel	61.3
Clinuvel Pharmaceuticals	60.0
Supply Network	60.0
Pro Medicus	46.7
NRW Holdings	38.9
CSR	37.0
PWR Holdings	36.4
Telstra Corporation	35.0
Nine Entertainment	33.3
Macquarie Group	32.3
Lifestyle Communities	31.3
REA Group	25.2
Reece	25.0
PeopleIn	23.8
Metcash	22.9
Objective Corporation	22.2
Pinnacle Investment	22.0
Healius	20.8
GWA Group	20.0
Hansen Technologies	20.0
Data#3	19.3
Cochlear	17.6
Altium	17.5
Collins Foods	17.4
Computershare	17.4
BHP Group	16.9
Jumbo Interactive	16.4
Perpetual	16.1
Premier Investments	14.3
Steadfast Group	14.0
Johns Lyng Group	14.0
Breville Group	13.2
Alumina	13.2
Servcorp	11.1

Pendal Group	10.8
Baby Bunting Group	10.6
Fiducian Group	10.4
JB Hi-Fi	10.1
Commonwealth Bank	10.0
Seek	10.0
Sonic Healthcare	9.9
Monadelphous Group	8.9
CSL	8.2
Technology One	8.0
Netwealth Group	7.8
Nick Scali	7.7
Bapcor	7.5
Harvey Norman Holdings	7.1
Smartgroup Corporation	5.8
ASX	5.7
Beacon Lighting Group	5.7
Medibank Private	5.5
Carsales.com	5.3
ARB Corporation	4.4
OZ Minerals	4.0
Codan	3.7
Brickworks	3.4
IPH	3.4
Reliance Worldwide Corporation	3.3
Credit Corp Group	2.8
Wesfarmers	1.1
AUB Group	0.0
Beach Energy	0.0
Globe International	0.0
IGO	0.0
IRESS	0.0
Schaffer Corporation	0.0
NIB Holdings	−8.3
Australian Ethical Investment	−14.3
Woolworths Group	−14.8
Magellan Financial Group	−15.2
Enero Group	−16.1
Super Retail Group	−20.5
Adairs	−21.7
Ansell	−22.2
Aurizon Holdings	−25.7
Platinum Asset Management	−29.2
GUD Holdings	−31.6
Fortescue Metals Group	−42.2
Clover Corporation	−60.0
Mineral Resources	−63.6

Table P
Five-year share price return

This table ranks the approximate annual average return to investors from a five-year investment in each of the companies in the book, as of September 2022. It is an accumulated return, based on share price appreciation or depreciation plus dividend payments.

	% p.a.
Pro Medicus	53.1
Grange Resources	46.5
Fortescue Metals Group	41.7
Objective Corporation	41.3
Johns Lyng Group	40.5
Jumbo Interactive	39.4
IDP Education	39.3
Wisetech Global	38.4
Australian Ethical Investment	38.0
PeopleIn	32.4
Mineral Resources	31.6
Lifestyle Communities	31.3
Globe International	31.0
PWR Holdings	30.3
Data#3	29.9
Enero Group	29.7
IGO	28.5
OZ Minerals	27.9
Pinnacle Investment	27.7
Altium	26.7
Supply Network	26.4
Clinuvel Pharmaceuticals	24.9
Codan	24.4
Baby Bunting Group	23.9
Elders	21.6
Technology One	19.4
Schaffer Corporation	19.3
NRW Holdings	19.1
CSL	17.8
JB Hi-Fi	17.4
AUB Group	16.4
Clover Corporation	16.2
Macquarie Group	15.8
Steadfast Group	15.5
Nick Scali	15.0
Collins Foods	14.2
BHP Group	14.0
Breville Group	13.9
Netwealth Group	13.7
Premier Investments	13.7
Wesfarmers	13.7
Rio Tinto	13.6
Reece	13.3
Carsales.com	13.1
ARB Corporation	13.0
IPH	13.0

Adairs	12.8
Metcash	12.8
Nine Entertainment	12.8
Beach Energy	12.5
REA Group	12.5
Beacon Lighting Group	11.9
Computershare	11.9
Sonic Healthcare	11.3
Brickworks	10.6
Ridley Corporation	10.4
ASX	10.2
Super Retail Group	10.2
Fiducian Group	10.1
Harvey Norman Holdings	10.1
Woolworths Group	9.8
Aristocrat Leisure	9.3
Commonwealth Bank	8.1
Hansen Technologies	8.1
Bapcor	7.4
NIB Holdings	6.7
Medibank Private	6.3
Telstra Corporation	6.3
BlueScope Steel	6.2
Michael Hill International	5.7
Cochlear	5.6
Ansell	5.0
Healius	4.7
Seek	4.5
CSR	4.4
IRESS	3.4
Reliance Worldwide Corporation	2.9
Credit Corp Group	2.6
National Australia Bank	2.6
McMillan Shakespeare	2.5
Iluka Resources	2.1
GWA Group	1.6
Aurizon Holdings	–0.6
ANZ Banking	–0.7
Alumina	–1.6
Monadelphous Group	–1.9
GUD Holdings	–2.1
Magellan Financial Group	–2.1
Smartgroup Corporation	–3.0
Servcorp	–4.8
Perpetual	–5.2
Pendal Group	–7.2
Platinum Asset Management	–17.0

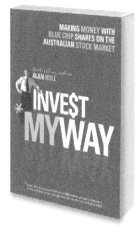

Best-selling author Alan Hull presents the complete
sharemarket solution for novices to experts. Whether
you're managing your portfolio, trading tactically on
the sharemarket or investing in blue chip shares,
Alan Hull explains the ins and outs of investing and
trading in easy-to-understand and engaging language.

Available in print and e-book formats

Printed and bound by CPI Group (UK) Ltd, Croydon, CR0 4YY

22/02/2023

03194234-0002